HOW TO
COOK
A MOOSE

HOW TO
COOK
A MOOSE

A Culinary Memoir

By Kate Christensen

ISLANDPORT PRESS

How to Cook A Moose

Islandport Press
PO Box 10
Yarmouth, ME 04096
books@islandportpress.com
www.islandportpress.com

ISBN: 978-1-934031-47-6
Library of Congress Catalog Number: 2014959692

Dean L. Lunt, Publisher
Book Cover Design by Teresa Lagrange
Interior Design by Michelle Lunt
Cover photo copyright © GMVozd
Back cover photo copyright © dbrskinner

Printed in the USA.

For Brendan, who brought me here

Other books by Kate Christensen

Non-fiction

Blue Plate Special: An Autobiography of my Appetites

Fiction

The Great Man
The Astral
The Epicure's Lament
In the Drink
Jeremy Thrane
Trouble

Contents

Editor's Note

My grandparents kept a farm along the York River in Maine for over sixty-five years. They raised four children, a bunch of sheep, some chickens, pigs, cows, and, every now and then, a horse.

A horse killed my grandfather in the field off the front porch when it bucked him off a hay rake. He hit his head on a stone and the rake ran over him. If you've ever seen a hay rake (it looks like a curved steel comb with tightly spaced, sharpened teeth), you will know that getting run over by one is not something one survives. My aunt, who was twelve at the time, found my grandfather's body around supper-time, when the sun glints gold off the river and the air gets very still. My grandmother watched her from the porch. The horse had run off into the woods.

Fifty years later, when my grandmother died (at ninety-four), we celebrated her life at a big family dinner spread out on that very same porch. Four generations of my family came together at the farm to share potato salad, cuts of beef from our own cows that had been stored in the deep freeze, corn, beans, and a blueberry pie made from blueberries that grew out back. That was three years ago, and today my generation owns the farmhouse and much of the land that sur-rounds it. Our dream for the farm is similar to the one shared by so many who live in these parts, or who want to live here: to protect and serve a way of life that speaks to the core of what it means to live in a meaningful way. A life that feels more in balance with natural rhythms and essential work. A life that adds more than it takes.

But it ain't easy.

Like my grandfather, the people in these parts who make a life from nature's bounty—an environment that is more often than not stingy, bitterly cold, and stubborn—bleed for it, maybe not with actual blood, but certainly with sweat and tears and a lot of dirt. It's true: Real, authentic joy abounds, the kind that can't be bought or facsimiled via technology, but it comes with a constant side order of hardship and labor. People do it because generations before them have shown it to be the healthiest way to live, and because it is necessary for their community to survive. In these perilous days, going backwards to move forward is starting to feel a lot like the answer.

A narrative like this was going through my mind almost constantly about two years ago. Michael Pollan had told us all to eat more like our great-grandmothers; I wanted to find a way to save the planet by *living* more like them, too. I sweated over who in the future would know how to hunt and fish and sew and forge tools and churn butter. I briefly explored turning the farm into a center for the pre-industrial arts. I kept thinking about a book I had read many years before that transformed my ideas about survival and grace in times of real deprivation. It was M. F. K. Fisher's *How to Cook a Wolf*. I wanted to find a new voice to write a similar book that would help to address our current dilemmas—one that didn't just bemoan our fate, but actually presented some useful advice on what to do, how to keep your sense of humor, and, importantly, what to eat.

That summer, I went with a writer friend to our local bookstore in Portland to hear an author read. I had a notion of this particular novelist's work because she had written six critically acclaimed novels, and now a memoir—an ambitious act for a woman, who at my first sighting I thought could not be older than thirty-two.

It turned out she'd lived a bit longer and a lot harder than I first thought; she'd taught herself how to write, cook, travel, live, speak French, and love with such unabashed, openhearted ardor that I recognized her in a way that I can only describe as familial. I sat there listening and all I could feel was, *Ah, there she is.* As she read, revealing a book so full of delight and wisdom (and *recipes!*), I began to vibrate with excitement. I knew with certainty that I had finally found the voice I'd been looking for. My only question was whether or not I could convince her to write the book I had in mind.

I don't remember what I said to Kate Christensen that first memorable evening, because I think it spilled out in one long rush of praise, description, and demands. She was off to teach at the Iowa Writers' Workshop the next day, so she scribbled her e-mail address under her signature and said WRITE ME underneath it, with a seriousness that made me think I wasn't crazy. Like maybe she wasn't just handling an overexcited fan, but that she had actually heard what I was asking, and was interested.

In fact, it turns out she was more than interested.

Kate had recently moved to Maine from New Hampshire (via Brooklyn, as you will find out), and had begun her own love affair with our history, its people, its funky wildness, and its food. She was also as twisted-up as I was about the state of the planet, and had already proposed a similar book to her other big-city publisher. When I mentioned *How to Cook a Wolf,* she almost jumped in the air. It was, honestly, the only AHA moment I've had in my life outside of college, and I will say, gauging her reaction, one of hers, too.

Kate took about a nanosecond to decide that, like the slow-food movement and the buy-local movement, writing a book for a local small publisher was a fitting way to put her money where her mouth—and heart—is. And her other publisher had enough respect for Kate's integrity to agree. Our Kate is no phony. In this book, she pays tribute to a band of people and a way of life that she and her partner, Brendan, embody every day. Her joy has been tempered by her own fair share of hardship, and she has earned her right to be, as Wendell Berry says, "of this place."

There's a sense of relief one gets when one reads a book that just makes some damn sense, just as there is a welcome feeling when one finally finds those people who got lost through the ages amid the shuffle of mortal coils. Kate and her work occupy both those places for me, and it is my hope (and hers) that this book will resonate for you, whether you live in New England or elsewhere. We hope you will find comfort in its pages, and be inspired to find the people in your own corner of the world with whom you can share great friendship, spirited conversation, and a simple, sustaining meal. With those ingredients, Kate and I believe we'll muckle through, whatever comes down the way.

Genevieve Morgan
Senior Editor, Islandport Press 2015

I would really rather feel bad in Maine
than feel good anywhere else.

E. B. White

Introduction

Cooking and Eating at the End of the World

Maine has inspired many, many writers. Maybe it's the combination of the wild, beautiful landscape, the narrative drama of extreme seasons, and the human struggle to survive in such a rugged place, but there's a long literary tradition of people who've written books about their experiences of moving here, growing up here, coming back here, homesteading here, or living off the grid in the far remote North Woods.

And aside from the intrepid natives, this place also seems to be filled with people like me, people who came here "from away" and fell in love with Maine's strong sense of community and fierce work ethic, granite and hemlocks, cold north Atlantic, marshes and coves: people who arrived as newcomers and stayed because they felt a deep sense of belonging here, of being at home.

I grew up in the Arizona desert and always felt alienated by that stark, grandiose, arid land. Its beauty was undeniably awe-inspiring, but my soul craved trees, shadows, dark places to balance the light, texture and contrast. I love the seasons and climate in New England, the geography and fauna, the changing light, the big, dramatic sky above and the intimate, invitingly human-scaled land below. I love the ghosts here, the powerful old worn-down mountains, scoured and rucked up by an ancient gigantic glacier more than a mile thick, and the rural roads cracked and bumpy with frost heaves, echoing the geography in miniature. My ancestors were all Northern Europeans—English, Norwegian, German—which might be part of why I feel so at home in this briny, rough, cold state. Maybe it's in my blood, maybe it's something else, but love begets obsession, and obsession is what makes books happen.

Hand in hand with my love for this place comes an obsessive, life-long love of food. I'm not a foodie—I'm an eater: I'm hungry. I'm a girl from Arizona who grew up on hot dogs and Cheerios as well as my mother's homemade breads and soups. I love good food, and I don't care if it's high or low; in fact, I am not even sure what that means. Oysters used to be workmen's food, cheap and plentiful and sold from street carts. Lobster used to be considered a trash fish, back when enormous cod and haddock thronged the Gulf of Maine. Provençal, Roman, and Tuscan food, once the local, homespun fare of peasants and farmers, are all gourmet and expensive now, their ingredients sold in specialty shops. But if you cook those cuisines at home, they're as homey as they used to be, back when paysannes and nonnas cooked over open hearths in farmhouse kitchens.

Eating well and simply is a way of life I consider both a luxury and a necessity. I don't mind spending money on good ingredients or restaurant meals. Some people splurge on new clothes, trips to the spa, power tools, beauty items, cars. . . . I spend all the money I can afford on food and consider it well spent, and I never look back. When I'm not treating myself to a meal at one of Portland's 537 (at last count) astonishingly good restaurants, I prefer, and try to buy, local, organic produce, fish that isn't endangered and/or filled with toxins, and meat that didn't have to fly around the world to get to my kitchen, from animals who were fed only foods they'd evolved to eat and who were raised and slaughtered as humanely as possible.

For everyday eating, I cook and eat simply, nothing fancy or overly ambitious. My favorite dishes tend to involve just a few ingredients: in summer, pasta with a sauce of fresh tomatoes, garlic, and basil, or a caprese salad of ripe tomatoes with buffalo mozzarella and torn-up fresh basil leaves, or chicken thighs poached in garlic, white wine, and olive oil with asparagus and boiled potatoes. In winter, at least once a week, I make a fantastic recipe I call Peace Chicken from Ottolenghi's *Jerusalem* cookbook, a chicken and basmati rice and onion one-pot stew with cinnamon sticks, cloves, cardamom, dill, cilantro, parsley, then yogurt on top at the end. If I'm in a hurry, I throw together a savory pureed vegetable soup in cold weather, a salad of fish and vegetables and cold boiled potatoes in hot. And one of my favorite summer suppers is a big plateful of nothing but zucchini—fresh off the vine, small and tender—cut into chunks and sautéed with plenty of garlic and good olive oil until it's velvety and luscious and melts on the tongue.

I'm a food populist, a curmudgeonly traditionalist, but emphatically not an elitist. In fact, I get something like a brain rash when I think about food snobbery. How dare anybody be a snob about food? We all eat to live; at its very foundation, it's the fuel of our lives. But in a larger sense, if we're lucky, it can be a source of community, joy, pleasure, and celebration. Eating well is the key to health, and health is the key to well-being. It's a sensual as well as a social and nourishing pleasure—a triple source of happiness.

This passion for eating well but simply seems to be something I share with many new and old Mainers. In recent years, Portland, Maine, has earned a culinary reputation that rivals that of any larger city in the country. But unlike many bigger cities, the feeling here is down-to-earth and authentic. If they want to survive here, the local restaurants, no matter how esoteric their culinary vision or highly trained their chefs, have to hew to the native Maine honesty, which I would sum up as "no bullshit, no cynicism, no art for art's sake." In other words, people here are serious about food in a traditional rather than a trendy or overt way. This seriousness takes the form of a respect for the old ways: Maine farmers and lobstermen, brewers of beer and mead, and bakers alike all look to the techniques and patterns of the past. Maine's climate and geography are tough to wrest a subsistence from; the knowledge and hard work of the people who came before, who grew crops in Maine's rocky, thin soil and who pulled a living's worth of fish out of the treacherous tides of the gulf, inform the people who are still doing it now. And so, even though I'm "from away," and this is a place of long-standing generational continuity and ingrained, and wholly understandable, suspicion of outsiders, Mainers are my kind of people, and Portland's "hunted, fished, foraged, and farmed," local-and-seasonal ethos is my kind of eating.

In 1942, the great food writer M. F. K. Fisher published a treatise on how to survive poverty and hardship called *How to Cook a Wolf*. Written during the wartime era of rations, shortages, and scrimping, the title refers to the proverbial beast with open jaws that shows up, slavering with hunger, in times of need and poverty, privation and sacrifice. To keep the wolf from the door means to have enough money, barely, to eat and live. Throughout the book, Fisher provides techniques and recipes with limited ingredients for surviving the lean times the country had fallen into in the 1930s and early '40s. These recipes have humble names like Quick Potato Soup, War Cake, Addie's Quick Bucket-Bread; there's also a very basic but serviceable Boeuf Tartare. Chapter headings include "How to Keep Alive," "How to Comfort Sorrow," and "How to Be Content with Vegetable Love."

It's an unusually (for Fisher) straightforward, didactic book about "living as decently as possible with the ration cards and blackouts and like miseries of World War II." But her tone is anything but grim, or rather, any grimness it contains is undergirded with humor. In the introduction, Fisher writes, "War is a beastly business, it is true, but one proof that we are human is our ability to learn, even from it, how better to exist." Her optimism is as comforting as any I've ever found in literature, as is her final chapter, "How to Practice True Economy." The title is ironic; she ends with the most luxurious, decadent recipes she can think of: Shrimp Pâté that calls for butter and mayonnaise and four pounds of fresh shrimp; savory Eggs with Anchovies, which involves quantities of eggs, cream, mushrooms, and Parmesan; and a fabulously rich Colonial Dessert, made of two cups thick cream, four egg yolks, and one cup brown sugar, that sounds like a sort of American crème brûlée.

In one of the book's final lines, Fisher writes, "I believe that one of the most dignified ways we are capable of, to assert and then reassert our dignity in the face of poverty and war's fears and pains, is to nourish ourselves with all possible skill, delicacy, and ever-increasing enjoyment."

This last sentence echoes one of my own most deeply held convictions: that eating both well and wholesomely, insofar as it can be done within one's budget and means, with elegant balance and the occasional indulgent luxury, is an expression of hope and dignity as well as a cause of happiness.

Fisher was writing about wartime deprivations, a bygone era when food was scarce and money was tight. But when the Great Depression hit the United States, people in Maine were largely unaffected, or rather, they'd always been in a depression, a perpetual three-hundred-year one, so they had already developed their own means of combating and surviving it. A book like *How to Cook a Wolf* would have taught these Mainers nothing; they had been cooking the proverbial wolf for centuries. And long before the first Europeans settled here in the 1600s, the native Indian tribes who lived in this barely habitable northeastern corner of the country had eked out a subsistence with seasonal migration, moving inland, where they hunted deer, moose, and smaller mammals, then back to the ocean, where they caught fish, porpoises, seals, and mollusks.

Up here in the northeast corner, life is hard but sweet. Happiness is simple when you don't need much in the way of material possessions or glitz, when you work hard for what you have and stay true to your roots, your community, yourself. As I wrote this book, I came across a lot of amazing people, some natives, some "from away," many of them young, all of them interesting, smart as hell, and down-to-earth. I talked to them and ate meals they'd cooked and saw how they live and work—chefs, fishermen, farmers, and "ordinary" New Englanders who know as a matter of course how to forage for mushrooms and oysters, grow and can vegetables, tap maple trees, hunt and fish, build houses and chop wood, and get through a long winter without going nuts. I loved meeting them all.

This region is populated by people with a resourceful ability to make do in hard times, to figure out solutions to seemingly insoluble problems, and to survive. For me, the people themselves are the greatest resource in this abundant and generous place. I'm honored to be able to live among them and to write about them.

The things I've learned here can be applied many other places, too, of course, and the people I've met have their counterparts in many other regions: New Mexico, Minnesota, British Columbia, and Georgia, for example. I moved here from Brooklyn, New York; even there, in that urban hotbed of hipster cool, people are going back to the old ways: pickling, canning, growing vegetables, fishing, hunting, and cooking food from scratch, with whole ingredients that are as local and seasonal as possible.

Common sense is returning to American food and eating habits after decades of prevalent, glamorous, easy, cheap junk-food technology, packaged chemicals that mimic real food. Even so, it's not so simple to combat the entrenched and super-powerful forces of corporate food and agribusiness: The wolf is back at the door these days, but this time, he's howling and hungry for food that's not only cheap, but also delicious, nourishing, and not unduly harmful to the ecosystem and natural environment. In the face of the complexities of balanced decision-making that go into every meal I shop for or cook or order, I find myself asking, in general, "What should I eat?"

I think I've found some answers here in Maine.

Chapter One

Landing in New England

The wolf was usually at our door when I was growing up in Arizona in the 1970s. However, by dint of various scrappy techniques Fisher would have lauded, such as economical cooking and thrift-store shopping and a knack for joy and festivity that made mealtimes fun, no matter what hardships we were facing, our mother got us through our childhood in good health and spirits. She mixed powdered milk into real milk, disguised cheap, tasty beef tongue in stews, and served beans in every way, shape, and form. From my mother, I learned how to dine well on very little. I also learned that, while it's preferable to have plenty of money, being poor can be an adventure if you have the right attitude about it.

Even so, as a little kid and on into high school, during all those years when my family was poor as hell, I wanted very badly to be rich. In fact, I yearned to be an English aristocrat, a character in a Jane Austen novel, maybe, a more contemporary version of one of her beautiful, vapid heiresses; being stupid seemed like an okay trade-off for the wealth I'd have, as long as I was gorgeous as well. I dreamed of living in a palace or mansion or great hall, with servants, a canopy bed, a breakfast room, balls and parties. I didn't see why this shouldn't be; it seemed unfair that I hadn't been born a duchess, a cruel trick of fate. I had the aspirations of a child who devoured heaps of books about rich people, past and present, and instinctively craved the opulent trappings of luxury, but whose real-life circumstances and family philosophy ran counter to her tastes.

Part of the problem was that I never felt like a Westerner. As a bookish, non-religious, violin-playing would-be writer, I felt out of place in the Arizona desert, the suburban, staid, Christian Southwest of the 1970s. I had no sense of belonging to a community or even an extended family; my mother and two little sisters and I were estranged from most of our relatives on both sides, for various reasons. We didn't go to church or belong to any social groups or clubs. We moved every year or two, so once again I'd have to make new friends, be the new girl.

What appealed to me in the novels I read was that often they were about place as much as character. I learned from books about tightly knit villages, the gossipy goings-on of the upper and lower classes, the severe repercussions of going against your place in tradition and society. In the 1970s, these things were being systematically dismantled without a solid replacement for them; I was fascinated by the literary evidence that they existed, as my own life went on being fractured and uprooted. To soothe myself, throughout my childhood, I planned my future as a novelist, vowed to find my own place somewhere in the wide world.

Even as a ten-year-old, when I wasn't wishing I lived in Victorian or Edwardian England, I dreamed of living in New York someday, that glittering metropolis of movies and novels. But when I finally arrived there in 1989, twenty-seven years old and fresh out of graduate school, some of my father's extreme Marxist values must have asserted themselves in me, to complement my mother's cheerful romanticism of scrappy survival. In other words, I discovered that I deeply disapproved of rich people. I was flat-out horrified by the conspicuous spending, material accumulation, and financial striving I saw in the city; I looked askance at the countess I worked for as a personal secretary, the Wall Street traders I overheard in bars talking about swaps and derivatives, anyone who seemed to have more than his or her fair share, whatever that was. I even not-so-secretly disapproved of my Choate- and Georgetown-educated WASP boyfriend from Connecticut, James, and also, wholly unfairly, of his easygoing, generous, fun-loving millionaire uncle, who struck me as a shallow, nouveau-riche layabout whose Rhode Island McMansion was badly built and falling apart.

I remember, one cold fall afternoon when I was twenty-eight, taking the subway from the sketchy, skeevy neighborhood deep in Brooklyn where I lived to the Upper East Side of Manhattan to meet James, his uncle's wife, and some of her friends in the Carlyle Hotel bar. I walked into the Carlyle in my ripped thrift-store coat, wearing a black miniskirt, a moth-eaten sweater, cheap tights, and Frye motorcycle boots, an outfit that worked perfectly well in the East Village. But here, in the hushed, ornate Carlyle bar, I realized that I looked like a pauper, an upstart, an urchin. I felt so out of place, I might as well have been in a country where I didn't speak the language, where I had no passport or money and knew no one.

James's aunt, who lived in Madison, Connecticut, and played tennis and had a shining blonde pageboy hairdo and a permanent sharp, intelligent, amused expression, saw me first. "Kate!" she called, waving. I approached their table, suddenly intimidated, feeling monstrously out of place. I looked around at her and her friends, their tasteful makeup, effortlessly correct clothes, glowing burnished skin, impeccable hair, and then I saw James, who looked perfectly at home among them in his navy blazer, Brooks Brothers shirt, and khakis.

He gestured to the empty chair next to him. I wanted to get the hell out of there, run and never look back. Instead, I hung my unspeakably terrible coat on the chair's back, exposing the rip in its lining, and sat down.

"Did you really mean for me to come here?" I blurted, loudly enough so that everyone heard.

"Of course," said James, his eyes flickering over my face in the general laughter at my gaucheness.

But I didn't believe him. I ordered a vodka on the rocks and sipped it, seething, uncomfortable, furious at him for making me come here where I didn't belong. It was as if he had forgotten who I was, momentarily mistaken me for someone who would fit in in a place like this. Then, as the vodka loosened my brain and diminished my anxiety, I watched them all talk, as curious as an anthropologist among a foreign tribe whose lifestyle she finds arcane and louche and exotic. They seemed so thoughtlessly self-satisfied, these wealthy Easterners, so polished and reserved.

Later, when I worked as an office temp and then a corporate secretary for several years, I watched the people I worked among the same way; these lawyers, executives, all the corporate types, were completely foreign to me. I'd mostly only known outliers growing up— hippies, politicos, suburban and provincial Arizonans, artists, spiritual crackpots, then college professors and Oregon outdoorsy types and intellectuals, then fellow writers and friendly, unpretentious, middle-class Midwesterners. Rich people and corporate types were far more foreign to me in their way than the countless nationalities of people I rode the subway with, jostled against on the streets. I was one of the aspiring poor of the city, and the aspiring-artist class is generally allied with the immigrant strivers. People who had money, either inherited or earned, seemed to exist in a rarefied bubble all their own, a privileged inner sanctum sealed off by several airlocks from the hubbub and chaos I lived in with my bodega beers, the well-used black pleather ankle boots I'd bought off a blanket on Avenue A for two bucks, the easy patois of half-heckling banter I was learning to speak with taxi drivers and deli cashiers and bartenders, the language of the aspirers.

The privileged, ruling-class people's language was radically different. At the table in the Carlyle, everyone spoke in low tones, understated, with calibrated pauses and significant eye contact, an elaborately developed shorthand. I didn't understand anything they said, caught none of their references, missed all the subtext and innuendo.

My half-alienated, half-fascinated disapproval of James and his family and their ilk did not, however, prevent me from buying a $70 round-trip Amtrak ticket, as often as I could, to go to Rhode Island to spend a three-day weekend with James in his uncle's empty house in Jamestown. For the year and a half before I became an office temp, I was the personal secretary to a countess on the Upper East Side, ghostwriting her spy novels and organizing her busy schedule of functions, fund-raisers, and galas, so "going to Rhode Island" meant escaping everything I dreaded and feared, and luxuriating in everything I loved. James and I lounged up on the house's widow's walk at sunset with glasses of wine, sat on the railed wraparound porch in the sun, rode our bikes to the old fort with a picnic for an afternoon, and hitchhiked into Newport to spend a day on the Cliff Walk and at First Beach or to go to music festivals or tennis matches.

I learned to love the food of New England—but not the famously bland WASP meals, imported straight from England, of turgidly gummy clam chowder and Saltines, or tuna salad with no mayo on a limp iceberg leaf with a pallid tomato slice, or overcooked chicken breasts drowned in thick sauce with a side of gray overboiled vegetables. In Rhode Island in the summertime, I discovered fresh, local food, and I never looked back. We bought smoked mackerel and fresh striped bass at the little fish place across the bridge, squash and lettuce and corn from the local farm stand. We drank cold, fizzy, robust vinho verde from the Portuguese store in New Bedford.

And I also discovered excellent restaurant food. When James's uncle came up from Connecticut for a night or two, which he only occasionally did, he took us out for expensive sushi dinners in his Jaguar; we sat at a table in the window of the Japanese place in Newport. Uncle Jack always ordered an enormous tray of fish, "the sushi boat," plus as much cold sake or Tsingtao as we could drink, and extras— unagi, or sea urchin with a raw quail egg, or a side of sashimi. He was rich; we were poor. He was generous; we were beholden. I couldn't ask for anything, and neither could James. We gobbled every piece of fish we could get our mitts on and tried to be charming and lively during dinner, and afterwards, we thanked him profusely. It made me uneasy. I wanted to be the one ordering and paying, the one who was generous. It seemed like an infinitely preferable position to be in.

Going back to the clanking, stifling, stinking, crowded city to my difficult job was excruciating after those heavenly weekends in Jamestown. All the following week, I craved the clean intense blue of Narragansett Bay, the washed-out greens of the sea grasses and beach plum bushes, the clapboard houses, and the briny, clean, sweet air. I had only been in New York for a year or two, but I was already dreaming of moving to New England. If I could have afforded it, I would have, but I was too poor. I had to make my way in the city, or not at all.

It was the early 1990s, and money seemed to be everywhere except in my bank account. It made me feel prim and judgmental: The real romance, I remembered from my childhood, was in making a lot out of a little, or meeting adversity with a sense of adventure and derring-do. I thought defiantly of my mother's Friday-night suppers of homemade applesauce with Farmer's Fritters, thin, tangy cottage-cheese pancakes, doused in Aunt Jemima, eaten in candlelight in our small Tempe cinder-block house while we told stories around the table. I thought of the platefuls of cut-up raw jicama, green peppers, and carrots that she gave us to snack on before dinner, her home-cooked plain nourishing meals, the way she managed to feed us festively and well on almost no money; I felt that we were akin to the March family in *Little Women*.

That was what being rich meant. Not the countess's gilt-and-marble foyer, not the tailored suits of Wall Street, not the stretch limousines that cruised along Park Avenue. Real wealth was found in literature and music, the joy of owning one's own soul and mind, a healthy body, the ability to laugh. Wealth was pleasure and adventure: fleeting, ephemeral, but all-important. Also, real wealth was access to good food.

I revised my childhood plan. Suddenly, I didn't want to be rich anymore; I just wanted to be able to afford to eat well. Actually, eating well struck me not as a luxury, but a basic human right. I'd never really thought about this before. Why couldn't I eat in good restaurants, too? For the first time in my life, as I ordered the greasy $6.99 Early Bird Special at BBQ or counted my change to leave a tip for my veggie burrito at Life Café, I began to aspire to all the amazing food I'd never had, "fancy" stuff made by "real" chefs. I wanted to eat in a place with an interesting, pricey menu and linen tablecloths and a sommelier and subtle lighting . . . I imagined ordering steak tartare, or venison, or exotic dishes whose names I couldn't pronounce. I walked by beautiful restaurants and gazed in their windows and daydreamed and schemed. Someday, somehow . . . But for years, I didn't dare go in. And I couldn't afford to.

ele

And then, in 1992, I fell in love with a man who taught me how to cook and how to eat in restaurants, and offered to support me so I could work hard at my writing and not squander all my time in dead-end jobs. We got married in 1994, and for the next twelve years, we lived together in north Brooklyn, the epicenter of hipsterdom. I begin to publish novels and essays and reviews; I dove into the world of food. During those years, except for the occasional trip to Mexico or Europe or to visit family, we seldom left New York; it was hard to leave, even for brief spells. The city exerted a powerful centrifugal force. There was always a full calendar of social events that made getting away impossible. If I left, I might miss something! For most of those years, I loved the city with a deep, committed passion—first, the way one loves a golden, enchanting, glamorous but complex lover, and then, after September 11th, as one loves a fragile, damaged, suddenly elderly spouse. I understood then how deeply I belonged to, and in, the city.

Those were heady years. My former husband and I, from the start, observed a mutual pact to live as if we would always have money, even when things were tight. We were lavish, freewheeling, generous, and we loved to eat and drink. Neither of us cared about clothes or possessions or things. We loved to live well, loved adventure and pleasure. We ate everything, everywhere, all over town. We threw dinner parties and cookouts for our friends. Our shared passion for food and drink made our marriage fun and enabled me to ignore the fact that we weren't fundamentally connected.

Until it didn't; until it wasn't enough for me . . . although we were good friends and comrades, we were out of sync in many ways, and, at the very heart of things, I was wrenchingly lonely with him; no matter how hard I tried to bridge the emotional gulf between us, I was unable to connect deeply with my husband. And I craved this connection so desperately, I finally realized I couldn't live in a marriage without it. Whether or not I'd ever find it with someone else, I remembered what my mother had told me throughout my life: "It's always better to be lonely alone than lonely with someone else."

In the fall of 2008, I moved out of our house in Greenpoint, Brooklyn, into a nearby sublet, then when that ended, I rented my own apartment in the neighborhood. That winter, I became thin and weak from too much wine and grief and stress and not enough food, sleep, exercise, or fresh air. Lying in my bed alone on cold gray mornings listening to garbage trucks grinding and roaring, inhaling smoke from neighbors' cigarettes, I felt myself planning to leave New York, pulling away, the same way I had left my marriage, with that same resigned sadness. Even New York's food no longer held the same excitement for me. I didn't feel hungry anymore; I felt bilious and exhausted. I longed for a new life, somewhere else, somewhere clean and quiet.

Someone must have been listening, or else I just got lucky, because that spring, I went on a date with a native New Englander. Brendan and I had met briefly in New York two weeks after I left my marriage, in October of 2008, but no matter how strong the spark was between us, it was much too soon then for me to think about falling in love again or even having a fling. We kept in touch sporadically by e-mail throughout the winter, while I lived alone in my apartment in Brooklyn, and Brendan, a poet, filmmaker, and musician, lived alone in his family's farmhouse in the White Mountains of New Hampshire, writing poetry.

Then, in late March of 2009, we had dinner at El Quijote on W. 23rd Street in Manhattan. We sat at the bar for five hours, drinking sangria and eating tapas, turned toward each other on our stools, talking until the restaurant closed. I hadn't expected anything much to come of this date, my first since my marriage had ended seven months earlier. After all, he was so young (he had just turned 27, and I was 46), and he lived so far away. But nonetheless, here he was: my own true love. And from that night on, we have been inseparable, despite the fact that I was, and always will be, almost twenty years older than him.

For our second date, he invited me up to his farmhouse in the White Mountains, a couple of miles from the Maine border. He had been born and raised there; it was mostly empty now, because his family lived out West. Once I arrived, I never wanted to leave. We lived in an idyllic bubble that spring, a couple of mad writers in swooning love. I rediscovered my passion for New England, remembered why I'd loved it when I'd visited James in Rhode Island all those years ago. I could not believe that I'd found such an amazing man who'd been born here and belonged here and had a place here and was excited to share it with me.

Brendan and I have been together for almost six years as of this writing. We own a house together, we're deeply committed to each other. We're planning to get officially married when we get around to it, but we've been married in the truly authentic sense of the word for a very long time. Brendan doesn't worry, on the whole, that I'm ahead of him, career-wise; he has plenty of time to catch up, and he's working as hard as he possibly can to fulfill his own ambitions. What's more, he doesn't want kids, and never has; that's a relief to me, since at my age, it's pretty much moot. Our age difference is, if anything, a source of strength for us. It keeps things interesting. Never mind that we're sometimes in danger of going broke, never mind that I have twenty years' more life experience, including a whole marriage. The externals don't matter to either of us.

I've never felt lonely with Brendan. One of the things I love most about him is that we can have any conversation, anytime, anywhere: driving home from a memorial service; at three o'clock in the morning in bed; sitting in a restaurant; or walking our dog. Even if I say something oblique and out of the blue, he takes a leap of willing and curious comprehension toward me, and I do the same for him. When I'm angry, I say so. When I want something, I ask for it. When I'm overwhelmed with adoration of him, which happens a lot, he reciprocates unhesitatingly, and he's often overwhelmed, himself. I'm humbly grateful to be able to love another person so fully and wholly, without being blocked or stymied, without having to suppress any part of myself.

This is all so basic and simple, I can't believe it's so rare. But it is, and it feels so precious to me and so hard-won, that as soon as I understood who Brendan was and what we had together, I held on to him and could not let go.

ℓℓ

Pasta with Pea Sauce

This is the pasta equivalent of chicken soup. It's a traditional, typically Roman sauce, the base for osso bucco and many other dishes. Brendan makes it on raw late-autumn nights, or after a long car trip, or when I'm feeling under the weather. A big, rich, savory-sweet bowl of it never fails to warm my heart and bones. To me, it tastes like love.

Make a soffritto: Mince 2 peeled carrots, 2 celery ribs, and 1 large white or yellow onion.

Heat olive oil in a heavy saucepan and add the vegetables. Sauté them on low heat until they're tender, about 15 minutes.

Turn up the heat, add half a 10 oz. bag of frozen peas, and 1/4 cup vegetable broth. Cook 5 minutes until peas are tender.

Add 1 1/2 cups Pomi chopped tomatoes, salt and pepper, and crushed red pepper. (It should be smelling deeply good by now.)

Let it simmer on medium-low heat for 15 more minutes, until it's thick.

Toss with 1 lb. freshly cooked hot pasta (fettuccine or penne is best) and serve with Parmesan cheese.

Serves 2 with leftovers; cures everything.

ℓℓ

By the fall of 2011, the facts suggested that I had left New York for good: For the past two and a half years, I'd been traveling a lot and otherwise living with Brendan in New Hampshire. Leaving New York had been a protracted, bittersweet process, and there were still times, even though I was deliriously happy up here, when I missed New York—dinner parties, late nights in good old bars. Most of my friends lived down there.

But I didn't want to go back. I loved our life up here. I loved how isolated and wild it felt, not seeing any lights at night. I loved how pristine it was, the wild animals, the nearby lake. We drove our trash to the dump ourselves, and that was just fine with me, because I didn't miss the early morning din of garbage trucks. It felt strange in the best way to live in such quiet. By the time I left New York and moved up here, my entire being felt as if it had shaped itself around the familiarity of urban life, so completely I'd hardly noticed any of it anymore—traffic noises, sidewalks full of crowds, strong smells, twenty-four-hour lights, the crash and squeal of the subways, the constant sense of millions of people around me. Now I felt all my internal muscles relaxing with relief; I hadn't even realized they'd been so tense and clutched.

But after two decades in New York, it did take a while for me to become accustomed to this region's ways and mores. Needless to say, the White Mountains are an entirely different country from New York City. The landscape was foreign to me at first, even exotic: wild, open vistas, thick woods full of spirits, farm stands, inns, and ski slopes bald in the summertime on nearby mountains. The people are English, Irish, Scots-Irish, Acadian—noses are sharp, hair blond, as often as not. English is spoken here, as it is in New York, but it's not Yiddish-inflected, it's not undergirded with the three most urgent questions of New York parlance: How much rent do you pay? What do you do? Who do you know? In New York, I spoke a rapid shorthand patois. After I moved up here, I slowly learned the local dialect: wry, under-stated, with a quick, merry fatalism that feels nineteenth-century. The questions undergirding conversations here seem to be: How do you heat your house? Who's your family? Working hard, or hardly work-ing? (This last is apparently a hilarious local joke that never gets old.)

In New York, I was a writer among my own kind, a pigeon com-peting for bread crumbs, perched on windowsills with the other pigeons united in a throaty, guttural, communal recitative about edi-tors, advances, bad reviews. In New Hampshire, the people I first met—I couldn't call them friends because I hadn't been here long enough to have made real friends; that takes years—were doctors, woodworkers, lawyers, and what used to be called "landed gentry," as well as a few painters and musicians.

Besides Brendan, I knew only one other writer, a playwright who came for vacations and sabbaticals. In the White Mountains, we few writers seemed to be treated as a slightly dangerous exotic species. Several times, I heard half-jokes about not telling me anything, or it might end up in a book. People here struck me as fiercely private; they minded their own business and trusted that you would do the same, which was a soothing relief after the relentless gossip of the city.

Sometimes, staying in the isolated farmhouse with my true love, I caught myself feeling as if I were living inside a children's book—a happy one. The view from the table where we sat working together all day was wondrous: long, wild meadows surrounded by stone walls, stretching down in two directions to dense old shaggy woods, a lake, a beaver pond, and mountains stretching back to the sky.

Out on the porch one spring morning, I saw a robin redbreast in the crab-apple tree over by the lilac bushes. It was hard to believe the things I well knew were happening all over the world, hard to reconcile this pristine, preserved, seemingly unchanged place with the terrible things going on "out there"—the massive-scale insanity of hydraulic fracturing and Tar Sands oil, the plastic and trash deposit in the Pacific Ocean the size of Texas and growing, Manhattan-sized chunks of ice falling and melting into oceans at the poles, so many animals endangered and extinct.

Then, as I was thinking about fracking and ocean trash, the sunlight slipped through the clouds and lit the grass and gilded the trees. The crickets were humming. The clouds cast shadows on the mountains' furry green blanket of trees.

ℓℓℓ

Chicken à la Ding

When I moved up here, I brought my dog with me. His name is Dingo. He's a midsize, now-elderly former Brooklyn street mutt, a handsome, bat-eared, extremely well-mannered gentleman. He'll go anywhere I go; as far as I can tell, there are very few things in the world that Dingo loves more than he loves me. (And by "loves," I mean, "expresses enthusiasm for"; who can know what lurks in the heart of a dog?) One of these things—now that I think about it, maybe the only thing—is chicken. In fact, it has occurred to me that if I could magically turn into a chicken, Dingo's life would be complete. Given that this is not going to happen, or so I hope, he'll have to be content with the second-best thing: I invented a chicken stew to add to his kibble. He doesn't get it all the time, although I don't think he could ever get tired of it.

The first time I made it, one night in the farmhouse, he somehow knew it was for him. While it simmered, he sat by the stove, his entire attention laser-focused on the pot. When everything was cooked and soft, I turned off the flame. While it cooled, I went back to work, sitting at the table. He hovered by my knees, resting his chin on them in a way that had nothing to do with affection; every now and then, his chin tapped my knees to inform me that he wanted that stew. I tried to explain that it was too hot, but he couldn't grasp that concept. By the time his dinner hour rolled around, he was in a hair-trigger state of monomaniacal jonesing.

I stirred a cup of stew into his half-cup of kibble and gave him his bowl. Less than two minutes later, he had licked the bowl clean and was gazing up at me with adoration, licking his chops. I was tempted to laugh about this, but I resisted the urge, because this is exactly what we human members of the household do. Every day, we anticipate our dinner, talk about it, plan it, make it, drool over the cooking smells, load up our plates—and then it's gone.

3 large boneless, skinless chicken breasts, chopped
1 lb. carrots, chopped
1 cup green beans, chopped
1 cup broccoli, chopped, with peeled stems

Place all ingredients into a big pot and cover with water, plus one inch. Simmer, partially covered, stirring occasionally, until the chicken is cooked and the vegetables are soft. Let cool before serving.

Store in an airtight container. Keeps for 5 to 6 days in the refrigerator.

ℓℓℓ

Chapter Two

My First Moose
and the Yankee Palazzo

Every day in the farmhouse, Brendan and I walked Dingo along the dirt road by the lake to the main road, four miles round trip. On a very busy day, six or seven cars might drive by in one hour, most of them locals but some of them strangers taking the shortcut to Maine. "We have to get this road taken off GPS," we griped, half-joking. "This is too much traffic."

And then, suddenly, one early summer day, there it was, headed down the dirt road, straight toward us—my first moose.

"Look at that tall, fat horse with spindly legs," I murmured to Brendan, not wanting to scare it away. "It looks like Don Quixote's spavined nag and Sancho Panza rolled into one."

"That's not a horse," he whispered back with a laugh.

I had lived in California, Arizona, France, Upstate New York, Oregon, Iowa, and New York City, and I'd traveled all over the world, but moose were in some ways more foreign to me than polar bears, penguins, or sloths—I'd seen the first two in zoos and the third in the

Costa Rican jungle, at least. Yes, I'd seen photographs of moose, but it took me a minute to recognize this as such. First of all, I was startled by its size. I hadn't realized they were so tall, so enormous, but in fact, they're the tallest mammals in North America. Males can weigh as much as 1,800 pounds, and their antlers can span as much as six feet.

This one was female, but she was still huge. Fortunately, I didn't know yet that moose, when startled or threatened, can be aggressive; she seemed peaceable enough. Also luckily, Dingo hadn't noticed her yet. He was behind us on the road, sniffing at a clump of weeds, as usual, oblivious to everything but the thousand and one smells his quivering black wet nostrils were inhaling and parsing out.

The moose looked back at us. We'd evidently interrupted her meditative constitutional. We stood quietly, very still, to show her that we weren't going to bother her any further.

She had a long, narrow face with a big upper lip like a camel's and a big dewlap under her chin, ears like a jackalope's, and a big, slightly bulbous nose. Her eyes were far apart, a liquid, reflective brown. There was a hump high up on her shoulder blades. Her fur was dark brown and looked almost fluffy. Her gentle, intelligent expression, rather than being supercilious like a camel's or adorable like a deer's, was mournful and introspective.

After a moment, this tragicomic, lovely, improbable creature lumbered off on her spindly legs down toward the lake and disappeared into the woods. I watched her go, feeling as if we'd been visited by an otherworldly being.

ella

As much as we loved our idyllic life in the White Mountains, we had to find a permanent place to live. The farmhouse wasn't ours. It belonged to Brendan's family, and on the occasions when they were living there, we felt acutely that we needed a place of our own.

In the spring of 2011, we began house-hunting in earnest. I'd moved out of the very cheap shared apartment in New York I'd been using for occasional brief visits back. At first, we thought of buying a tiny pied-à-terre in Brooklyn. Then, when I decided that I no longer wanted to live in the city and couldn't afford a decent apartment there anyway, we looked at a few houses an hour's drive up the Hudson River from the City. But the Hudson Valley is a dark place, even on the brightest days, and that close to the City, it's basically an extended suburb.

Finally, we realized we didn't want to leave New England. At first we fantasized about renovating the old barn by the farmhouse, but that proved to be too complicated in terms of Brendan's family. Then we looked at a few houses in small towns nearby, Sandwich and Tamworth, New Hampshire. But it seemed crazy to buy another house in the rural White Mountains when we already had one standing empty most of the year, and we didn't necessarily want to be buried in the deep countryside for the rest of our lives. We wanted to live in a town.

In retrospect, the perfect solution was there all along; we just had to tumble to it in our own slow way. But as time went by, as we traveled in and out of its easygoing little Jetport an hour and fifteen minutes away from the farmhouse, with lobster and moose on the WELCOME HOME signs, we slowly but definitively fell in love with Portland, Maine. We started coming into town more often, eating in the excellent restaurants, admiring the old brick buildings in the small downtown, the seagull-bustling wharves, the long gorgeous views over Casco Bay on the East End, the quiet tree-lined streets of the West End.

With zeal and zest and a clear sense of purpose for the first time since this whole process began, over the course of the summer and into the fall, we looked at a total of twelve houses on the peninsula, in Munjoy Hill, the West End, and neighborhoods in the middle of the city, near the Old Port.

The thirteenth house we looked at wasn't for sale; the downstairs apartment was for rent, but Brendan, who had found the listing, insisted that we go and see it anyway, on a hunch. When we first walked in, we were struck by its beauty and elegance, although it was worn and shabby.

"We can't afford this place," I said sadly, dazzled by the original plasterwork, the white fireplace mantels with decorative carving, the tall, graceful staircase with its newel-post light. "There's no way they'd sell it to us even if we could."

Thanks to Brendan's persistence, it turned out that the owners did want to sell, after all, and their asking price happened to be exactly the outer limit of what we could afford, thanks to the money my ex-husband had paid me to buy me out of our house in Brooklyn. And so it came to pass that, on an updraft of optimism and faith, in the fall of 2011, we bought a nineteenth-century brick house in the West End, just off Congress Street. It had been divided into two apartments early on. The downstairs apartment included the first floor and the front half of the second floor, and our inherited tenants lived in the other apartment, the back half of the second floor and the whole third floor.

We moved in to the downstairs apartment as soon as the deed was in our hands, having never spent a night in Portland before, knowing no one. It was a raw, blustery, rainy November evening. There we were, in our drafty, unfamiliar old house. We sat on the couch, which was the only furniture in the living room besides the double mattress, surrounded by all my boxes and stuff that had arrived that afternoon in a moving van from my two storage spaces in New York, looking around at all the work that needed to be done, asking ourselves, "What the hell are we doing in Portland, Maine?"

"I'm hungry," said Brendan. "What should we do for dinner?"

"I don't want to cook," I said. "Do you? None of our kitchen stuff is unpacked, we have no groceries, and I don't want to go out. It's too wet and cold out there."

We sat there for a moment.

"Wait a minute," I said. "Of course."

In the farmhouse, when I'd found myself homesick for cheap, good, fast ethnic food, I realized that, if I wanted pork dumplings, sesame noodles, or pizza, instead of dialing the local place and waiting twenty minutes, I had to make them myself. And so I did.

But now, I simply got out my laptop and googled local delivery places. A Vietnamese place called Saigon delivered, and on the menu was beef pho, to my joy.

I first fell in love with pho in 1989 at a place called Pho Bang on Mott Street. Pronounced *fuh*, it originated in Hanoi at least a hundred years ago, probably more. Pho was always a treat when I lived in New York, since I never lived near a place that served it, let alone delivered it. "Going out for pho" was a pilgrimage, a mission, a search for exciting comfort and nourishing satiation in a stressful, huge, chaotic city. Pho was something you had to go and get; it didn't come to you.

But now, evidently, I could summon a vat of it whenever I wanted, in exchange for ten bucks and a phone call.

Twenty minutes later, a paper bag arrived, containing two plastic containers of broth, piping hot and fragrant with spice and meatiness, accompanied by all the fixings. We squeezed in some lime juice and added cooked rice noodles, then thin slices of beef, which cooked instantly, then thin-sliced raw onions and other additions. We fell on it with chopsticks and spoons, too impatient to wait for it to cool. The broth was rich and beefy and very clear, full of the delicate flavors of roasted exotic spices. The basil, cilantro, and bean sprouts were fresh and crunchy. This was real pho, excellent pho, the pho of my dreams.

We ate it all, slurping the satiny noodles, splashing Saigon's house-made hot chili sauce on the thin, tender slices of beef. Brendan had a cold, and I felt like I was getting one. After we ate, we both felt cured, nourished, and so much better about this town and our future life here. The house suddenly felt warmer.

We slept well that night on our mattress in the living room, and the next day, energized and cheered, we dove straight into the long, slow process of restoring our half of the house.

We had already half-jokingly nicknamed it the "Yankee Palazzo," because, despite its shabbiness, the high ceilings with their original plaster medallions made us feel like New England lords and ladies. But the truth was, our house had a checkered history. It had been a Goodwill house for adults with Down syndrome as well as a school. In the past ten years alone, it had gone through several owners, and more than one of them was apparently (according to our next-door neighbor) completely batshit. Its colorful history was manifest in all the terrible things that had been done to it: ugly, cheap, disfiguring fixtures and hideous wall-to-wall carpets, institutional paint, and worst of all, a cold, dark kitchen.

My ex-husband and I had renovated our Brooklyn house mostly by ourselves; having done that once, I felt no need to do it again, and Brendan didn't try to talk me into it. And so, during that first winter, we stayed in the farmhouse much of the time while our house was being restored, as much as possible and as much as we could afford, to its former loveliness.

Once a week, we drove into Portland to meet with our contractors, Patrick, Jeff, and their Landmark Construction crew. We'd find them painting the new built-in bookshelves in the upstairs study or framing out the new shower in the little bathroom, and spend an hour going over the work still to be done: insulating the basement, painting the stairwell and foyer and rooms, putting a tile inlay into the foyer floor where the old cold-air exchange was, installing in our bedroom the vintage claw-foot bathtub that we found in the basement, a longtime dream of mine. Dingo sat at my feet and yipped at me every so often, demanding to be told what we were doing in this strange place.

Then I went over for a class at the nearby Springboard Pilates studio, which in those days was in the high-ceilinged, bay-windowed parlor-floor rooms of a lovely, solid nineteenth-century house. The mats and machines sat on old wood floors next to carved fireplaces with ceramic hearths. My Pilates instructor, Meredith, was impressively strong, curvy, and beautiful, and had the same dark, punchy sense of humor that our contractors had; clearly, it was a Maine thing. She was constantly reminding me to breathe into my ribs, button my buttons, stay long and focused. I tried, but then she picked a piece of lint off my sock or cracked a joke about slutty hips or demonstrated a move I couldn't quite do, fluidly and gracefully, but with comments so funny I couldn't follow her because I was laughing too hard. I was sure laughter somehow strengthened the core, and it was a trick of hers to get me in better shape. Pilates is extremely difficult and complicated, especially if you do it right, which I couldn't do yet, not even close, but my hour was always up before I was even aware of the time, and then it was time to buy groceries and go back to the farmhouse.

ele

The history of this city is one of constant erasure, change, and reinvention. Portland, Maine (Portland, Oregon, was named after it), covers almost seventy square miles, about a third of which is land and two-thirds, water. It sits on a hilly peninsula on Casco Bay on the Gulf of Maine and the Atlantic Ocean. The Abenaki, or Wabanaki, tribe, who lived all over New England before any Europeans arrived, called the peninsula Machigonne. In 1623, an English naval captain named Christopher Levett tried to found a village here on six thousand acres granted him by King Charles I, which he proposed calling York, after his hometown. He left a settlement here of ten men in a stone house he'd built (I can only imagine what their life was like), then he went back to England and wrote a book about his new town called York, hoping to drum up money and other settlers, but apparently no one in England wanted to invest in or move to Machigonne. The ten men left behind vanished into the fog of the historical unknown. There's a fort named after Levett here, but little else.

Then, in 1633, just a decade later, a fishing village was established on Casco Bay. This was the first permanent settlement of Europeans on the peninsula. The town was called Casco at first by the fishermen who lived there, but it was renamed Falmouth in 1658 by the Massachusetts Bay Colony, who took control of Casco Bay (as they were fond of doing, forcibly, to various regions of Maine through the decades and centuries).

In 1676, the Wabanaki destroyed Falmouth in a raid. The village was rebuilt in 1678, and then it was destroyed again in the Battle of Fort Loyal by a combined army of French and Wabanaki. The town wasn't resettled until after the 1713 Treaty of Falmouth, which established peace with the Wabanaki. But then the settlement was demolished and burned yet again, in the Revolutionary War, when the British Navy bombarded it for nine straight hours on October 18, 1775, leaving three-quarters of the town in ashes.

The surviving citizens were, understandably, hell-bent on independence. In scrappy Maine fashion, they rebuilt the town and established it as a shipping port, and so it came to pass that, in 1786, it was given the name of Portland, which finally stuck.

Then disaster struck again: Portland's fledgling shipping economy almost collapsed twice—first in the Embargo Act of 1807, which prohibited trade with England, and then in the three-year War of 1812, when the British blockaded the Atlantic Coast.

In 1820, after suffering and withstanding the sovereign entitlement and greedy land claims of both Massachusetts from the south and the English Crown by sea for two hundred years, as well as brutal attacks from the northern armies of Canadians and Native Americans, Maine finally became an official state. Portland was the capital for just twelve years, then it moved to Augusta, where it has remained.

The "Maine Law," otherwise known as Prohibition, was passed in 1851 in Maine, and shortly thereafter in eighteen other states. Portland became a hotbed of protest, especially among the immigrant Irish population of the city, who felt personally attacked by the law. The Rum Riot took place in 1855 against the mayor, Neal S. Dow, the "Napoleon of Temperance," whose historically landmarked house, with its plaque bearing Dow's name, is near Longfellow Square on Congress Street, right around the corner from our house and next door to a 7-Eleven.

Dow was rumored to have stockpiled a shipment of $1,600 worth of booze. He had, in fact, arranged for the shipment for pharmacists and doctors, since liquor was permitted under the law only for "medicinal and mechanical" purposes, but this fact wasn't widely reported. A mob of a few thousand protestors gathered; one man was killed by the militia in the ensuing violence, and seven others were injured. Dow was later prosecuted in court when his own alderman sued him for not having properly authorized the shipment. Dow was acquitted, but, largely because of the Rum Riot and the lawsuit, the Maine Law was repealed in 1856.

Meanwhile, Portland's economy had rebounded from the embargo and war. The Grand Trunk Railway was built in 1853, which made Portland the primary ice-free winter seaport for Canadian exports, which lasted until the hub moved north to Nova Scotia in 1923, and the invention of icebreakers. The town was booming.

Then came the Great Fire of 1866, which was ignited during Independence Day celebrations on the first Fourth of July after the Civil War. A firecracker or cigar ash ignited a building on Commercial Street and it spread to a lumberyard, then a sugarhouse, and then throughout the town. It finally burned out up on Munjoy Hill. Only two people were killed, but most of the commercial buildings, hundreds of houses, and half the churches of Portland were destroyed, 1,800 buildings in all, and 10,000 people were made homeless. Most of them took refuge in a tent city on Munjoy Hill on the East End, overlooking Casco Bay. (This area later turned into a working-class neighborhood that housed cannery workers; these days, as things always seem to go, it's the most hip, happening, desirable neighborhood in town.)

An old photograph of Portland taken just after the fire shows ashy rubble and drifting smoke. The poet Henry Wadsworth Longfellow, who was from Portland, wrote, "Desolation! Desolation! Desolation! It reminds me of Pompeii, that sepult city." But once again, the town was rebuilt, this time, luckily, with brick. The Cumberland and Oxford Canal was built in 1932 to allow commercial shipping inland to Sebago Lake and Long Lake. During the ensuing building boom, which lasted through the 1930s, mansions sprang up on the West End, designed in grand style by famous nineteenth-century architects, most notably John Calvin Stevens: Federal, Queen Anne, Victorian, Romanesque, Gothic. The West End is now a quiet, tree-lined neighborhood of meticulously preserved and renovated houses on wide, clean streets, many of which, ours included, have been split up into apartments and condos.

When the Maine Mall was built in South Portland in the 1970s, downtown Portland and the Old Port fell into decline and abandonment. Businesses closed; Congress Street was shuttered and vacant. But then, in yet another reversal of fortune, thanks to a combination of the city's architectural preservation laws and the Maine College of Art, which opened in the 1990s, the peninsula boomed again with restaurants and businesses and shops. And now, downtown Portland is alive and well, full of tourists, locals, and students.

The population of Portland proper is just over 65,000; the "greater Portland area" has about half a million people, which is more than a third of Maine's total population. (What a vast and empty state, stretching way up north to tuck into the sheltering wing, or armpit, maybe, of Canada.) Still, it feels very small. And yet, for such a small city, I'm amazed by its diversity and cultural life, the overall sophisticated excellence of its many restaurants, and by the pervasive feeling here of belonging to the greater world. Portland isn't a backwater, but it does have a marked sensibility, a collective tough-minded, resourceful fatalism appropriate to a city that's been, over the centuries, seized, bombarded, rebuilt, burned, rebuilt, economically sunk, deprived of booze, burned to the ground again, rebuilt, economically sunk again, and revived. The city motto is *Resurgam*, or "I Will Rise Again"; the city seal shows a phoenix rising, of course, from ashes.

ele

It's an hour and fifteen minutes' drive, door to door, from the farmhouse through Maine to our house in Portland. The drive is entirely on small country roads through woods and tiny towns and farmland, past lakes and rivers, down from the mountains to the coast. Almost the only businesses we pass are old, unique—the Mediocre Deli, Kate's Bait and Tackle, an old 1950s diner in a brightly painted saltbox house, Smiling Hill Farm (which has a sign advertising Ice Cream Lunch). Even the gas stations look homey and singular. There are almost no chains except Dunkin' Donuts, few fast-food franchises or signs of the present-day corporate ubiquity.

Driving into the city itself is a continuation of this cozy, time-warp landscape. When we first moved to Portland, it felt permanently 1987 here, in a good way. One discreet Starbucks tucked in the old brick downtown and the superstores hidden down on Marginal Way—Trader Joe's, Whole Foods—were almost the only indications of this new millennium. All the other coffee shops, bars, and restaurants, all the businesses, were what used to be known as mom-and-pop—run by the actual people who owned them.

The people likewise looked as if they'd been airlifted in a time ship from 1987. Almost everyone smoked. Skateboards and dread-locks and piercings abounded, and almost everyone under forty-five was heavily tattooed. Men wore plain denim jeans and plaid shirts, sweatshirts, jean jackets, leather jackets, and Nikes. Women wore leggings, denim skirts, vintage dresses with boots. In the bars, there was a sense of unforced, easy warmth; people here all seemed to know one another. When someone came in, he or she was greeted by one or more of the big, friendly groups gathered hugger-mugger around small tables.

It struck me right away as the kind of place that sneaks up on you. Or maybe it's a self-selecting town where the people who move here all seem to really want to be here; I've never heard any resident say a negative thing about Portland. It's all passionately understated joy with an undertone that says, "We get it." If you're not Portland's type, it lets you move on down the road without a twinge. If you are its type, it gets its hooks in you so gently, so gradually, you don't know it until you find yourself as happy here as everyone else.

But it took a while for me, used to big-city attitudes and rapid-fire competitive one-upmanship and in-your-face, nosy, hotheaded aggression, to understand the dark, wry, wacky sense of humor and the fierce but quiet work ethic of Mainers that is somehow never puritanical or self-righteous, as well as the lack of judgment, the mind-your-own-business attitude, and the fierce pride of place.

In 2011, the social posturing and intense, self-conscious attitudes of my old stomping ground, North Brooklyn, had not yet found their way this far north—not even close—and I hoped they never would, despite the fact that, as soon as we moved here, we were barraged by people telling us that "Portland is already over, it's too late, it's being ruined by hipsterization" . . . To which I could only say, you've never lived in North Brooklyn. But of course, places change. And Portland is catching on as a place people want to visit, and even move to. (The fact that I'm contributing to the trend has not escaped my notice.)

But so far, Portland is a haven from all that for me. In fact, having lived in both places, I have the strong impression and suspicion that hipster culture was borrowed from the north by early adopters who imported it to the urbanized south—from Alaska to Seattle, from Maine down to Brooklyn. That's the only explanation I can understand for all the current coastal-urban facial hair and plaid shirts and artisanal charcuterie and small-batch beer and hand-crafted jerky and flash-pickled ramps, fiddleheads, scapes . . . hipsters' yearning for authenticity and a return to the old ways is reflected in their imitation of the people who actually *do* wear those clothes and look like that, who actually do make these things, because they can't afford not to (plus, beards are warm). Mainers do it themselves because no one else is going to do it for them. They're not aware of being trendy; they're doing the best they can with what they have, according to the old ways.

Even on the sidewalks, watching people walk, I see how unstudied they are, how idiosyncratic, as if the furthest thing from their minds is how they might appear to anyone watching. A simple thing: Everyone walks naturally here, probably because they're all too busy thinking about what they're doing to worry about how they look.

ele

In New York, I had a handful of favorite bars, among which were a hipster bar, a hotel bar, a secret bar, a neighborhood hangout, and a faraway bar. Like most people I knew, I felt possessive, passionate about, and proud to know these places. I felt the same about my friends in New York, who were just as carefully selected and highly cherished. Instead of a group of them, I had individual close friends. I preferred to see them all alone, on "dates," so we could hunker down face-to-face and really talk. And so, drinking in bars was, for many years, a nighttime, one-on-one thing for me, in a favorite place with a favorite friend.

And now, once we'd moved to Portland, it still was, but only because Brendan was the only person I knew in town. During our first winter here, we spent a lot of time alone together in a place around the corner from us; it was big and airy but cozy, full of couches and comfortable tables, with an open kitchen in the back and a full menu. It was comforting to have other people around us, thronging the couches and tables, greeting one another, but we had yet to find a tribe of our own, or even a friend. Luckily, we loved each other's company, because that was all we had for months.

Finally, in early May, a Brooklyn novelist friend who was temporarily homeless came to live with us for a few weeks. She took stock of our sorry lack of a social life and intervened.

"You need friends," she said. "I'll introduce you to my writer friend Ron and his girlfriend, Lisa."

I've always been slightly leery of other writers, as well as friends of friends. I'm afraid they'll be competitive and/or standoffish, and that I won't like them as much as I should. But I couldn't afford to be leery of meeting anyone right now. In fact, I leapt at her offer like a hungry dog catching a thrown tidbit.

The next night, while Brendan was out of town, she and I met Ron and Lisa at the place around the corner. I liked them instantly. Ron was a novelist and Lisa worked in local politics; they both grew up in a small town north of Portland called Waterville. They were friendly, charming, low-key, smart, and (it must be said) extremely good-looking. The four of us chattered the night away.

Happy as I was to meet them, they were her friends, not mine. And then, after she went back to Brooklyn, Brendan and I spent most of the summer in the White Mountains, writing in his family's farmhouse, while contractors banged and sanded away in our Portland house.

So that might have been that. But in September, when we were back in town, we got an e-mail from Ron, inviting us to come and meet some of Portland's other writers at a bar called Sonny's. Improbably, this was to take place on a Wednesday at the astonishingly early hour of five p.m.

When I lived in New York, I rarely met anyone for a drink earlier than seven-thirty (except, of course, for brunch dates). Dinnertime was generally around ten p.m., so to me, five was arguably still lunchtime. Nonetheless, we accepted Ron's invitation with gladness in our hearts.

When Wednesday came around, I closed my laptop at four-thirty and walked downtown to Brendan's café and picked him up from "work." We walked together around the corner to Sonny's, which is housed in the former Portland Savings Bank, a high-ceilinged antebellum building on Exchange Street in the Old Port, tucked into a corner of Tommy's Pocket Park, a tiny European-feeling square where street musicians congregate on benches under the old trees.

It was still light out. Tree leaves rustled in an ocean-scented wind. Seagulls shrieked on updrafts above mansard roofs. The brick of downtown glowed in the sunlight. It felt far too early, too nice out, to duck into a dark bar.

Then, through the plate-glass window in front, we caught sight of Ron with some other people at a big table. He saw us, too, and waved. In we went, feeling half-shy.

We entered through red velvet curtains into a foyer that wouldn't have been out of place in a Victorian bordello, which I mean in a good way: brocade fainting couch, low-hanging fringed lamps. The bar had exposed brick, vaulted ceilings, tile floors, stained-glass windows. The booths and tables were clearly designed to blend in and look as if they'd been there forever. There was an old bank-vault door high over the bar.

That first Sonny's night, in addition to Ron, we were joined by two female novelists, two guys who ran the local indie bookstore, as well as an old friend of Ron's from Waterville. We sat around that table until after eighty-thirty. (We would come to appreciate that in Portland, this is late, just as we'd come to appreciate getting home by nine p.m. after a big night out on the town.)

Throughout the fall and following winter, Wednesday night at Sonny's turned into a semi-regular thing. More writers and their spouses were folded in. One night, so many of us showed up that we took over the long table in the back room.

Several years later, Sonny's nights have become a social regularity. We all generally have two or maybe even three drinks over the course of an evening, enough to relax us but not enough to send us off our rockers. We're a warm, convivial, cheery bunch. We laugh a lot and have much to discuss. And this is New England: We create zero psychodrama—no contentious spats or pissing contests, no factions, backbiting, or bitchiness. We talk shop, commiserate over hardships and setbacks and struggles, congratulate one another on books begun, finished, published, or good reviews, prizes won, and plum assignments.

And the thing about Sonny's itself, and our group of friends in Portland, is that we didn't choose them. They happened to us, just as we happened to them. But we couldn't have chosen a better bar or better people. Sometimes life is just lucky that way.

Our meetings have expanded to cocktail parties at our various houses, smaller dinner parties, individual friendships, and—gasp—occasional meetings at other bars in town. But Sonny's is still the writers' bar of Portland, Maine. And it's always a Sonny's night in my mind when we all get together, wherever we are.

ℓℓ

Buckwheat Blini with Crème Fraîche and Salmon Roe

Acadians in northern Maine and Canada have a long tradition of eating crepe-like buckwheat pancakes called ploye*. Every Thanksgiving and Valentine's Day, I make blini for breakfast. I use Acadian buckwheat flour fine-milled by Bouchard Family Farms in Acadia, all the salmon roe I can afford to buy from Browne's Trading Company on Commercial Street in Portland, and thick, buttery crème fraîche that comes in a little pink tub. I serve these crepes with mimosas made of cava and blood-orange juice. They are festive and delicious, filling but light, the perfect kickoff to a day of occasional eating, and a tip of the hat to Maine tradition.*

2/3 cup buckwheat flour
1/3 cup gluten-free baking flour
1/4 tsp baking soda
1 tsp sugar
1 tsp salt
1 1/2 cups buttermilk
2 egg yolks
2 egg whites, beaten till stiff

1 T melted butter

Combine the dry ingredients and mix well. Add the buttermilk and egg yolks and stir until it's a smooth batter. Fold in the egg whites, then stir in the melted butter.

Drop spoonfuls of batter into very hot butter in a skillet to make small, thick, round pancakes. As soon as you drop the dough in, turn the heat down to low and let the pancakes sit until they bubble on top, then turn and cook them till browned. Slather crème fraîche on top and garnish with plenty of salmon roe and chopped chives. Serve them 3 to a plate.

Serves 4, with a few blini left over for snacking on later with cheese.

ello

One day, on our way back to the farmhouse, we stopped in at the Portland Whole Foods for a week's worth of groceries. At the checkout, I said jokingly to the cashier, "Did you notice how healthy our food is?"

Instead of joining my self-mocking incredulousness at the heap of organic produce, the organic free-range eggs, the organic red rice and gluten-free organic pasta and organic steel-cut gluten-free oats, locally caught monkfish, free-range bison, organic free-range chicken thighs, and so forth, he said earnestly, "Oh my God, yes—doesn't it feel good to buy a bunch of food like this and go home and eat it?"

Caught off guard by his fervor, I laughed.

"Yes," I admitted, "it does."

The same cognitive dissonance I feel on those beautiful, pristine mornings in New Hampshire, when my thoughts turn to dire environmental crises, also intrudes naturally into every decision I make about food. Food is not a simple thing. Deciding what to eat carries implications that go far beyond our own mouths and stomachs. Grocery shopping has become possibly more powerful than voting. And I am resolutely, unquestioningly nonjudgmental in almost all things, except other people's shopping carts. I can't help it. When I see a conveyer belt heading for the cashier loaded with individual plastic-wrapped, high fructose corn syrup–laden, GMO-heavy, processed, corporate-stamped dreck, I blanch like a Victorian maiden aunt whose niece is running out of the house in rouge and a plunging neckline. "There goes the world," I gasp to myself with the hand-fluttering futility of the overly well-informed first-world consumer.

I'm not judging the people—just the terrible food, and the corporations that make it, and the political systems that give them so much power.

Even now, good, healthful food is scarce for many; money is tight; the environment is degraded and changing fast; sea levels are rising and the oceans are acidifying and warming and polluted with plastic and emptied of life by wide-scale dragnet fishing. Agribusiness pollutes the earth with pesticides and herbicides; Monsanto's genetically modified monocrops crowd out diversity and threaten organic farmers. Likely because of the widespread use of industrial-strength agricultural pesticides, bee colonies are dying out, which threatens food production, since much of the produce we eat depends on bees for pollination. It takes a hell of a lot of oil and gas to fuel the trucks and ships that transport great quantities of food vast distances, around the globe. And so on, and so on.

As catastrophe appears to loom ever closer, and in many ways feels as if it's already arrived, the question I keep coming back to time and again, the one I find myself wrestling with constantly, is: How should we eat in such a world? And *what* should we eat? For example, I try to buy so-called sustainable and non-threatened wild-caught fish—monkfish, mackerel, sardines, Alaskan salmon—but who knows if they're really okay, given the state of the oceans? It's terrible that something as simple as buying fresh fish has become so fraught, but there it is. Farmed salmon? Full of PCBs. Tuna, swordfish? Loaded with mercury, and endangered. Sea bass? Endangered. Haddock, hake, cod? Overfished. What the hell? Who knows if anything is okay anymore? And who knows how much longer our infrastructure can sustain such luxury and impracticality?

Michael Pollan writes in his introduction to *The Omnivore's Dilemma,* "'Eating is an agricultural act,' as Wendell Berry famously said. It is also an ecological act, and a political act, too. Though much has been done to obscure this simple fact, how and what we eat determines to a great extent the use we make of the world—and what is to become of it." I find myself shopping in Whole Foods with mixed feelings, both guiltily seduced by and indignantly aghast at the piles and mounds of perfect, beautiful fruits and vegetables that have come from around the world, out of season, trucked and flown in and wrapped in plastic. Avocados from California, red peppers from South America, fish from Alaska, lamb from New Zealand. This can't last, I've always thought; it's not possible. As it is, only the relatively wealthy can afford to buy even conventionally grown green peppers from Mexico at $3.89 a pound.

Aside from growing your own vegetables, one excellent solution, of course, is to get them from a local farm stand or farmers' market. But the best thing to do might be to buy directly from the farmers and fishermen. CSA (community-supported agriculture) shares are widely available all over Maine, thanks to the strong ties between farmers and their local communities. Black Kettle Farm, half an hour's drive outside Portland, delivers weekly boxes full of freshly picked seasonal produce to the city's Eastern Promenade from spring (asparagus) through fall (squash). And there are also similar shares in fishermen's weekly catches: Salt & Sea is one such seafood-share program, called a CSF (community-supported fishery), and all the seafood you get is local, freshly caught, and sustainable, "from the docks of Portland's working waterfront to you."

Maine has a bounty of food, right here; you just have to be willing to grow it or find it. No need to eat an overpriced pepper shipped all the way from Mexico if you're willing to wait until they're in season here. And "local and in season" is not a trendy urban catchphrase in Maine; it's the best and most sensible way to eat, even in this region with its famously long winters, since the arts of preserving and canning and freezing never died out, because many people have always depended on them to get through the winter without starving.

However, that day in Whole Foods, being new to this area, not having committed to a CSA share yet, we paid $264 for five sacks of food and wine, loaded it all into the Subaru, and drove the hour and fifteen minutes back to the White Mountains. That night, putting on a pot of Jacob's Cattle beans to soak for the next day's baked beans, I kept thinking about what the fresh-faced, wide-eyed young guy at Whole Foods had said. He really meant it, earnestly, without ironic hipster self-mockery or smug hippie self-righteousness: "Doesn't it feel good to eat this way?"

Yes, sweet, wholesome checkout man at the Whole Foods in Portland, Maine, it does, and I'm very, very grateful that I can.

℮℮

Wicked-Good Lamb Burgers

Because the local farm near the farmhouse had no lambs that year, we bought some ground lamb at Whole Foods, flown all the way from New Zealand. We also bought Canyon Bakehouse gluten-free hamburger buns, which are from Colorado and are the best I've ever found. Brendan picked a handful of mint from right outside the door; that, at least, was local.

To 1 lb. ground lamb, add:

1/2 large onion, minced
8 garlic cloves, minced
a small handful each of minced fresh mint and cilantro
1 T harissa spice mix
1 tsp each of salt and black pepper
1 T olive oil
a dash of Worcestershire sauce

Form 4 patties. Fry in oil over medium heat, about 7 minutes a side. Serve on toasted buns with a sauce made of the following ingredients, mixed well:

2 T mayo
4 T ketchup
a dollop each of apple cider vinegar and Worcestershire sauce
2 tsp harissa spice mix or Sriracha
a small handful of minced cilantro

Eat with oven-roasted red potato wedges and a French lentil salad with grated carrots on a bed of red-leaf lettuce. Serves 4.

ello

Chapter Three

A Tale of Two Kitchens

Right away, when we first moved to Portland, I noticed the large numbers of homeless and mentally ill and drug-addicted and hard-scrabble people on the streets. Walking Dingo through our new neighborhood, I saw a lot of strung-out-looking people talking to themselves with unselfconscious intensity as they took refundable bottles from recycling bins, as well as couples screeching at each other, enraged and incoherent, often many feet apart on the sidewalk. Every time we drove to buy groceries, passing by a series of homeless shelters on and near Preble Street, I'd look out the window of our warm car at the faces of the people standing there, huddled groups of down-and-out men and women, a few black but mostly white, hunched in wool pea coats and hats with earflaps, or watch caps and down jackets, rubbing hands together, kibitzing and standing around waiting for the soup kitchen to open and exhaling cigarette smoke as if it had warming properties.

I thought about my own good fortune, my unexpected happiness here in this small seaside city. I was in my secondhand but hardy Subaru, on my way to buy (reusable, cloth) bags full of groceries and wine at Whole Foods, that bastion of elitist consumption; meanwhile, I was eating well in the local restaurants. I had a job I loved, writing books and essays and reviews, teaching and giving readings and talks, which sustained this way of life, at least for now. And I was healthy, at least for now. I knew that I was very, very lucky to have this life of happiness and luxury and well-being and pleasure. I didn't take any of it for granted; I was constantly, deeply grateful for all of it, but that didn't feel like enough.

Maine has always been a place of poverty and hardship, and during the country's current economic downturn and recession, Portland has fared worse than a lot of the rest of the country. People who were already struggling tipped into a state of real emergency. Whole families became displaced and homeless. New immigrants, many of them parents with children, couldn't find jobs and found themselves on the streets and in the shelter system.

But, unlike New York City, whose relationship with its homeless is both historically and at present a complexly harsh one, involving cruelly draconian bureaucracy, bad conditions, and a catch-22 of contradictory, whimsical rules, Portland is unusually generous with its homeless population. In 1987, when a homeless encampment arose at City Hall in protest of a shelter's closing, Portland implemented a policy, which still holds, of not turning away anyone seeking shelter. It's worth noting, it seems to me, that around the time I moved to New York in 1989, then-mayor Rudy Giuliani became notorious for closing homeless camps, most notably the one in Tompkins Square Park in the East Village, and exporting countless numbers of homeless people elsewhere. No doubt a certain number of them ended up in Portland, Maine, because of its reputation for being homeless-friendly. In New England, people take care of their own, even when they have little themselves. It's a long, honorable tradition.

Recently, because of this policy and the recent economic hardships, Portland's shelters have been strained to their breaking point. In an article in the *Portland Press Herald*, published in October 2013, when the city's homeless population hit an all-time high of as many as five hundred people seeking shelter a night, Randy Billings wrote, "Only 272 beds, cots and sleeping mats are available each night in the six shelters run by the city and nonprofit groups. When the shelters are full, 75 additional mats are placed in the Preble Street Resource Center to handle the overflow. When that is full, an additional 17 mats are placed in the city's general assistance office. And when that is full, people in need must sit in chairs in the city's refugee services office." The city also rents motel rooms for the overflow, particularly families: "The number of families seeking emergency shelter in Portland increased 19 percent this year from a year ago, and a tight rental market is forcing people to stay longer and overflow the city's family shelter. Portland spent more than $61,174 on motel rooms for homeless families during the past year, more than triple what it spent in fiscal 2012."

For another article in November of 2013, Billings interviewed a Coast Guard veteran named Chris Wagner who had been living in a tent in the woods on the outskirts of the city for two years after he'd lost his apartment. He and his partner had just found an apartment downtown. As Wagner told Billings, "Portland is known as a place where the homeless can find services such as shelter and health care, as well as help restoring their independence. If you want to help yourself, you will get help."

And so, on one particularly cold day in winter, as we drove by the Preble Street shelter for the umpteenth time, I looked out the window at the orderly but desperate-looking crowd smoking outside and decided to volunteer in a soup kitchen. That night, I filled out the online application. When it was accepted, and I was assigned to

Thursday lunches at the women's shelter kitchen, I felt oddly thrilled, as if I'd been deemed worthy of service. I had few illusions about my reasons for doing this; I knew that volunteering would benefit me far more than it would any of the homeless women I served. Giving always feels better than receiving. Volunteering was a luxury I could afford, and I was the lucky one, not them.

ele

On my first day, Brendan dropped me off at Florence House, a women-only shelter down on Valley Street at the bottom of the Western Prom. I was fifteen minutes early. I went in at 10:15, nervous but glad to be there. I told the women at the front desk who I was and what I was there for. A staff member led me back through the dining room, which had floor-to-ceiling windows leading out to a big deck. We went into a clean, large kitchen with an enormous gas range, stainless-steel shelves and countertops, and a roll-down window by the service area. As I signed my name in the register in the little office, I heard Nick Drake on the CD player ("Three miles from sundown, Jeremy flies"), saw a Julia Child quote on a banner ("You don't have to cook fancy or complicated masterpieces—just good food from fresh ingredients"), and smelled something good cooking on the stove.

I was meant to be here. I was suddenly in tears.

I wiped them away and introduced myself to Monica, the kitchen supervisor. She was only twenty-six, fresh-faced, with an ebullient, easygoing, laughing nature I would come to love and admire. She had been a chef at one of the most popular restaurants in town. When she realized that she wanted to make a difference in the world rather than pursue a career as a chef, she applied for the job running the Florence House kitchen, and got it. She was from an old Maine family, but her parents were peripatetic; she and her brother had grown up all over the country before her family returned to Maine.

She was also an amazing cook; I was almost twice her age, but during the year or so I worked my Thursday lunch shift at the Florence House, I learned a lot from her about both cooking and life.

She put me to work right away. I assembled about sixty cheese sandwiches and toasted them in butter on the grill and set the container into the steam table, loosely covered, to await lunch service. Then I peeled and diced a box of carrots and stored them in the refrigerator in a "fish tub." I learned that local supermarkets had donated almost all the ingredients in the kitchen—Hannaford, Trader Joe's, and Whole Foods. Much of the produce was organic, and it all looked fresh.

From twelve to one p.m., I stood by the steam table and served two kinds of soup, both made from scratch (broccoli cheddar and tomato basil), along with the sandwiches I'd made, while Kim, my fellow new volunteer, served the salad she'd made, and Monica started the prep work for that night's dinner.

Kim and I talked while we served. I learned that she was a Jersey girl, a former heroin addict and rock guitarist. She'd moved to Portland after rehab to live in a halfway house with several other female recovering addicts and start a new life, far from her old druggie friends and copping places. She seemed raw and vulnerable, not quite sure what to make of this northern seaside town where she found herself alone and sober. She was funny and quick-witted and warm, and I rooted for her to succeed here. I never found out what happened to her; after that shift, she had a job interview. She must have gotten the job, because I never saw her again. She was the first of several recovering addicts I worked with at Florence House. Volunteering was clearly curative for us all. My suspicion that it did us more good than them was confirmed over and over.

During that first lunch, Monica told us that the other volunteer on that day's shift, Diane, had just been given the Volunteer of the Year award; it was not hard to guess why she'd been awarded the honor. Diane spent the entire shift washing dishes in the corner. Every time I needed more, there she was, restocking soup bowls and sandwich plates by my elbow. She did this with immense cheer, unobtrusively.

I stood in my apron and dished up lunch for all the women who came shuffling up to the service window. Some of them didn't make eye contact. Many of them looked as if they had been through terrible things, formidable struggles. A few of them had black eyes, bruised mouths. Several were obviously strung-out or tweaking. Some limped badly, sat in wheelchairs, used canes. Others hunched in their coats, huddled into themselves, almost catatonic.

Even so, they knew what they wanted in their lunch, and they were not shy about demanding it. One of them said, "Not that sandwich; give me one that's not so burned." (None of the sandwiches, it must be said in my own defense, was burned, but possibly some were a bit more well-done than others.) Several of them asked for seconds, even thirds. They all loved the broccoli cheddar soup.

At the end of lunch service, Monica went out and made the rounds, sitting at each table, talking and laughing and lending a sympathetic ear. They all clearly loved her.

The Preble Street shelter system, I learned from Monica, had a strong ethic of service, or "mission," as they called it, that wasn't religious or didactic but was humble, without ego or judgment. One of the rules of the place that I agreed to observe when I volunteered was not to reveal identifying details about anyone there. This is not a writer's favorite promise to make, especially because the singular details and specificity of people are a novelist's bread and butter. Even so, I could see the usefulness of protecting the anonymity of women in a shelter. But as I stood there dishing up their lunches, I was dying to know all their stories, their histories. I would be lying if I pretended otherwise. But they didn't owe me that, or anything.

ele

Every week during the time I volunteered at the soup kitchen, Brendan and I were working (which is to say, writing) ourselves into puddles of melted butter to be able to pay for the renovations on our house. The upstairs two bedrooms and bathroom and the downstairs foyer had been restored to a stripped-down elegance; the old claw-foot tub we'd found in the basement was installed in a corner of our bedroom; the original pine-plank upstairs floors had been uncovered under many layers of linoleum, carpet, and tar paper, and had been refinished; and all the walls were freshly painted in warm colors and off-whites instead of the awful institutional pale blue we'd inherited. Now, in the second phase of the Yankee Palazzo renovation, our entire kitchen and dining room had been gut-demolished down to the joists and beams and brick.

When we bought the house, the kitchen was all pink granite counters and white melamine cabinets, white appliances and a horrible Brazilian cherry floor, and the walls were painted the same cold sky blue as the rest of the house. The huge side window was Sheetrocked over, so the room was dark. We hated that kitchen, hated cooking and eating in it, and it seemed to us that the house chafed and protested against this bullshit with every joist and beam; we could almost hear it.

To help offset the cost of the new kitchen, we sold the old, clinical melamine cabinets, the cold-as-tombstones granite countertops, and less-than-stellar appliances on craigslist; people came and carted them away and gave us a lot of money for them, which struck us as an amazing deal.

In their place, we envisioned old wood everywhere, a copper bar top, butcher-block countertops, and a Mexican tile backsplash. While Patrick's guys banged away in there for weeks, taking down the old posts from the wall that separated the dining room from the kitchen, we drove around southern Maine and scoured the Internet, hunting for materials. It was a great adventure from start to finish. Brendan found a hardworking, straight-talking guy up in Poland Spring who took barely used appliances out of rich people's summer houses in Cape Elizabeth or Bar Harbor when they traded up for new ones, and resold them on consignment out of his barn for a fraction of what they would have cost new. One thrilling day, he delivered our butter-yellow Viking stove with gas burners and electric oven, plus a Bosch dishwasher whose didactic beeping mechanism he'd dismantled for us, and a beautiful stainless-steel Viking fridge with a bottom freezer drawer and luxury of luxuries, an ice maker (I'd never had one before).

Most of the materials we used were old—"repurposed," as they call it. Brendan found the 1880s tin ceiling tiles for sale online in Ohio and had them shipped here; we bought the wide, weathered first-growth pumpkin-pine floorboards that graced an old 1770s barn wall from an old-wood purveyor in South Portland; and the stacks of hundred-year-old maple boards, which were used to build the kitchen cabinets, the base of the bar, the refrigerator encasement, and the wainscoting in the dining room, had served as the flooring in an old mill in Biddeford. All these materials were full of history, rich with age. It was exciting to see them installed in our old house instead of the soulless new crap that had been there when we'd bought the place. We felt as if we were restoring the house's beauty and character.

The contractors never once quailed at these materials, never complained about the unorthodoxy of using them. In fact, we felt, and they evidently did too, as if we were all collaborating on an interesting project. They seemed to approve of our choices, our vision for the house, because we were restoring it, using as much old material as possible, rather than trying to make it into something it hadn't been intended to be. Also, we were obviously not rich brats dripping with money; we made a point of waiting for each subsequent step in the renovation until we'd earned and saved enough so we wouldn't fall behind in our payments. We tried to make decisions knowledgeably and decisively and change our minds as little as possible. And we respected the fact that nothing can happen overnight; we trusted them to work at their own pace.

If we upheld our end of the deal, they exceeded theirs. They were fun to talk to, merry and funny and darkly wry, in that (by now familiar) Maine way. They embraced every challenge: they scraped and sanded and then painted the ornate old squares of ceiling tin they'd had to carefully jigger into place and cut to accommodate the overhead recessed lights; they planed and sanded and endlessly polyurethaned the rough, weather-beaten dimensional countertop planks into smooth, richly golden expanses. They weren't put off by the patinaed old copper from the 1906 bathtub Brendan bought from a guy north of Waterville. After scratching their heads and discussing the matter for a while, they flattened it overnight under heavy weights, then they cut it into separate sheets and siliconed them to the bar-top plywood with sandbags and clamps. They carefully cut out the old drain and made a beautiful medallion in the middle of the countertop and jointed the separate pieces neatly with copper nails.

By the beginning of summer, after months of hard, painstaking work for our contractors, our new kitchen was finally finished. Everyone had been remarkably patient and coolheaded throughout, maybe because we all knew we were creating something beautiful, and that doesn't happen overnight. On the very last day, the contractors grouted the Mexican tile backsplash, replaced the glass in the door to the mudroom, shaped the copper edges around the bar top and affixed them, and then they were done.

After they'd swept the wide-board pumpkin-pine floor and packed up their tools and driven away, we wandered around the big, airy, dazzling room, slightly befuddled, dazed with the joy of having our kitchen and dining room, which had been so coldly ugly before, be so warmly beautiful now, all one big room instead of divided, with two more windows and the brick chimney exposed, the walls freshly painted a warm neutral buttery yellow, everything gleaming and rich with history, every detail exactly what we'd wanted. The finished kitchen looked eccentrically, cozily resplendent, at least to us. There was wavy semi-opaque glass in the upper cabinet doors. The stained-glass window we'd designed and had built at a glass place on Forest Avenue was installed in the enormous side window the contractors had uncovered when they gutted the room. They'd also punched a fourth window through the newly exposed brick chimney, so the room was flooded with natural light. The (new) porcelain sink had been set into the countertop and hooked up. The tall wooden door with beveled glass and carved details that used to hang in the front entryway was now a swinging door between the kitchen and the foyer.

The kitchen felt as if it had been in the house forever; our aim all along had been to have people walk in and assume that, feel it instinctively, and say, "How lucky that you didn't have to renovate when you moved in!" Our house was old and tall and beautiful, and it wanted to feel comfortable and attractive in its outfit; it also wanted an outfit befitting its dignified age, its 1850s vintage. Ridiculous as it sounds, I couldn't help thinking that the house was rejoicing in its new duds, even preening a little, and I didn't blame it.

As for me, I was awash in a contented happiness so powerful it almost made me melancholy. After more than four fun, passionate, adventurous years together, Brendan and I had found our home and had made it our own, together, and now we had the amazing good luck to live here. The feeling was so unfamiliar, I had to think about it to parse out what it was. After a moment, I realized it was the utter rightness of where I was and the person I was with. I had never experienced this before in my life. My marriage, though good, had been fraught; the house my ex-husband and I had renovated together, doing all the work ourselves and fighting all the while, had always felt like it was his, not mine, because he had controlled the decisions. Now, I felt nothing but rootedness and contentment. Brendan and I had never once argued during the buying and renovating of this house; we hadn't lost our patience or good humor or mutual excitement about the whole process. It had been a joyful, fun experience, like everything we did together—exploring Maine, discovering Portland's restaurants, walking Dingo on the Eastern Prom, sitting and writing at the same table in perfect harmony, driving back and forth from the farmhouse, talking and singing and laughing, and, most of all, cooking together.

ﻬ

For me, the kitchen is the most important room in a house. I'm always happy at a stove, stirring something; there's no room for angst or self-doubt in a pot of chicken soup. When I'm anxious about something or stuck with my writing, chopping onions, carrots, and celery and sautéing them in a skillet is calming, centering. I love the feel of ingredients in my hands. I love to improvise, to invent and play and have fun. And I love feeding people.

But, until recent years, cooking was a solitary activity for me. Like writing, it's something I've immersed myself in alone. Being "in the pocket" at the computer or stove was my refuge, the introvert's escape.

My ex-husband and I used to joke that when one of us cooked, the other had to leave the kitchen. We could not cook together without a power struggle. (We were both firstborns, which might have been the problem right there.) For decades, my mother and sisters have lived thousands of miles away, so we've never had much opportunity to cook together, as a family. And I've only rarely ever cooked with my female friends, even though many of them are amazing cooks. We cook for one another, as an act of generosity and love, rather than collaborating on dishes.

I assumed from the start that Brendan and I wouldn't be able to cook together. Besides our twenty-year age difference, I was born on the West Coast, he on the East Coast. His family is old-world, traditional, proper; mine is bohemian, happy-go-lucky, eccentric. And our cooking styles were extremely different and seemingly incompatible. Both of his parents grew up in Italy, and he learned to cook from his father, who taught him a number of Tuscan and Roman dishes, like pork tenderloin with rosemary-prune sauce, peperonata, orecchiette with broccoflower and garlic, and pasta with tomato and pea sauce (my favorite, and the most soul-nourishing dish I've ever had, the chicken soup of pasta). And I, true to my own background, have always tended to either throw dishes together based on what's in the fridge and cupboard, or create something from an amalgam of six or seven different recipes after doing quick, hit-and-miss research.

So at first, we cooked for each other, winning each other's hearts through our stomachs. I loved watching him small-dice a soffritto, or tuck sprigs of rosemary and cloves of garlic into a leg of lamb, or roll the mezzaluna, an Italian two-handled, curved chopping blade, over a pile of steamed broccoli rabe before sautéing it in garlic. Brendan, likewise, was entertained and fascinated by my ability to figure out how to make something I'd never made before. He cheered me on as I made Vietnamese pho from scratch, applauded from the sidelines as I fried up crisp, light, gluten-free buttermilk-buckwheat blini, a recipe I'd devised myself, for Valentine's Day breakfast. He was gracious about my failures and excited to eat my successes.

But we were so inseparable, we were always in the kitchen together.

"I'll chop the onions," I said one night, stepping up to the cutting board with my glass of wine.

"I'll stir that for you," he said the next night, easing himself in at the stove while I chopped vegetables.

Soon we were waltzing around each other with oven mitts and knives and wooden spoons.

Then we collaborated on pork dumplings with scallion ginger sauce. I made the dough; he rolled it out. I made the pork mixture; he wrapped it. I steamed the dumplings; he fried them. I made the scallion-ginger sauce; he stir-fried shiitake mushrooms and baby bok choy to go alongside. This was the beginning of a beautiful kitchen romance. Since then, he's made me more aware of the value of traditional recipes; I've begun consulting and using them with increased respect for the cooks who've gone before me. And he's become more relaxed and inventive, learning to throw together a "cupboard supper," a concept he learned from me.

All my life, I felt lonely and alone, even in my family, even when I was married, even in the kitchen. I no longer do. Our harmony in the kitchen is a metaphor for the way we are together. We rarely fight; but it's not boring, it's soothing. We bolster each other and share a sense of purpose. We're both writers and inherently solitary people, but instead of going off to our respective corners of the house, we're able to sit at the same table and write side by side. We pass our work back and forth for edits, ideas, and feedback.

The whole issue of our vast and unconventional age difference was a little harder to solve, no matter how natural it seemed to us that we were together, how easy and inevitable our connection felt right from the start. At the beginning, in the first months or year, we were both a little self-conscious about being around other people in public. Would they treat us weirdly, look askance, make unflattering assumptions about us? In fact, they did, but interestingly, it was only people who knew us who did that—a few acquaintances, friends, and family members. Amazingly, in all these years, we have never encountered any awkwardness or judgment from strangers. Everywhere we go, when we meet people, they instantly seem to understand that we're together, and they don't seem to think anything is amiss about it. It's not that I don't look older than Brendan; of course I do. But no one ever mistakes me for his mother, or any relative at all. From this, I surmise that the way we are together is more telling of our connection than what we look like superficially, which I find both comforting and interesting.

Over the years, as we've grown closer and more rooted with each other, we've become out-and-out accomplices and collaborators in the kitchen. One summer day on the Eastern Prom, the amphibious tourist vehicle called the Downeast Duck trundled by at the top of the hill. A little while later, as we came along the trail above the bay, we saw it floating out in the water.

"I want to make a dish called Downeast Duck," said Brendan suddenly, after we'd been walking for a while in silence.

I am always up for a speculative discussion of a hypothetical future meal.

"What would you serve with it? What cuisine?" I said. "Chinese? With rice noodles? Ginger-cilantro broth? Hot and sour or barbecue sauce?"

"Downeast," he said. "So it would be Maine duck."

And that was that, because he is the native of this region, and therefore the authority on all things local.

We batted this idea around, trying as hard as we could to include some lobster in our vision: duck confit with lobster terrine? Too fancy and labor-intensive. Roast duck wings with lobster claws? Funny in theory but awkward on the plate. Duck and lobster jambalaya, risotto, or paella? Too much starch all around. We eventually jettisoned the lobster, or rather, saved it for another meal, and settled on the following simple feast: duck breasts, pan-fried until they rendered much of their fat, then a heap of cut-up potatoes, Yukon Golds probably, pan-roasted in the duck fat. The sliced crisp breasts would go on top of a mound of julienned zucchini tenderly poached in chicken broth and butter. And alongside, a simple salad of chopped blanched sugar snap peas in a dressing of champagne vinegar, hazelnut oil, and thyme.

Later, on the way home, the Downeast Duck drove by us yet again. We waved at the tourists, and they waved back.

That night, we made exactly the dish we'd envisioned on our walk: two big, juicy duck breasts pan-fried until the fat rendered; four medium Yukon Gold potatoes steamed, then cubed, then crisped and browned in the duck fat; three small julienned zucchini poached in butter and chicken broth; and snap pea salad with thyme vinaigrette.

I made a fruity Maine-ish glaze for the duck: rhubarb, blueberries, maple syrup, cognac, thyme, ginger, and red wine, boiled well and pureed in the blender . . .

We toasted the tourist bus as we ate, glad that we weren't tourists, glad that we lived here.

ele

The day after the renovation was finally finished, we unpacked the boxes of cooking utensils and pots and bowls, baking pans and cookie sheets and wooden spoons, glasses, cups, plates, and the bags of staples, rice and lentils and pasta. We slotted the spices into the indented maple ledge built into the back of the island, emptied the corner of the living room where all the kitchen stuff had been stored since February, moved the table and chairs back into the dining room, rearranged the couch and armchairs around the fireplace in the living room, vacuumed and mopped and dusted and hung pictures.

Our friend Rosie was coming from Brooklyn to visit us that weekend. This would be our first meal for a guest in the new kitchen. What should we cook, we wondered?

Rosie is a formidably accomplished, knowledgeable cook, a famous bartender and inventor of cocktails, but despite that, she's never intimidating to cook for or to mix drinks for, because she is impeccably philosophical. She wants to be pleased; she wants to enjoy our hospitality. A couple of years before, I had forgotten to trim the strings off some sugar snap peas I had sautéed with green beans to go alongside Brendan's roast, and my potatoes dauphinoise was too dry because I hadn't used enough cream. We ate our meal, picking peapod strings out of our teeth, putting away plenty of dauphinoise despite its flaws.

Mid-meal, I broke down and apologized.

Rosie shot back, "Julia Child said, 'Never apologize, never explain.' I never do. You shouldn't either."

And that was that.

Therefore, I knew that whatever we made, Rosie would not complain; she would eat enthusiastically and without criticism. But even so, I wasn't going to try anything new or complicated. I felt superstitious. It had to be good.

My mind kept drifting to a favorite standby, which is foolproof, easy, fast, no-fuss, comforting, and delicious: haddock fillets cut into bite-size pieces and marinated in lemon juice and harissa spices, then added to a skillet in which chopped chorizo and leeks have been sautéed in olive oil and white wine. The fish is poached till it's tender and cooked through; then this smoky, spicy stew is served over red rice cooked in chicken broth, with garlicky steamed red chard alongside.

I was already drooling at the thought of digging into a red-hued plateful that night; we'd light candles, open the windows, dim the chandelier.

And so it came to pass:

"This is Harissa Haddock, BBC News," I said in a fake British accent as I poured wine.

"Wait," Rosie shot back, "I thought Harissa Haddock was the tragic, much preyed-upon, oft-violated young heroine of an extremely long eighteenth-century novel?"

"That was Moll Flounders," said Brendan. We all laughed, and then we ate.

ℓℓℯ

Harissa Haddock

3 T olive oil
1 lb. fresh haddock (two good-size fillets)
2 T harissa dry spice mix
juice of 1 lemon
1/2 cup white wine, or more if desired
2 large leeks, cleaned well and chopped
2 fresh pork chorizo sausages

1 cup red rice
1 3/4 cups chicken broth
1 T butter

2 lbs. red chard, well-rinsed and chopped
8 garlic cloves
1 cup chicken broth

1 T olive oil
salt to taste

Cut 1 lb. of haddock fillets into bite-size chunks and put them in a
bowl with the juice of 1 lemon and harissa spices. Stir well and
leave on the counter to marinate.

According to the directions on the bag, simmer a cup of well-
rinsed red rice (I rinse it in a mesh strainer under the faucet for a
minute or two) in 1 3/4 cups chicken broth with 1 T butter.

Slit the chorizo sausages down the middle and remove the casings
so you're left with just the innards. Discard the casings or feed
them to the dog sitting avidly at your knee. In a big cast-iron skillet, heat the olive oil, then add the chopped leeks and chorizo sausage innards. Stir well, chopping the chorizo with the edge of the
spatula or wooden spoon to break it up. Add the white wine.
Sauté for about 10 minutes, till the leeks are soft and the sausage
is cooked through.

Add the harissa haddock with all the lemon juice to the leeks and
chorizo. Cover the pan and gently poach for 7 to 10 minutes. Stir
well.

Meanwhile, chop 8 cloves of garlic and add to 1 cup chicken broth
and 1 T olive oil in a huge pot. Steam the chard, covered, for
about 5 minutes, or until limp. Stir well, salt to taste.

Serve the haddock on top of the rice with the chard alongside.
Serves 4.

ℓℓℓ

The next Thursday at the soup kitchen, Monica asked me to make
an applesauce to go alongside some pork chops for a later dinner. I

filled a small plastic crate with a variety of red and green apples from the big fridge in the pantry, washed them in the small sink, took off the little stickers, then set up a big cutting board with a wet cloth underneath to keep it from slipping. All through my shift, whenever I had a spare several minutes, I stood at my little workstation, happily and steadily reducing that big box of apples to a smallish dice. I prefer to leave the peels on for texture; that's how my mother always made applesauce. Cutting them small makes the applesauce smooth and palatable. I also like dicing; I'll take any excuse to do it.

By the time my shift was almost over, I had filled a deep steam-table pan. I added a big handful of brown sugar, three bay leaves, some minced fresh rosemary from the plant in Monica's office, a good pouring of cinnamon, and another of salt. After I mixed it all together, I poured two cups of water over the pan, covered it in parchment paper and then foil, and stuck it into a moderately hot oven to bake for the next hour or two.

I left not knowing how it turned out; it didn't matter. I was so soothed and refreshed by chopping all those apples over the past couple of hours, I came home energized, smiling, almost euphoric.

The next week, I walked into the soup kitchen to find that I was the only volunteer that day for lunch, and Monica was on vacation. Her substitute, Jordan, ran the teen center. He had two premade chowders heating in the oven when I arrived—one corn, the other, fish.

"How do you feel about making biscuits?" he asked when I came in.

"I feel fine about making biscuits," I said, with private misgivings, which I kept to myself. I've known I was gluten-intolerant since I did an elimination diet in 2002 to determine why I felt so terrible all the time: depressed, bloated, foggy-brained, crabby. Since then, I've been rigorously gluten-free and no longer depressed or bloated. It's been worth it. But the machismo of the professional kitchen, even a merciful, charitable soup kitchen, does not allow for fear of wheat.

You have to cook what needs cooking. I resolved to keep my mouth closed while I made them, try not to breathe the flour dust, scrub my hands and sponge off my clothing afterwards, and hope for the best.

Jordan handed me a handwritten recipe he'd copied off the Internet for a large-enough quantity of biscuits for the day's lunch: 8 cups flour, 1/4 cup baking powder, 2 cups oil, 4 cups milk, but only 1 teaspoon salt. He went back into the office, where he was working on the teen center's weekly menu.

The oven was already hot, so I got out a big bowl and measured the flour from the huge sack in the pantry and carried the bowl quickly back out to the kitchen, leaving behind the inevitable puffs of flour dust in the air, trying not to breathe any of it. I rolled up my sleeves and averted my face as I stirred in the baking powder and a good shaking of salt, a lot more than the recipe called for, because one teaspoon of salt was not nearly enough for all that flour.

I considered the two cups of oil. If I used oil, I could stir the batter with a spoon and drop the biscuits onto the cookie sheet with a smaller spoon. I wouldn't have to touch the dough. I could get it done and into the oven quickly, and be safe from flour contamination.

But they wouldn't be biscuits. They might taste all right, but biscuits involve creating an alchemy of starch and fat that you can only get by rubbing them together by hand until they're blended.

The soup kitchen had no butter, only margarine. I took out a two-cup block, unwrapped it, and cut it into the flour mixture. Then, using my bare, clean hands, I rubbed and rubbed it into the flour. It took a while. Toxic, dangerous flour covered my arms up to my elbows, hung in puffs in the air in front of my face. I didn't stop until the magical alchemy happened and I had grainy, fatty, yellowed flour, ready for the milk.

I made an indentation in the flour, splashed in some milk, worked it into a paste, added more milk. I didn't measure the liquid—another secret of real biscuits. The flour will tell you how much it wants. When I had a ball of clean, firm dough, not too sticky, not too dry, I got out a big board and set it by the bowl. I filled the measuring cup with more flour, not even bothering to be prissy about it anymore; I was too intent on my project to care by now.

I floured the board and turned the dough ball out onto it.

"Jordan," I called, "is there a rolling pin in this kitchen?"

He emerged from the office. "You can just drop it onto the sheet with a spoon," he said. "They come out fine."

"I have to make them my grandmother's way," I said with a self-mocking laugh.

Did my grandmother even make biscuits? I have no idea. I was referring to some mythical grandmother, an old-fashioned Midwestern farm wife who got up at dawn to feed her hardworking family breakfast with real American biscuits.

I patted and pushed the dough with the flats of my palms until I had an inch-thick layer, which worked fine in the absence of a rolling pin. Then I took a drinking glass and cut out the biscuits one by one. I took the leftover scraps, patted them into another layer, and cut them out. I did a third round, and then they were done.

I arranged them on the sled-sized cookie sheet and baked them. They came out puffy, golden, moist, and light. I wished I could eat one; I was sure they were delicious.

Later, during lunch service, a tall, elegant black woman with a strong Southern accent approached the window.

"I'll take another biscuit," she said. "Girl, you made these?"

We smiled at each other.

"Yeah," I said.

"These are real biscuits!" she said. "Like my grandmother used to make. I haven't tasted these since she was alive!"

I gave her two more, and afterwards, I was hardly able to contain my elation as I climbed the hill up the Prom toward home.

That night, at home in my own new kitchen, inspired by the idea of cooking with soul, I roasted a chicken. I stuck a cut-up lemon and a handful of pitted olives into its cavity, squeezed lemon juice over its peppered skin, and put two big pats of butter on top. I surrounded it with whole peeled shallots and halved peeled carrots and parsnips set into a coating of olive oil, covered the pan with foil, roasted it at 500 degrees for twenty minutes, then uncovered it and turned the oven down to 350.

I made a broth with the pile of parsnip and carrot peelings and tops, the shallot peels and ends, the gizzards from inside the chicken, pepper, and salt, simmering it until it was sweet and earthy. I strained the broth and whisked polenta into it and let it cook until it thickened, then stirred in a lot of minced fresh basil and Parmesan cheese.

When the chicken was moist inside and crackling outside, and the root vegetables were soft and had begun to caramelize in the chicken fat, and the polenta was cheesy and savory and redolent of basil, Brendan and I ate.

Afterwards, I poured the chicken fat that was left in the pan into a coffee cup and put it in the fridge. The next night, I fried wedges of red cabbage in it until they were soft and browned and velvety, just like my mythical grandmother would have done.

ele

One of the last Thursday mornings I worked at Florence House, I walked into the kitchen to find Monica almost in tears, in a state of awe. There were ten or eleven boxes on the floor by the steam table full of the most beautiful produce I'd ever seen—lettuce, radishes, kale, chard, spring onions, garlic, broccoli, cauliflower, garlic scapes—glistening and alive and gorgeous and colorful. Florence House had just been awarded a grant worth $100 a week, which paid for a full membership in a farm-collective share. The collective is local, in Portland and right outside the city. And they train immigrant women to farm.

For several minutes, Monica and my fellow volunteer, Alison, and I stood there beaming at each other and at the vegetables before we got down to work. First, we had to use up all the vegetables that were already there to make room for this incredible new stuff. I augmented a steam-table pan of leftover fried rice with a medley of sautéed chopped carrots, onions, celery, and peppers, stuck it into the oven to heat, then made two big stir-fries, one vegetarian, one with many pounds of donated Whole Foods organic chicken.

When it was noon and time for lunch, Alison held down the serving while I did dishes and prepped radish greens. (For some reason, maybe because I'd never thought about it, I hadn't known that radish greens were edible. I tasted some as I worked. They're mildly peppery, a little like arugula.)

Meanwhile, Monica was breaking down the shipment of farm-collective vegetables. Then, using a fish tub full of vegetable scraps, she made a stock for a spring onion and potato soup. It always struck me, cooking with her, that she seemed never to waste anything: not food, not energy, not words. With Yankee (as I was coming to identify it) thrift and know-how, she used every scrap of donated goods and leftovers, moved around the kitchen purposefully and economically, and spoke thoughtfully, concisely. I found her quality of direction so easy to be around; I trusted her on an animal level.

I felt this way a lot with people I was meeting here—our contractors and neighbors, waiters and checkout people, the native Maine writers we'd become friends with. Whether it was cooking, writing, or building houses, there was a common thread of self-taught, organic integrity, a refreshing lack of didactic cant and cerebral showiness, a seat-of-the-pants ability to do what needed doing in the most direct, practical, commonsensical way that wasted the least amount of resources, whether it was installing ceiling tiles, making vegetable stock, or writing a sentence.

Since moving here, I'd found something else, something I'd always lacked: a strong sense of community, from which everything else flowed. It felt good to be in this kitchen with Monica and the other volunteers, to feed these homeless women nourishing, well-cooked food, and to work physically hard. I spent my days in a chair at a desk. At the end of a three-hour shift of nonstop dishwashing, pot-scrubbing, chopping, serving, and cleaning, I felt tired and relaxed, as if my brain had had a real break. Volunteering is profoundly and essentially different from working for pay.

I looked into the faces of the women as they took their plates of food, or as they returned their used plates to the dish window. I didn't know exactly what it was I was receiving from them. They always thanked me. I always thanked them back.

One of them, a tall, thin, quiet blonde woman I guessed was maybe a few years older than I was, stood near me as I wiped the tables after lunch.

"I'm moving today," she said, unable to contain her excitement. "I got an apartment. I've been homeless for seven months. I'm getting my own place. The landlord's an angel; she didn't ask for a deposit, a credit check, nothing. I can use the yard to plant a garden, she said."

I stopped wiping to listen to her. "That's fantastic," I said. "I'm so happy for you."

She and I exchanged a brief look, smiling, but there was something else, too: We were two middle-aged, white American women, on either side of an economic divide.

She said with measured insistence but no self-pity, "I owned my own house for years, you know? I raised eleven kids in it, I lived there forever. Then my husband—not their father, my second husband . . . because of him, I lost the house. He ruined me. I couldn't believe it. Then he took off. Suddenly I was alone and homeless."

"Oh my God," I said. I didn't ask why one of her eleven kids hadn't taken her in; it was none of my business.

"It can happen to anyone," she said. "I didn't understand that before, and now I do. You, me, anyone."

We exchanged another look. I recognized a warning in her expression, as if she saw something about me that needed addressing. Maybe she glimpsed the wayward, hungry, lonely street dog I had been for so many years and could very well be again someday. She had once had a home with people she loved, as I had now, and she had lost it all, as I could. Nothing was ever certain; I got her message loud and clear, right in my gut.

As I walked home, I felt yet again that near-melancholy sense of my own luck, my settled happiness. The melancholy came from an underlying and very real fear of losing it all. The woman at the shelter had illuminated that for me. This was the trouble with finding true love and a happy home: It couldn't last forever. Nothing could.

But that was the only trouble with any of it that I could see.

ele

Soup Kitchen Stir-Fry

From the vegetable fridge, take all the fish tubs of chopped or sliced vegetables and chop and slice up everything that hasn't been prepped yet. Assemble your flavorings: the carafes of teriyaki and soy sauce and the jug of corn oil and the jar of roasted pureed garlic and the little thing of five-spice powder.

When everything is ready to go, heat a giant drum pan over two burners. Pour in about a cup of oil. When it's hot, throw in a wad of garlic and a heap of aromatics: onion, carrots, celery. Stir. After two minutes, add chopped peppers, cauliflower, mushrooms, broccoli, zucchini, and summer squash. Stir, and sprinkle with soy sauce and five-spice powder until it smells really good. Keep stirring. Add a heap of well-washed, minced, farm-share radish greens. Stir like mad. The drum pan should be over half full.

When the stir-fry is cooked (but not overcooked), get someone to help you lift the pan to divide the contents between two deep steam-table pans. In one of them, leave room for the chicken. Put the pans into heated steam-table slots and cover them.

Return the drum pan to the heat. Add a cup of corn oil. Stir-fry all the chopped chicken, adding teriyaki sauce at the end. When it's cooked, add it to the vegetable stir-fry pan in which you left extra room, and mix together well.

Florence House also is home to a number of hardworking, well-trained service dogs, registered emotional-support companions. Make sure to leave enough chicken out of the teriyaki sauce for anyone with a dog who asks for it.

ℓℓℓ

Chapter Four

A Land of All Seasons

Often, when I tell others from away that I live in Maine, a fond, wistful look comes over their faces.

"Maine," they sigh. "I *love* Maine."

Invariably, what they mean is that they used to go to camp up here in the summers as children and teenagers, and now they have dreamy, blissful memories of lakes and canoes, rocky beaches and lobsters, hikes in pine forests, young love, first cigarettes, clandestine cans of beer, unforgettable adventures. I can see it all in their faraway expressions.

And then they look back at me, eyes focusing as something occurs to them.

"But what about the winters?" they ask. "How do you stand them? Aren't they awful?"

"I love the winters here," I say. "They're not so bad. They were much worse in New York."

And I mean it, for the most part.

The course of a typical year in northern New England provides so much intense drama and climatic variety, it's never the same place twice. People love to discuss the weather up here; it's the most fascinating and important topic imaginable. In fact, a local saying borrowed from Mark Twain goes, "If you don't like the weather, wait a minute."

Along with the northern Midwest and Alaska, whose winters are often colder, but no longer or more dramatic, the northeast corner of the United States has got some of the most interesting weather in the country. There's always a surprise: the January thaw, the late-March snowstorm, the occasional late-August frost. This land hosts tornadoes and blizzards, nor'easters and hurricanes. Spring rain gives way to golden sunshine gives way to sleet and fog in the course of a few hours, temperatures fluctuating accordingly.

Of course, in terms of the people who live here, there's very little variety. This region, apparently, is called by certain urbanites the South of the North, evidently because it's populated largely by the type of white people referred to as rednecks by city dwellers, who view them as uneducated, poor, backwoods-dwelling hicks who subsist on Walmart canned and junk food as well as hunting, fishing, foraging, and the occasional roadkill.

In all, the "non-Hispanic white" population here is 94.4 percent, the highest in the nation. The population is largely made up of people of French, Irish, and peasant English descent, with a very small smattering descended from Poles, Italians, Germans, Scots-Irish, and Swedes. Many families have been here since the seventeenth century and identify as simply American, or Mainers.

But weirdly, and disturbingly, after the demise of Jim Crow laws in the 1920s, the KKK established a highly active faction in Maine, the whitest state in the Union, persecuting the Irish and French Canadians, i.e., Catholics, the only "other" ethnicity around.

Despite the relative homogeneity, human nature being what it is, there's a certain degree of ingrained contentiousness among the various groups of people up here, groups that might seem fairly identical to the uneducated "from-away" eye. Most of New Hampshire lies cheek by jowl along its common border with southwestern Maine, and New Hampshire is tucked under Maine like a long neck supporting a big head, but despite their compatible and even corollary mottoes, "Live Free or Die" and "The Way Life Should Be," they're famously hostile, like Norway and Sweden, or those rival advice-giving identical twin sisters, Ann Landers and Dear Abby. Mainers tell a host of insulting off-color jokes about the degree of incestuousness and stupidity and low-life loucheness of New Hampshirites, who tell the exact same jokes about Mainers. Their hockey rivalry is legendary and ongoing.

As a newcomer, and a New Hampshire resident who owns a house in Maine, it strikes me that the more alike you are, the more you fight to distinguish yourselves . . .

ele

In 1652, the sparsely populated, hardscrabble land of Maine was annexed (unhappily) to the Commonwealth of Massachusetts until 1820, when it became the twenty-third state. Mainers' long-held distrust and dislike of people from Massachusetts stems from very deep, ancient resentments fueled by almost two centuries of entitled rich people from the south imposing their greed and laws on struggling poor people in the north. These class wars continue today in many subtle and not-so-subtle ways, beginning with the notion of "summer people" and extending to a general squinty-eyed disapprobation of "Massholes." Even so, Maine is chock-full of Red Sox and Patriots fans. It's complicated. (New Hampshire, as one of the original colonies, never having been ruled by Massachusetts, understandably feels a bit more warmly toward its southern neighbor.)

Maine's population of 1.3 million people is distributed in a wildly uneven way throughout the state. Maine is the least densely populated state east of the Mississippi, having an average of forty-three people per square mile. But this is misleading; in the enormous, heavily forested counties in the northern interior, there's an average of less than one person per square mile, as vast tracts of land up there are uninhabited and wild. Meanwhile, 40 percent of Mainers are crowded down in southern Maine, in and around Portland. Rural northern Mainers derisively refer to these southern urban dwellers as "flatlanders"; in other words, not really true Mainers at all. And so the population is further divided into "us" and "them." Most of the French Mainers live in the north. (Although the state is 28 percent Catholic, it's also the least religious state in the country.)

Geographically, the region is as interesting as the weather, and the two are almost certainly related. I can hardly imagine this, but during the Ice Age, all of New Hampshire and Maine was covered in a glacier almost a mile deep, thick enough to cover even the highest mountain peaks. Called the Laurentide ice sheet or cap, this unruly ice monster swept down from Canada and covered all of New England for 18,000 years or so; just a geological blink of an eye, but it was enough to change the entire landscape. When it receded, it left a mess behind. It rucked up rocks and swept many of them to the coast, where they remain in glacial moraines. The gazillions of rocks that stayed behind had to be plowed and removed from fields every winter by farmers through the centuries and painstakingly stacked to build New England's thousands of miles of stone walls.

New Hampshire has the shortest coastline in the country, but Maine's got the fourth-longest, after Alaska, Florida, and Louisiana, if you measure by all the coves, inlets, and jags: 3,478 miles of corrugated sea-edge in only 228 miles as the seagull flies. To travel up the Maine coast is to feel viscerally this folded-in, twisting sinuousness of the embrace of land and sea—cove after cove, inlet after inlet, creating one spit, peninsula, and tongue after another. Maine also has 3,166 islands, including freshwater. Land and water are intricately, complicatedly interconnected. Maine's Midcoast region rises steeply from the sea into hills and mountains folding back inland to the Appalachians. Katahdin, which the Penobscot dubbed "The Greatest Mountain," is the highest of these at 5,269 feet, and before the International Trail continued up into Canada, it was the northern terminus of the Appalachian Trail. And inland, the land-water dance continues: Maine has about 6,000 lakes and ponds; the much-smaller New Hampshire has 944.

New Hampshire's mountains are higher than Maine's. In the Presidential Range of the White Mountains, Mount Washington is the tallest peak in New England, at 6,288 feet. It's also where some of the worst weather in the world occurs, including the highest-ever recorded wind speed in the western and northern hemispheres, 231 mph in 1934. It gets almost 100 inches of precipitation a year, a lot of it very quickly, the record being 11 inches of rain in twenty-four hours. The lowest recorded temperature at the summit is -59 degrees F, the highest a balmy 72 F; all year, enormous storms rage on the mountain, which sits at a lucky confluence of Pacific, Atlantic, and Gulf weather systems and gets them all, all at once, in full force.

Down in the valleys, where we live, the temperatures and winds are milder, but no less interesting to a newcomer like me. Growing up in Arizona, I had little experience of seasons, except for the extreme summers, which were so scorchingly hot, we tried to stay inside a lot of the time. In the deepest winter, when the temperatures dropped into the 60s, we put on cardigans and turned off the air conditioner. Later, when I lived in New York, the seasons were dramatic but unconnected to the natural world, fundamentally human. Winter meant keen, street-focused winds, banks of rocklike, black snow and snarled traffic, and internal coat-hunched thoughts; spring meant an explosion of urban social life and a shedding of garments. Summer meant sweltering streets and frequent escapes to local beaches or wherever else you could go, and autumn meant a return to interiority, a back-to-school intellectual energy.

For the first time, living in New England has acquainted me viscerally with the connection between the weather and time of year and the natural world and food chain. This land of farmers has distinct cycles of planting, growing, harvest. Then there's a kind of patient regrouping during the very long, very cold, very quiet winters, which provide a deep rest for people and land alike; a state of hibernating renewal during which wild animals scramble to stay alive. Thin coyotes and hungry blue jays forage for fallen apples in the orchards; squirrels take refuge in warm eaves and people live on the harvest's stored root vegetables, canned garden produce, and frozen packages of meat; farmers pick rocks out of their fields and spend hours by the fire poring over seed catalogues dreaming of their spring plantings. And hermit writers hunker down, burrow in, and work.

On the whole, it's true, what I tell people about loving the winters up here. Up here, when it snows, everyone goes out and shovels and plows and throws sand and salt, and then we all get on with our days. In New York, life generally ground to a halt after a snowstorm for one perfect day of quiet and dazzling white, sledding in parks and snowmen near front stoops, and then the gears reengaged, the soot and grime descended, and the sidewalks remained frozen, treacherous obstacle courses of dirty snow-ice heaps until it all melted, finally, overflowing the gutters. In New England, snow is dealt with efficiently, without drama, as just another part of life. City sidewalks are clear, for the most part, and whenever it's possible, snowbanks are shoveled out of the way of pedestrians and traffic.

In fact, winter is in many ways my favorite time to be in the White Mountains, in the farmhouse with Brendan and Dingo, the three of us all alone at the end of the dirt road. Winter in the countryside is flat-out beautiful, even the bleakest, coldest days; the snow is white and clean, the air is crystalline and fresh. There is no better place or time to work productively, day after day, free of social obligations and distractions. Brendan and I sit writing at the kitchen table, looking out the window at the bare, white mountains, while Dingo guards the house on his window seat, ears tipped forward on full alert, eyes glued to what's going on out the window, which isn't much.

The outside world is muffled and still. Bare black branches drip in an icy rain or are covered in heavy snowfall. Fog hangs over the lake and shrouds the mountains. Snow lies in a thick blanket up to the first or second or third rung of the fences. The sky hangs low over the hemlocks on the ridge. But our daily walks are thrilling as we tromp through bracing, cold air on the frozen road. Often, the sun pierces the clouds and gilds the snow-furred hemlocks. The frozen lake creaks with otherworldly theremin-like moans and eerie shrieks. Sparkling snowflakes hang in the bright frigid air and fall in clumps from hemlock boughs. By the end, we're warm and sweaty, noses running, layers stripped off.

It's a very cozy season; since it's almost always dark, the distinction between day and night becomes a matter of perspective. One deep winter night, our whole household was up and awake at three in the morning. We humans woke up first. Brendan went downstairs. Optimistically, I tried to lull myself back to sleep just because it seemed like the thing to do, but then it dawned on me that it didn't matter if I got up now and then slept all morning. Suddenly hungry, I put on my bathrobe and went down to see what was happening. Brendan was sitting in the armchair by the fireplace, writing. He'd built a little fire, and the room was dark and warm. Dingo wasn't in bed anymore, either; he lay on his window seat. He looked at me, thoroughly befuddled: Why was it time to start his workday when it was still dark? Where was his breakfast?

I curled up at one end of the couch and started reading yet another engrossing Maine memoir. The room was aglow with firelight. Brendan tapped away at his keyboard. The logs crackled. Dingo snorted gently to let us know he was still wondering where his breakfast was. Outside, it was pitch dark. Inside, we were three solitary wakeful beings marooned together in a pool of light and warmth in a vast, sleeping landscape.

I read the whole book in three hours, then, yawning, my eyes almost shut, I climbed the stairs, got back between the flannel sheets, pulled the down comforter over my head, and fell into a deep sleep. I awoke to soft, snowy, late-morning light coming in the dormer windows and the smell of coffee.

ℒℒ

Although it's lovely and cozy, winter in New England is always full of unforeseen challenges. One early February day, the farmhouse furnace, which was about three decades old and had been limping along for the past five or more years on replacement belts and magic, was officially pronounced dead—or rather, it had cracked, and the carbon monoxide it was probably giving off would be dangerous, if the house had been better insulated, or insulated at all.

Meanwhile, our house in Portland was now home to four humans, two dogs, a cat, and an indeterminate number of squirrels. Over the winter, according to our upstairs tenants, the squirrel population had exploded and expanded. Before, according to them, they could hear the family of squirrels talking, fighting, having sex, giving birth, celebrating, and dying, leaving their excretions and carcasses within the walls of the house, and that was bad enough. But this winter, the squirrels seemed to have quadrupled in number and expanded from the walls into the ceiling. And now, they could also hear their vigorous chewing, of the house itself.

A dangerous, dead furnace and a rapacious infestation of squirrels—both problematic, potentially expensive, and time-consuming to deal with. Welcome to the northeast corner. A new furnace cost a small fortune. Exterminators charged as much as $75 per squirrel; who knew how many were up there? More were born every day, evidently.

When the guy from White Mountain Oil & Propane tested the carbon monoxide levels, by law he had to shut the furnace off, which left us completely without heat in the middle of February. There's a Jøtul woodstove in the middle downstairs room, but we were low on wood because we hadn't been here that fall to buy another cord; we only had a few sticks left. It was a warm 35 degrees, but the following week was going to bring another polar blast. We wouldn't be here, fortunately, so we could empty the pipes and shut off the water and skedaddle back to town, and our squirrel problem, but we were coming back to the farmhouse in mid-March, which would still be full-on winter. It was clearly time to replace the furnace.

Back in Portland, we debated what to do about those squirrels. I fantasized about camping out in a lawn chair with my .22 (I did not own a .22, but would have happily bought one for this purpose) and picking them off one by one as they came down the fire escape. I had no ethical problem with this, because I would then, equally hypothetically, dress, cook, and eat them. Friends who'd done so assured me they were delicious: squirrel potpie, braised squirrel stew, deep-fried squirrels with cream gravy—we could eat free-range, organic meat for weeks.

But, too bad, it was illegal to shoot a gun within city limits. And catch-and-release in the dead of winter is cruel; they would freeze and starve to death wherever we dropped them, far from their summer's worth of caches and stashes of food.

Ah, the joys of winter in the Far North! At least we had plenty of water and food. At least the farmhouse was nicely porous, so we didn't die from carbon monoxide poisoning while the old furnace was exhaling its toxic last breaths. And at least those squirrels hadn't chewed through any electrical wiring and set our Portland house on fire. Yet.

For the rest of the winter, we watched fat squirrels sitting outside the kitchen window, staring in at us, looking as if they'd taste delicious in *écureuil au vin*. Finally, in the spring, our tenants caught them one by one in Havahart traps and released them in a graveyard in South Portland, where the family was reunited, or so I liked to think.

And the farmhouse got a brand-new furnace.

ℓℓℓ

Spring came, finally, but our troubles weren't altogether over. This northeastern corner of the country is notable for dishing out the cruelest April I've ever known, breeding icicles out of the dead land, mixing ennui and irritation, stunting dull roots with unseasonable snow. Cabin Fever Month finally goes out with a soft exhalation of sunny updrafts that shake the new buds and cause the crocuses to bob like the heads of dashboard hula girls, and all is forgiven, but that doesn't mean I've forgotten any of its earlier depredations.

How many marriages up here have ended in divorce as a result of all the winter's many seasons and their ensuing challenges? There aren't just four seasons here, there are about ten: early winter, bleak midwinter, January false spring, deep winter, late winter, March false spring, and finally mud season. After that comes blackfly season, and then it's summer for a minute, and then it's fall again, tipping over into those seven or eight months of winter. It whirls around so fast.

Mud season might be the toughest of all to take. It's a cruel joke: Where is spring? The winter is over. Why isn't it warm and green yet? In April, everyone seems to go a little mad, but not in any romantic or transcendent way. Up here, the phrase "mixing memory and desire" from Eliot's "The Waste Land" might be more aptly phrased as "muddling nostalgia and craving." Memory and desire are more literary and refined, the sort of emotions a well-bred lady might swoon with, requiring smelling salts, a lavender hankie, or, at the very least, a thimbleful of sherry, a turn about the topiary garden. Nostalgia and craving are blunter, more animal and immediate, and therefore closer to my own experience, living here. They're also basically the same thing, except one is hunger for the past and the other is hunger for the future.

One mud-season morning in Portland, we awoke to yet another cold, rainy, gray day. We were all craving sun and spring. As I put my coat on yet again to take Dingo out, I thought, what season is this? Outside, I adjusted my expectations, put on my hood, tried to convince myself that spring would be here any day. I let Dingo trundle me around our block, jerking my arm as he suddenly stopped to pee, making me wait while he sniffed with full concentration. I scooped up his neat turds with a long-practiced swipe of the bag and carried it in the hand that didn't have the leash. Never do I feel more clear about the power dynamic of our relationship than on the morning walk.

The chilly air forced me to stay retracted into myself, like a prolonged inhalation, when I was jonesing to expand and turn outward and get the stale air out of my lungs. The trees and bushes in this town were just starting to bud, but barely, cautiously; I was sure they all felt the same way I did, as well as the bulb flowers, which were getting a late start in recently thawed dirt.

The enormous old ash tree in back of our house, which puts out leaves much later than the trees around it, was showing no sign of renewed life yet. Everyone was walking around hunched into warm clothes, looking askance at the sky, griping to anyone who would listen, marveling at how disappointed we all felt after such a brutal winter to be denied a warm, sunny spring. It felt unnatural and cruel. Our bones were cold and our timbers were shivering.

Later, Brendan and Dingo and I took our usual mid-morning walk on the Eastern Prom as the foghorn lowed, the high tide slapped and sucked against the stone seawall, the pavement and gravel and grass all sopping wet. It was too foggy to see the bay or islands. The rain slid down, greasy and cold, not a spring rain but a chilly one, with malicious intent. Up on the cliffs, the still-bare branches dripped. The only people out besides us were two groups of men, none of them up to any good: a couple of wild-eyed hobos drinking hooch and puffing cheap cigars on the stone steps up to the trail ("Happy spring! Beautiful spring day!" they trumpeted at us as we climbed up past them, cackling as if this were the best joke ever made), and then a group of three preppy, athletic-looking teenage boys in blazers and khakis. They ambled by us on the mucky path, not making eye contact, trailing the smell of skunky ganja. They looked like sweet-natured, well-bred high-school seniors cutting school.

And then the weather changed again.

One day in late April, back in the farmhouse, the sun was fiercely bright, and the sky was a mad, deep blue. We emerged from the house blinking like underground rodents in sudden klieg lights. The air was so mild, I stripped down to a T-shirt by the end of our walk. My snow boots sank into the soft, mushy, wet skin of the road. The streams were all running again. The air smelled like water; that dry-ice quality of deep winter was gone. The remaining snow was all porous ice from melting and refreezing and melting. Dingo's fur looked mangy, clumpy; he was about to blow his thick winter undercoat.

There was a kind of bird I called the taxi bird—because they were as ubiquitous as taxis in New York—and when I first came to the White Mountains and was so urban I couldn't identify a single bird or bush, that was my primary point of reference. And now the taxi birds (phoebes, I now know) were back, singing their two-note descending call from treetops all along the dirt road.

Right outside the window by the table where I spent the afternoon working, the little maple tree had buds on it, very little and very hard, but buds nonetheless. I looked out at them frequently and smiled. In the late afternoon, I knocked off work and went out with a glass of wine and sat on the porch in my jeans and socks and T-shirt and bathrobe, my winter writer's uniform. This had always been my favorite time of day, but today was especially nice. Dingo lay next to me, ears and nostrils all aquiver, but there was nothing going on for him to bark at. The sun was setting and the air was absolutely still.

After days of howling winds and lowering fog and dripping eaves, the serene silence felt as shocking as the sudden warmth. The grass was turning a soft young green; crocus spears were finally poking out of the dirt.

All day, in my head, I'd been reciting the e. e. cummings poem that starts,

in Just-
spring   when the world is mud-
luscious the little
lame balloonman

whistles   far   and wee

and eddieandbill come
running from marbles and
piracies and it's
spring

when the world is puddle-wonderful . . .

I couldn't stop thinking the words *mud-luscious* and *puddle-wonderful* over and over, and the rest of it sort of filled in chockablock with a galumphing joyful rhythm around those two words, along with "far and wee."

ele

Two or three weeks later, the mania of full-on spring infected our hermetic little threesome. Dingo bounded around outside all day like a humpy rabbit, barking at snow drip-melting off the roof and fluffing his copiously shedding fur in the breeze and sunlight. After an uncharacteristically studious, intent winter of hard work and concentration, Brendan and I reverted to our punchy and goofy and amorous selves. I felt scattershot and addlepated with unfocused disorganization: What was I working on, again? Eight different things, it turned out.

All night one night, the full moon blazed in through the bedroom window and lit up the long fields of snow and dark, shaggy woods with its silver, dramatic glow. The fact that wild solar flares were hitting Earth made sense; my dreams were absurd and rich with peril, upside-down logic, and Loki hilarity. And the next morning, the air had turned suddenly warm.

I woke up very early, let Dingo out into the sunny snow-blind morning, and fed him. While I drank an enormous cup of strong coffee, I sat blinking over my correspondence, unable to write anything coherent to anyone. At eleven a.m., creatures of clockwork habit, we three took our usual four-mile fast walk up and down the hilly dirt road, which streaming with runoff, was muddy. The lake and much of the snow had melted. The soft dirt road was strewn with squished baby frogs who'd gotten in the way of the ten or twelve cars, mostly Subarus, of course, that drove along the road each day. The lake was a rich steel blue, choppy in the fresh breeze, shading to black around the edges. The mountains were cobalt hulks under a cloud-dense, abruptly sunny sky. Down at the beaver pond, we counted two new dams, making a grand total of five; their population was thriving, exploding even. A gosling swam behind its parents as they came bustling over to check us out. The little protruding hummocks near the shore had newborn, spindly stalks and greening moss.

We came home with wet feet; Dingo's entire undercarriage had to be toweled off. While I rubbed the grit and sand and snowmelt from his stomach and legs and hindquarters, he smiled goofily at me and panted in my ear and leaned against my shoulder in a manner I can only describe as flirtatious.

The best thing to do in these transitional seasons, winter to spring, especially, is to give in to animal instinct. In early spring, that means acquiescing to any and all seductive urges, sleeping a lot, drinking all the wine you want and plenty of water, and going outside into the sunlight in short sleeves and moving around. It's good to eat lightly but decadently, food that's good for you (because the change of seasons is a shock to the system) but which also satisfies a sudden intense itch for variety, change, novelty, adventure.

Instead of deeply flavored stews, root vegetables, and potato-based fry-ups, my appetite was suddenly laser-focused on ruffled fresh green lettuces and—it pains me to say this out of compassion for my vegetarian friends—baby lamb. It's a frank hunger for the sweetness of new life—little leaves shaking off dew and standing upright, the tender savory flesh of very young animals.

Popcorn Cockles and Asparagus
with Fenugreek Sauce and Mango Salsa

This is the perfect antidote and accompaniment to spring fever. Cockles are better than clams for this dish, but very small, tender clams will do if no cockles are available.

Steam 20 young asparagus spears until just soft. Plunge into ice water, remove, and pat dry. Drizzle with the following mixture:

2 T mayonnaise
1 T lime juice
1/8 tsp ground fenugreek

Steam 3 dozen very fresh cockles in their shells just until they open. Remove the cockles from their shells (they will be wet with their own liquor) and immediately coat them in finely ground corn-meal. Heat 1 inch of peanut oil in a skillet until it spits when you flick a drop of water at it. In batches that just cover the bottom of the pan, fry the cockles, covered to minimize spatter, for several minutes, till their crusts are golden. Remove and arrange alongside the asparagus. On the other side of the cockles goes a mango salsa:

In a bowl, mix:

1 ripe mango, chopped small
1 to 2 T finely minced cilantro
2 T lime juice
1 minced medium or large garlic clove
1 to 2 jalapeno peppers (depending on how hot you want it), minced

This recipe serves 4 as an appetizer, in theory, but has been known to serve 2, just barely.

One late afternoon in May, we decided to go up Foss Mountain.

Going up Foss is a very old ritual for Brendan, one that long pre-dated my arrival in the White Mountains. In a small knapsack, we packed a cold liter-bottle of hard cider and a bag of roasted cashews, as well as water and a treat for Dingo. We all got into the car and drove a few miles back through the woods on dirt roads, through the tiny mountain hamlet of Eaton with its clean lake and nineteenth-century town hall, and then we headed upward.

Foss Mountain Road has a few isolated houses with old barns and a working llama farm. The road is so steep, the car occasionally tipped and jolted upward as the engine strained to heave us over the hump to the next flat spot. It was rutted from frost and snowmelt, as grooved and corrugated as a dry streambed in places. We jounced slowly up through dense woods for a good long time. When we came to the tiny turnoff, we parked and got out of the car and hiked up through a big, scrubby privately owned blueberry field (PLEASE DO NOT PICK THE BLUEBERRIES, said many signs posted along the way) that took us to a narrow path through a small birch wood. This path is studded with boulders, and on this afternoon, was slick with fallen leaves and wet from an underground spring, so we had to tread carefully and occa-sionally grab a branch or walk on higher ground. Above the wood, we hit the huge granite outcropping and scrambled up it to the top.

The summit of Foss affords a 360-degree view of the White Moun-tains and their valleys and lakes and woods. It could be 1802 up there, or even earlier. There are three or four houses visible in valleys far below, but no roads, no traffic sounds, no other signs of civilization. Once in a while you hear the distant *thwack* of a hunter's shotgun. Otherwise, it's pristine and silent on that granite roof, just the wind rustling in the blueberry shrubs, the giant rushing peace of wilderness, the imperceptible ticking of sunlight on the rocks.

Every time we go up Foss, it's a different landscape, depending on the season, the weather, the mood of the place. Sometimes on a hot, sunny summer early evening there's a small crowd, kids picking ripe blueberries, running in a pack down the paths through the meadow, dogs forming their own pack and milling around, drinking from rain pools in the rocks and sniffing one another, adults gawping at the view, mostly silently, sometimes with quiet talk.

On this late afternoon in May, Brendan and Dingo and I were the only ones there. It was a chilly, lowering sort of day, with a brisk fresh breeze and thick low clouds, but we could feel summer coming, just around the bend. When we got to the top, we were quiet for a moment, in frank awe. The land had a blue tinge, a strange cast, almost like an old photograph of itself. Suddenly, a sunbeam slipped through the clouds and lit the slope below Mount Washington with a powerful shaft that made a distant lake shine like mica.

It felt like being in a giant cathedral, a reverent hush, an indrawn breath, mystical and strange.

We sat on our usual outcropping and opened the backpack and popped the cork out of the hard cider and had a swig each.

"I've never seen it this beautiful here," I said finally.

"Me neither," said Brendan, who'd been going up Foss for thirty years.

Dingo lay at my side, not saying anything.

The cider we'd brought was made from local apples, similar to the apples that grow on the old, gnarled little trees in the orchard around the farmhouse, sour, flavorful, tiny things that look like weird stones. The dry, deep, tart taste of that cider always reminded me of Foss; or rather, that was the only place we ever drank it.

(Someday, during a year of sufficient bounty, we plan to make our own cider from the apples that grow on the dozens of apple trees around the farmhouse; there's an old cider press in the barn. Some of the trees in the orchard were planted over a century ago. They're gnarled, and most of their apples are as small as gumballs, but according to Brendan, they're fantastic for regular cider. His attempt to ferment the cider last time he made it, years ago, didn't work so well, but there's always next time.)

The mountains were layered one after another back to the horizon all around us in every direction, in shades of gray and blue and blue-gray and dark blue, like a roiling, turbulent, wild sea in a storm. Mount Washington turned into a massive giant wave about to send our little craft up its towering flank. We both saw it and shivered together in that pleasurable make-believe fear.

The wind died down. The sun stayed hidden. The granite we sat on felt warmer than I'd expected it would. It was dry up there—no rain pools in the rock for Dingo to lap at.

A flock of nine little birds, tits or pipits, maybe, starlings, the tiny kind whose silhouettes look a bit like Piper Cubs, lifted all at once out of the meadow just below us. They hurled themselves into the air high, high above our heads and, in a game of follow-the-leader, flew in a big circle, swooping and soaring around us, and coming to ground again, back where they'd started. A moment later, they performed the whole air show again.

After that, it was time to go. We hiked down to the car, nosed it down the vertical road, and headed home slowly with the windows open to let the fresh cool air stream in.

ℓℓℓ

Maine is a true paradise in the summertime, one sweet golden-green-blue day after another, unfolding gently and without fanfare. After the long, dark, cold winter, the summer is a blissful return to light and warmth and the bright/earthy smell of plant life. Everyone seems to burst forth into the fresh air to make the most of it as long as it lasts—people, dogs, cats, squirrels.

In New York during the summertime, people ran air conditioners, sweated profusely, stayed inside to avoid the suffocating heat. But in Maine, for that brief and shining season, the temperatures are perfect. Almost no one has air conditioners; it's a pleasure to walk around town without being dripped on by the condensation on window units, which happened on every block in New York. I measured summertime there by having to swerve on sidewalks to avoid the icy drips that reminded me of Legionnaires' disease and landed splat on my hot scalp. Up here, summer is serene. Instead of the ubiquitous humming of air conditioners, there's the cawing of seagulls and the whoosh of the breeze through treetops.

Seagulls aren't always conducive to serenity, however. By mid-June, when it's warm enough to sleep with the windows open, the neighborhood gulls caterwaul overhead, screaming bloody murder at one another in the sky, waking me up out of a deep sleep. City seagulls! They sound like Southie mothers shrieking, "SEAN, you betta not end up like ya fuckin FATHA!!" and "Bobby O'Houlihan, if I catch ya I'm gonna SKIN YA ALIVE!"

One morning, as I stared sleepily out the window into the blue predawn light, I could see one of them on the rooftop across the street, strutting along the peak, shrieking its head off, probably at another gull on another rooftop, waiting for a response, then shrieking back.

The British weren't coming. They had no predators to warn one another about, that I knew of. The sun wasn't even up yet; what urgent news could there have been to impart? How was this productive? How did this advance their cause in the world? Why weren't they down by the water, catching fish and nourishing themselves?

Seagulls were mysterious, I concluded. Then I put in earplugs, pulled a pillow over my head, and went back to sleep.

Later that morning, after our walk, we went to the farmers' market down in the park, by the fountains, under the trees. There was a bounteous array of food for sale, as well as a tightrope walker, a bluegrass band, and many calm and friendly dogs (as are all the dogs here; Portland has none of that weird Brooklyn neuroticism of both animals and owners). It felt like a nineteenth-century country fair; matter of fact, here we are. We bought some organic chorizo, rhubarb, lettuce, soft cheeses dusted with spices, big ripe tomatoes, zucchini—whatever was fresh and in season, until we ran out of cash.

At home, I washed and trimmed the rhubarb and cut it into four-inch pieces. I mixed two cups total of apple cider vinegar and rice vinegar with maple syrup, honey, salt, peppercorns, fresh sliced ginger, cardamom pods, sliced serrano peppers, and cloves. I let this mixture boil for five minutes, then turned off the flame and added the rhubarb. When it had cooled, I packed the rhubarb into a container and poured over it as much of the liquid as it would hold.

This was my first time ever making pickles; I was unreasonably excited by how easy it was and how good they were. The next day, Sunday, we packed a picnic and took it to the Eastern Prom—the rhubarb pickles along with deviled eggs, three kinds of cheese, flaxseed crackers, a bottle of chilled rosé, and dessert: an apple for Dingo and chocolate-covered strawberries for us.

We sat, all three of us in a row, on a picnic table overlooking Casco Bay, sheltered by the trees, warm in the sun, looking out at the sailboats trundling over the blue water and the shaggy green islands beyond as we feasted, feeling as if we had that corner of the world almost to ourselves, although it was a bright, warm, sunny holiday. Everyone had, no doubt, decamped for the beaches north and south of town. We sat on the picnic table, soaking in the briny, clean, grass-scented air, basking in the mellow sunshine, sipping our wine and feeding scraps to Dingo, who lounged happily in the shade. After lunch, we packed everything up and took a good, long, fast walk up and around the headlands.

Later, at home, we fell instantly into a triple coma of a nap. I regained consciousness in the evening to find Dingo fed and walked and Brendan hard at work. Down in the kitchen, by some miracle, hungry yet again, I hauled out the farmers' market chorizo and a string bag of littleneck clams and opened a bottle of cold Orvieto.

In olive oil, I sautéed a lot of garlic, two medium leeks, two tomatoes, a jalapeno, and a red pepper. I stirred in two diced potatoes and the chopped chorizo, then added a cup of the white wine and a cup of chicken broth and two bay leaves, and simmered it until the potatoes were soft. Then I squeezed in the juice of one lemon and stirred, arranged the clams on top, covered the pot, and let it simmer till the clamshells opened. I added a big handful of minced Italian parsley, and we feasted for the second time that day.

The thick, tender chowder was rich with spicy pork fat and the sweetness of the clams and the mealy cubed potatoes; the cold, crisp white wine cooled our tongues.

Early the next morning, our bedroom flashed and banged with thunder and lightning, an intense electrical storm. Dingo crept in and we all huddled together, feeling safe in our house. When I took Dingo out, the air was humid, cool, dark, and sweet-smelling. The soaked dark sidewalks were strewn with vivid pollen and petals. I felt that by-now-familiar bone-deep happiness, feeling at home here, in this place.

ele

The only trouble with summer in the Far North is that it's so short. Because Brendan and I are writers, not farmers, we make our hay in other ways. Like everyone else who lives up here year-round, we still have to work in the summertime, but we give ourselves over completely to the evanescent sweetness and light, knowing what's coming in a few short months.

One unusually hot summer morning in the farmhouse, Brendan and I put on our bathing suits and set off toward the lake. We turned off the dirt road onto the steep path to Brendan's aunt's dock, dashing downward through clouds of horseflies that bit us freely and without restraint. At the lake, we stripped off our clothes and ran to the end of the dock and plunged into the clean, chilly-then-warm water, which was full of little wavelets and covered with a thin scrim of pollen.

By the time we got back to the house, we were hot all over again. We took cool showers and dressed in as little as possible and tried not to move. As the sun went down and we got hungry, we tried to imagine what we could possibly want to eat on such a day.

"I know," said Brendan, whose parents grew up in Italy, and who learned to make many traditional Italian dishes from his father and his grandmother's Tuscan cook. "I have the perfect thing."

He put a big pot of water on the stove and poured us each a small glass of Rioja with several ice cubes. When the water boiled, he plunged ten medium-size ripe Roma tomatoes into it for three or four minutes, until their skins split, then he took them out and peeled (but did not seed) them. Meanwhile, he peeled and chopped a heap of garlic.

In a deep skillet, he poured some of the olive oil from the stash of bottles in the cupboards over the fireplace, which came from his family's olive trees in Tuscany, and for which I thanked all the gods, every time we ate it.

I sipped my wine, looking out at the mountains, while Brendan sautéed the garlic for a scant minute, then added the chopped tomatoes along with all their juice and some salt and pepper and a smidgen of crushed red pepper. He let the sauce cook down for twenty minutes or so until it thickened, then added a handful of chopped fresh basil at the very end and tossed the sauce with a pound of penne rigate.

Meanwhile, I threw together a simple salad and poured us some more Rioja over ice. We sat at the table in the pressing heat and devoured everything. It was the best pasta of any kind I've ever had, hands down, silky and rich and garlicky. I moaned *Yum,* and made other guttural animal noises as I ate. The cook took this as the highest praise, as he should have. We ate until the pasta dish was empty and all we could do was run a finger along its bottom to dredge up every molecule of that sweet, savory, beautiful sauce.

After dinner, cool air started to blow in with far-off thunder and lightning. We went outside and sat on the porch for a while and watched the dragonflies troll through the air like beautiful, predatory machines, eating mosquitoes. Over the fields, fireflies were winking and glinting.

The storm was slow in coming, and its approach was dramatic. As the darkening sky became saturated with electricity, echoing booms of rolling thunder and white-hot lightning cascaded through the high clouds, blinding explosions of streaking brachioles of light illuminating everything for several beats before fading.

I had never seen a lightning storm like this before. Naturally, I couldn't help but wonder whether this was a result of climate change; whenever the weather does anything extraordinary or extreme, it's the first thing I think. No matter how beautiful it is, no matter how exciting, it's always tinged with a sense of impending doom. I try to enjoy the beauty nonetheless, to let it win out over the sense of loss. All of life is like this; I think it always has been.

I put my arm around Brendan, and he put his arm around me, and we leaned into each other and watched the light show. Neither of us said a word. The hair on our arms prickled from the combined chill and electric charge in the air.

The next morning, we went kayaking on the lake, paddling past the rocky, piney little island where Brendan camped as a little boy with his brother and friends.

"This island seemed so big and far away back then," he said.

We dove in and floated in the bathtub-warm water, low from drought, but still clean and sweet-smelling and silky on the skin.

We played Scrabble all afternoon in the summer barn, the windows open to the thunderstorm. At sunset, we sat on the stone bench down in the meadow and watched the light change on the mountains.

All summer long, we bought bags of fresh vegetables, local wine and cheese and ice cream, homemade sausage and blueberries from the farm stands just across the border in Maine. We went to the biodynamic farm nearby and bought eggs, lettuces, tomatoes, whatever else was on hand. We took deep, quiet, late-afternoon naps, sprawling barefoot on the couches. We climbed Foss Mountain's short, steep trail at sunset to look out over the whole mountain range and valley; we sat on the slab of granite at the top and watched two little boys pick blueberries, eating more than they managed to save.

ell

Spite & Malice Pizza

On a cool late-summer evening in the farmhouse, after playing Spite & Malice all afternoon with two worn, soft decks of cards we found in the summer barn, we poured ourselves some red wine, added an ice cube to each glass, and then made pizzas for supper with amiable cooperation, between deadly rounds of cards. The oven heated up the house, but we opened all the windows and let the cross-breezes cool it again. When the pizza was hot and bubbling and starting to brown on top, we pulled it out and sliced it and ate it with more hot red pepper flakes and grated Parmesan, with a crisp green salad alongside. Then we resumed our cutthroat card playing. (We both had a touch of indigestion in the night, but some-how I don't think it was from the pizza.)

2 pizza crusts (we used premade gluten-free crusts; you can use any you like)
2 cups shredded fresh buffalo mozzarella

For the sauce:

1 1/2 cups Pomi strained tomatoes
1 T olive oil
3 T minced or 1 T dried fresh basil, oregano, and/or tarragon
salt, pepper, and red pepper flakes to taste

For the roasted vegetables:

1 bell pepper, cored and thinly sliced
1 red pepper, cored and thinly sliced
1 large red onion, halved and thinly sliced
1 cup sliced mushrooms
8 to 12 medium cloves of garlic, peeled
2 T olive oil

For the meatballs:

1 cup ground turkey (or chicken, beef, veal, lamb, or pork)
1 small white onion, minced
1 T minced garlic
1/2 tsp cumin
1 egg
2 T ketchup
1/4 cup heavy cream
1/2 cup bread crumbs
salt, pepper, and hot red pepper flakes to taste
oil for frying

Optional additions to the meatballs:

1 to 2 minced jalapeno or Serrano peppers, depending on your taste for spiciness
3 T grated Parmesan
3 T toasted pine nuts

Preheat the oven to 475 degrees.

Mix the strained tomatoes in a small bowl with the fresh herbs, salt and pepper, and olive oil.

In a larger bowl, mix the cut-up vegetables and the olive oil. Spread on a cookie sheet in a single layer and bake for 20 minutes, or until soft and beginning to caramelize.

Combine all meatball ingredients. Stir lightly till mixed. With oiled hands to prevent sticking, form the mixture into small, gumball-size meatballs. In a large skillet, heat the olive oil. Drop the meatballs into the hot pan and fry them in batches, flipping them after a minute or two when browned and transferring the cooked ones to a plate.

To assemble the pizzas, spread half the tomato sauce on each crust, then the mozzarella, divided, followed by the roasted vegetables and then the meatballs. Bake on a pizza stone or large cookie sheet for 30 minutes, or until hot and bubbling.

ele

And then before we knew it, it was autumn again, that time of smoky nostalgia and lucid reckoning as well as new beginnings and optimism. In a way, the weeks following Labor Day are the best time to be a resident of Maine. After Labor Day, the summer people and tourists depart Vacationland, leaving it once again to the natives and "year-rounders," as the natives call us people from away who live here full-time, as a kind of grudging upgrade. September is glorious: golden days, nights with a chill in the air. Indian summer in October brings everyone outside again for a few days, a week, for one last hurrah.

And after the summer-long verboten banishment, you can walk your dog off-leash on the beaches any time of day again. No massive white cruise ships hulk in the harbor, dwarfing every building in town, disgorging thousands of passengers who throng the Old Port. Street traffic trickles to its normal state of easy passage. Post–Labor Day, it's an empty, heavenly country up here, suddenly private and quiet, as the year-round residents hunker down and head into the magical autumn.

In late October and early November, of course, the leaf peepers show up. And all winter come the skiers. The economy depends on them, so it's a good thing, but during that sweet, empty time from early September until mid-October, it feels as if the world has gone away from this northeastern corner, and those of us who are left up here feast on roast squash and watch our dogs run on empty beaches, barking at seagulls.

Chapter Five

Mock Turtle Soup and Terroir

During the kitchen renovation, when eating out became a necessity rather than a luxury, we were very glad that Portland has more good restaurants per capita than any other American city.

We had struck gold. For passionate eaters, this town turned out to be something of a Shangri-la, and most of our favorite places happened to be within blocks of our house: the funky, tin-ceilinged brick-oven pizza place on the corner; the Japanese noodle place with luscious sushi rolls drizzled with house-made mayo and toasted almonds, or a bowl of silky, spicy rice noodles with julienned vegetables and a fresh egg from the chef's own chickens; not one, but two homey, stylish, slouchy, glam hipster bars offering healthy home-cooked-style food; the New Orleans joint with the killer chicken wings and the so-so (you get what you pay for) dollar oysters at Happy Hour, classic Louisiana grub, and a tray of different sauces and pickled peppers on every table; an Italian-French place with cozy booths and an excellent wine list and a seasonally changing menu of Mediterranean-inspired dishes; a Thai "street vendor–inspired" tapas-and-skewer bar whose night-menu (as opposed to day-menu) pad thai was the best in town; and finally, our favorite, a classic corner bistro with perfect steak frites, perfect steak tartare, perfect simple salads, perfect pot de crème, and perfect service, decor, and everything else.

All this, within four blocks! There were other, equally excellent restaurants, five or seven or ten or twelve blocks away, like the dumpling place, the other pizza place, the upscale oyster place, and the hipster tapas place, but with such bounty, who needed to walk so far? Even during the two decades I lived in New York, no matter what neighborhood I was in, I never had this variety and quality of culinary excitement so close by.

A large part of my pleasure in all of these places was the fact that every one of them had a gluten-free menu and a friendly, concerned, helpful wait staff. Waiters in New York had always generally acted as if they had something much better to be doing, somewhere much better to be, and one or two of them even affected ignorance of the very existence of gluten, staring blankly at me as if I were speaking a foreign language they didn't comprehend. It was maddening, even though I understood: I'd once been one of those who scorned people with special dietary needs. I was a pain in the ass; I knew that. But it still bothered me.

A couple of years after I'd moved to the White Mountains, I went back to my old city on a book tour. As soon as I arrived, I made a beeline for my favorite bistro, a famous place in Soho beloved by natives and tourists alike. I ordered steak tartare without the bread; I thought I'd made my gluten situation very clear to the waiter.

However, when my lunch arrived, two slices of bread were perched on top of the chopped raw meat. I couldn't just whisk them off; my symptoms, damn it, can be triggered by a stray crumb.

"Oh, sorry," the waiter said with a bored moue when I finally got his attention and pointed this out. He took it back to the kitchen.

Another plate reappeared. I slid my fork into the savory raw meat and took a bite. In the luscious mix of fresh raw hamburger combined with raw egg yolk and condiments and minced aromatics, I tasted something suspiciously breadlike; then I saw the bread crumbs all over my food. The waiter had gone to the back, expediently whisked the bread off the steak tartare, and served the plate back to me.

Listen. I am an eater without tender scruples. I will happily eat raw meat, raw egg yolk, raw anything, any part of any animal, and I've never been sick from any of it, but gluten turns me almost immediately into a human lump of depressed, bloated, foggy-brained wreckage. I won't die from it, but I can't tolerate it. That's that.

Well, I'd already eaten the gluten, so it didn't matter, because any amount will do the trick, so I ate the rest of it, but my joy—in being back in my old favorite restaurant, in my once-beloved New York, in this much-yearned-for perfect steak tartare—was vastly dimmed.

That was, I think, the moment when the scales fell from my eyes, and I saw the cynicism and weariness of the city too clearly to ever turn back.

I felt as if I'd discovered a whole new culinary world up here. In Portland, I wasn't a demanding, persnickety, irritating freak; I was among friends. Every restaurant had a gluten-free menu, even the sports bar in the Old Port, and the waiters were all willing to consult with the chef if they weren't sure about something. Not only could I eat out with confidence and fearlessness in my new town, but we quickly came to realize that, as a matter of course, most of the restaurants in town used as much organic, local, free-range, cage-free, hormone- and antibiotic-free, wild-caught, sustainable, seasonal ingredients as possible. The menus often included lists of local farms and sources of meats and seafood along with brief descriptions of provenance; this wasn't trumpeted smugly, it was mentioned as a matter of interest, as if to say, "Here's where your food came from. Bon appétit!"

Restaurants here don't need to trumpet anything, smugly or otherwise. Maine's restaurants are great in large part because the food grown and raised and caught here is great, and smart chefs know not to gussy it up too much or tamper with its essential perfection. The word *terroir* is bandied about quite a bit these days by food writers and cooks, to refer to the essential taste of a place, the particularity of a region's geography, climate, soil, seawater, and air, and the way these elements combine with plant genetics to produce a particular, local flavor, which informs an organic and essential cuisine. In this place of long harsh winters and short lush summers, spring mud and autumn leaves turning to mulch, granite and sea and forests and acid soil, and abundant precipitation, the terroir is so rich and consistently excellent, it's practical common sense to cook ingredients that are local and in season, the fresher and closer to home, the better.

Eating in a good Maine restaurant is—in its most sublime sense—like being in someone's house, at their table, if that someone happens to be an amazing chef with access to the best imaginable ingredients. Maine's back-to-the-land movement was in full swing in the 1970s. Many new organic farms were created and established, which gave rise to plenty of available year-round organic local produce, which, in turn, over time, gave rise to the indigenous excellence of the restaurants here. Maine chefs tend to design menus according to the best available ingredients at hand, letting them dictate a dish with visceral instinct rather than combining foods from wildly disparate locales and cuisines with cerebral abstraction and culinary school doctrine. This smart practicality and inventive simplicity makes the food here as exciting as the cuisines of other regions with a similar approach to cooking, like California, Italy, or France.

∂∂

There were a few misses during our months of eating out, of course, but we learned to steer clear of those, aided by one helpful telling ingredient. Inexplicably, in our first year or two in Portland, truffle oil had suddenly become ubiquitous in fancy restaurants around town that were trying too hard to be trendy instead of making honest, nonsense-free food, the kind of food I'd learned to expect as a matter of course. It was splashed on salads, beaten into eggs for omelets, drizzled over a perfectly good hamburger (I just made that up, but it could have been).

For a while, I didn't notice, but after Brendan got violently sick from the truffle-oil popcorn at the bar of one tony restaurant (and could only mutter, "I'll never eat truffle oil again. God damn that fucking truffle oil!"), it occurred to me that yes, he's right: That stuff is disgusting. A few days later, there it was again, hidden in our lobster sushi. The aftertaste, now that I'd been made aware of it, lingered unpleasantly for hours.

A casual investigation, conducted by me on Google after one such disappointing dinner out, revealed that truffle oil is not made of truffles at all; rather, it's a synthetic amalgam of something called 2,4-Dithiapentane, which doesn't sound very appetizing or wholesome to me, plus organic aromas, sometimes from actual truffles, in an olive- or grapeseed-oil base. Why would you want that on your baked fish—or anything, for that matter? *Truffle oil* looks fancy on menus, but it's sheer food snobbery, which always makes me weary.

Truffles themselves, as everyone knows, are outrageously delicious, wickedly expensive, hard-to-find mushrooms buried near trees, sometimes found by trained pigs and, more recently, dogs. Brillat-Savarin called them "the diamond of the kitchen." The whole point is that they're rare. You don't eat them in everything the same way you don't wear diamonds every day; they're for special dishes and occasions, a luxury. Shaved, with olive oil, chives, and a little parmesan, black truffles elevate humble linguine to a gourmet feast.

At another restaurant, one of the most gushed-over, highly touted establishments in town, we were handed a "tasting menu" as the only option and a wine list with nothing under $40 anywhere to be seen on it.

For the next two hours, we nibbled our way through a series of small plates with even smaller bits of food on them, all of it over-thought, self-congratulatory, fussy, pretentious, and overly complex. I've forgotten every single thing we ate, but I have a visceral recollec-tion of a series of luridly colored emulsions smeared here, precious tiny garnishes draped there; incompatible, incongruous ingredients, like, say, a thin slice of roasted turnip, a leaf of mint battered and fried like tempura, and a quivering lump of burrata, that trendy, ubiqui-tous former peasant cheese, plunked side by side in a didactic chal-lenge to common sense and taste; or possibly an insultingly tiny coinlike tenderloin of undercooked duck arranged just so on a meager "bed" of corn porridge cooked with lots of fat and salt, like an invalid on a hospital gurney, covered with a gummy plum-colored salty sauce; desserts designed much like the high-heeled, elaborate shoes men wore in the court of Louis XIV.

I tried and failed to figure out why the tasting menu was the only dinner they offered. It cost $130 per person and contained not one dish I would have ordered voluntarily. We left feeling still hungry and pissed-off and went home for a nightcap of our own $8 Rioja and a filling snack of leftover roast chicken.

Another night found us at a farm-to-table Italian restaurant up in the Midcoast region; having heard nothing but raves and paeans about the place, we had decided to pay it a visit. The restaurant was in an old Victorian house on a hill overlooking the ocean. We arrived just as it opened, in hopes of getting a table in the upstairs café without a reservation. The place was so popular, people reserved tables in the main, downstairs dining room months in advance.

We were in luck; only a few couples were ahead of us, a well-heeled, prosperous-looking bunch, all in their sixties or thereabouts, the women in linen shorts and pashmina shawls and espadrilles, their hair shining pageboys, mostly blonde, the men in khaki shorts or pants and casual-leisure polo shirts and boat shoes.

We were seated upstairs by the bar at a cozy table for two. We looked around: The place had been expensively, meticulously renovated to resemble what struck me as a louche brothel, circa 1935. Everything was perfect, luxurious. It was very dark in here, even though outside it was a sunny, bright, late-June early evening. The atmosphere seemed promising; we rubbed our hands together, excited about the meal to come.

The waitress appeared: young, wholesome-looking, wide-eyed, and rabidly fanatical about the menu. "Downstairs, Chef Melissa is offering some whole fresh-picked *ceci*"— pronounced *cheh-chee*—"for seven dollars, roasted in our pizza oven and coming with sea salt." She said it as if she were offering us something rare and precious.

"*Ceci* is a pretentious way of saying unshelled chickpeas," Brendan told me after she'd gone away to let us deliberate. "Any Italian would laugh at that."

We laughed ourselves, shaking our heads at her earnest smugness. (Then, of course, curious to see if it was as special as our waitress seemed to think it was, we ordered it, and of course we got a handful of Italian edamame. We felt like chumps.)

Our dinner at this place in Midcoast Maine felt the way eating at another widely beloved restaurant had, a decade or more ago when my ex-husband and I were in Berkeley: like a high temple of culinary correctness, without a whiff of hedonism, gluttony, fun, or pleasure. The food was bland and sub-par; our waitress, breathless with awe at the *ceci*, seemed self-serious, zealous, and judgmental of any customer who didn't seem worthy of the food.

They made it known that they were very proud of the "working farm" in back that supplied their kitchens; after our mediocre, puzzling dinner, which cost well over $200 for two people, with wine, we walked through this small farm and saw pigs and chickens, but no shit, and perfect, obsessive-compulsive rows of vegetables, but no weeds. It was gorgeous and clearly highly functional, but I was feeling bilious and in no mood to like it.

"It's Foodsneyland," I said. "Like a picture-perfect cartoon farm."

"The parking lot is full of SUVs," said Brendan. "And the restaurant is full of rich people who have no idea that Tuscan chicken isn't overcooked hen in a bland tomato sauce."

"*Ceci*," I said, laughing.

"Why was that meal so expensive? It was food from their garden, yes, and it probably costs more to produce it yourself than sourcing from local farms, but the servings were too small for the price, and it wasn't even that good."

We went home filled with something that felt like class rage.

But the next day, I thought hard about why I'd reacted this way to what is by all accounts a universally beloved and excellent restaurant, run by a chef renowned for her hard work and philosophy of growing as much as possible of what she serves. I determined that I'd likely been unfair to the entire endeavor; the reason it was so expensive was that it's tremendously labor-intensive to do. The wealthy-seeming clientele was not the chef's fault, in other words. The economic reality dictated that those customers would be the people who'd eat there on a summer Saturday night: summer people, from away, with disposable income. I forced myself to question my ancient suspicion of rich people. They were supporting this worthy, earnest bastion of real food instead of taking their money to a restaurant that served cynical crap. And every restaurant has an off night. Clearly, we needed to go back and give it another chance.

Also, these disappointments were the exceptions, and they stood out from our usual experiences in Maine restaurants. Up and down the coast, we found places we were thrilled to discover: a simple pub in Damariscotta with fantastically light, fresh, gluten-free fish and chips and local oysters, the best I've ever eaten; a harborside local hangout in Camden with fat, clean steamers and kickass coleslaw; the lobster truck in Fort Williams Park, whose lobster salad was perfect.

On a special occasion, we decided to go out for dinner as a splurge and a celebration, so we chose our restaurant carefully. Vinland might be New England's answer to Noma, the Copenhagen shrine to local and seasonal molecular cooking which was recently voted the best restaurant in the world. Vinland's owner and chef, David Levi, even staged at Noma for a summer. He's from away, but he's forged deep relationships with local farmers and fishermen. The name of the place comes from the mythic New World land where the Vikings found wild grapes growing; Maine is as likely a potential spot as anywhere else.

David Levi's got an idealistic manifesto, a stringently quixotic but admirably consistent take on local, seasonal, and organic. The restaurant serves no olive oil, for example, since there are no olive trees in Maine; the same goes for chocolate. And because lemons and limes don't grow here, instead of citrus in cocktails, they use whey—the astringent dairy by-product of cheese making. Adorning the spare walls are birch logs. The tables are handmade; the dishes are made of natural materials—stone, clay. The menu proclaims that it's gluten-free, Paleo-friendly, and "100 percent local, down to the salt." It's the New Nordic Cuisine raised to an art form.

"How's your dinner?" David asked us, coming by our table as we dug our forks into astonishingly fresh, delicious salads with emulsified blue cheese and apple vinegar dressing. He was young and thin,

Italian-Jewish, with an earnest, very awake expression. He was wearing a bandanna around his head that said EAT LOCALLY. He asked as if he deeply wanted to know.

"Amazing," we told him honestly.

We'd ordered a feast: lobster with wild black trumpet mushroom emulsion, strip steak with whey-poached parsnips and hen of the woods, radicchio with potato and cheddar, monkfish with shiitake, spinach, and the tenderest sunchoke we'd ever eaten, Brussels sprouts with roast delicata seeds. As dish after dish appeared, we noticed that the portions were about half the size of a normal restaurant, but we got full quickly. At the end, we felt totally satisfied, but not bloated or stuffed.

Over a digestif of house-made dill and fennel aquavit, I asked David to expound on his philosophy.

"It's the culture of a place reflected in the cuisine," he said. "Because food is the basis of culture. It's the Native American pre–agricultural revolution ways of eating, according to the seasons, the climate, combined with modern craftsmanship, the precision of molecular gastronomy and French cooking. I think of it as meta-indigenous."

"Meta-indigenous," I repeated happily, polishing off the last crumbs of the cheese plate with oat crackers. "I love that."

Maine is—in many ways—the ideal place for a restaurant like Vinland, replete with thriving organic farms, sustainably caught local seafood, and the centuries-old traditions of hunting and foraging. The thin, acidic soil of the region and the short growing season make the state unprofitable for industrial agriculture. In the past this might have been considered a negative, but in fact it's been beneficial. Maine's native agriculture has been preserved by its marginal nature, pushed in a positive direction out of necessity to embrace and preserve old traditions.

"There's more local food in Maine," said David. "Farmers show up at restaurant doors with fresh organic produce. It's so easy to get." But even in a restaurant community known for a heavy reliance on local food, Vinland stands out for its strict adherence to its local-only mission.

What would he say to those who call this mission radical? Even extreme?

"I hate being called extreme," David stresses, with quiet vehemence. "Extreme and radical are relative terms, relative to a given norm, used as an objective state of being. We live in a very tragic time, a radical, extreme culture relative to the community of life. We are destroying the earth rapidly, horrifically. Relative to that, I'm radical and extreme. Relative to the natural world and traditional societies, I'm very conservative. I deeply believe in immense precautions to preserve the natural world and communities."

I found myself rooting for David Levi to succeed here in stalwartly down-to-earth Maine, even though he's conceptually rigorous, even though the inspiration behind his food is more cerebral than visceral. No matter how weird it may be to have whey in a Dark & Stormy instead of lime juice, that meal was flat-out delicious, creative, and interesting. Levi's intensely rigorous cuisine of local-only ingredients, down to the salt, turns out to be a lot of fun to eat in the hands of such a brilliant, adept chef.

After dinner, we drove through an early snowstorm to the White Mountains. The next morning, I awoke to a fresh, snowy, sunny landscape. I felt rested and energetic and clear-headed. We took Dingo out for the usual fast four-mile walk, admired the shadows the sun cast through clouds on the mountains, inhaled the crisp northern air. A birch branch had fallen into the creek. Snowflakes sifted down through bright air from hemlock boughs. The lake was as steely-blue and choppy as a fjord.

We came home to hot steel-cut oatmeal with wild blueberries, maple syrup, and cinnamon. My Nordic heart was singing. This region, so Scandinavian in so many ways, is a place where Noma's culinary ideals as interpreted by an earnest zealot like David Levi can flourish.

ℓℓℓ

Before the back-to-the-land movement, which started in 1952 with Helen and Scott Nearing's move to Cape Rosier to found the now-famous Forest Farm, and exploded in the 1970s as young people came north in droves to meet these gurus and emulate them, restaurants in Maine used to serve what I think of as "horrible New England cuisine": stodgy, "fancy," oddly garnished dishes of dubious origin.

The Maine Historical Society has a collection of vintage menus from the olden days. According to an entertaining piece by Meredith Goad, published in the *Portland Press Herald* on September 11, 2013, local restaurants used to feature such delicacies as "mock turtle soup" (made with organ meats or calves' heads, rather than turtle), "baked halibut Manhattan," and "boiled ox tongue with piquant sauce." Tomato juice cocktails were popular. Weird garnishes abounded. A dish called "banana scallops," according to Goad, contained no scallops, but was rather "a retro [for us] recipe of coated, fried bananas that were often served like a vegetable."

The Preble House's extensive menu (pronounced "bad and disgusting" in 1868 by none other than Charles Dickens) included "fried smelts served with tartar sauce and French fried potatoes, breaded lamb chops with tomato sauce, oyster patties, apricot fritters with wine sauce, roast chicken with giblet sauce, tenderloin of beef and mushrooms, Roman punch [a tart, boozy rum and lemonade concoction with a dollop of meringue on top that was commonly used back then as a palate cleanser], roast partridge with game sauce and Saratoga potatoes, and on and on, until the meal is finished with coffee and cigars."

ℓℓℓ

Mock Turtle Soup

From *The Home Comfort Range Cook Book,* circa 1900

Boil half a calf's head with the skin on until soft; cut the meat into small pieces; also the tongue; prepare from the yolks of two hard-boiled eggs round balls the size of marbles, and chop up the whites; take of soup stock two quarts; then fry in one ounce of butter a medium-sized onion and add one ounce of flour and brown the same; then add the stock, a teaspoon of Worcester-shire sauce, pepper and salt, the juice of one lemon, and let simmer for ten minutes. Pour over the meat and imitation turtle eggs and serve hot, adding the chopped whites of the eggs.

ℓℓℓ

This was, evidently, the state of public dining in Maine until the summer of 1974, when a young, unseasoned Sam Hayward sliced open the belly of a thirty-pound cod from the Gulf of Maine and looked inside. "It was chock-full of 1 1/2-inch baby lobsters," he told Mary Pols and Meredith Goad of the Source section of the *Portland Press Herald*. "Lined up, all facing the same direction, stacked up."

Although he had no formal training, Hayward had just been hired by Shoals Marine Laboratory on Appledore Island to cook for the teachers, students, and the construction crews and engineers finishing up the lab's new buildings. He was relying heavily on his copy of Julia Child's *Mastering the Art of French Cooking*, but it was the enormous cod he'd sliced open that made everything leap to life for him: There it was, the food chain, laid out in front of him.

"Suddenly you start to see interactions in the community in the Gulf of Maine," he told Pols and Goad. "It became an object of fascination for me that I still feel. How do we connect the dots?"

That summer, he developed a passionate interest in local ingredients. Then he opened a restaurant in Brunswick and forged a bond with a local farmer, Frank Gross, taking whatever produce he had, a relationship that continues today. In 1996, he opened what is now arguably Portland's most famous and beloved restaurant, Fore Street. Hayward is widely hailed as the father of Maine's farm-to-table movement; all around him now are restaurants whose chefs have been inspired by what he started forty years ago—a whole posse of self-taught native Maine cooks up and down the coast and inland.

One of the most visible and exemplary of Hayward's culinary descendants is Erin French. I had heard amazing things about her restaurant, the Lost Kitchen, located in the small farming hamlet of Freedom. It had only been open since July of 2014, but it was already booked well into the future. When *Food & Wine* magazine asked me to go up and interview her, of course I leapt at the chance, and of course I brought Brendan with me. And it was there that I found the quintessential young Maine chef I'd been looking for.

To eat at the Lost Kitchen, first we had to find it. From Belfast, we drove inland on a two-lane country road through seventeen miles of snowy, windswept, mountainous farmland. The sign for Freedom was so small, we nearly missed it. A quick left on Main Street, and there was the Mill at Freedom Falls. We took the last parking spot and walked across a narrow bridge over a rushing stream. It was early December, snowy and icy, but that night's dinner was fully booked. (At that time, the Lost Kitchen served a multicourse prix fixe menu on Saturdays, family style; on three other days, they offered a full and ever-changing menu, and on Sunday, Monday, and Tuesday, they were closed.)

In the stone-walled wine cellar downstairs from the restaurant, Jess, the sommelier, was wrapping bottles in brown paper bags and tying them with twine for the diners. While we waited, we browsed her small, beautifully curated collection of wine on open shelving. (There were no liquor licenses to be had in tiny Freedom, but you could bring your own wine or buy it there.) When it was our turn, we asked what went with that night's main course, which was described tantalizingly on the menu as "tea-brined duck breast with root vegetable hash and caramelized onion jam."

"Are you from Maine?" I asked Jess; she had a distinct New York accent, but I never presume.

She laughed. "Do I sound like I'm from Maine? I'm a Jewish girl from the Bronx."

We bought the bottle of Gamay she recommended, as well as a half-bottle of port, then went up to the restaurant, which was in a large, airy room with barn-board walls, sanded plank floors, and a ceiling of exposed beams with suspended mill trestles. A wall of windows looked out onto the stream and bridge; the handmade tables were spaced far apart.

We sat at the polished concrete kitchen counter. Erin and that night's crew of four other young women (the only guy working in the place was the dishwasher) prepared and served the first of a succession of small plates, each better than the last: marinated herbed olives with crusty bread, butter, and watermelon radishes; luscious scallop crudo, the first of the season, with olive oil, shallots, and lemon; crunchy fried smelts with aioli; and the pièce de résistance, a succulent fried Pemaquid oyster in its shell on a bed of seaweed with piquant raw beet slaw and horseradish aioli.

After the appetizers, Erin stepped out from behind the counter and gave a toast, thanking us all for finding the place and making it possible for her, a self-taught cook—"I feel weird being called 'Chef,'" she told me the next day; "I'm just a girl who loves to cook"—and a local girl, to realize her dream.

Next, warm roast carrot soup was swirled from Mason jars into bowls of crème fraîche and honey. Then came a crunchy, textured salad of late season lettuces, with slabs of shaved Pecorino tucked in here and there—and then the duck: brined in Lapsang souchong for a smoky richness, perfectly cooked, rare in the middle and steak-like. The caramelized onion jam was addictive; I wanted a jar full of it and a spoon. And the root vegetable hash was rich, savory, dense with flavor. And finally dessert: parsnip cake with salted caramel whipped cream and hazelnuts; the whipped cream was as addictive as the onion jam.

Every dish consisted of just a few local, seasonal ingredients; all were plated with fresh herb garnishes on vintage dishware. The crew moved from fryer to counter to tables in a well-rehearsed dance. The feeling in the room was calm, festive, and homey, all at once.

Erin sent everyone home with a bag of freshly baked molasses cookies, her grandmother's recipe that she'd tweaked with pieces of candied ginger. We drifted across the bridge to the parking lot, happy and sated, and drove back to our seaside hotel in Belfast.

ele

Erin French's Fried Oysters with Beetroot Slaw and Horseradish Aioli

12 oysters

For the fry batter:
1/2 cup flour
1/2 cup semolina

For the slaw:

1 small shallot
1 large red beet
1 T seasoned rice wine vinegar
3 T olive oil
salt and pepper to season

For the aioli:

1 large egg yolk
1/2 cup olive oil
1 1/2 tsp horseradish
1/4 tsp lemon juice
1 tsp water
salt to season

4 cups canola oil for frying
seaweed and kosher salt for garnish
special tools: mandolin, deep-fry thermometer

To prepare oysters: Shuck the oysters into a small bowl along with all of the oyster "liquor," discarding the flat top shell, retaining the rounded-out bottom shell. Refrigerate the oysters until ready to fry. Wash the retained bottom shells, scraping out any remaining oyster pieces, and set aside to dry.

To prepare the fry batter: In a small bowl, combine the flour and semolina. Set aside.

To prepare the slaw: Finely chop the shallot, place in a small bowl, and top with vinegar. Let stand for 15 minutes to macerate. Add the olive oil to the mixture and whisk to combine. On the finest matchstick tooth blade of a mandolin, grate the beet. Add the beet to the shallot mixture. Mix to coat and season with salt and pepper. If the slaw seems dry, add a bit more olive oil to suit. Set aside for flavors to incorporate.

To make the aioli: In a small bowl, beat the egg yolk with a hand mixer on high speed. Add a few drops olive oil and continue to beat. Continue to add the olive oil, one drop at a time, beating constantly until the mixture is thick, pale, and fluffy. Add the lemon juice and water to thin. Stir in the horseradish. Season with salt to taste.

In a 12-inch cast-iron skillet, preheat the fry oil to 375 degrees over medium-high heat. Meanwhile, prepare the oyster "baskets." On a large platter, scatter a bit of seaweed for garnish. Pour 12 small mounds of kosher salt and top each with a clean oyster shell. Fill each with a bit of beet slaw. Now, fry the oysters.

To fry the oysters: Dredge each oyster through the flour and semolina mixture. Drop into the preheated fryer and fry until golden brown, about 15 seconds. Remove with a slotted spoon and blot on a paper towel. Season with a pinch of salt. Place an oyster on each slaw-filled oyster shell and top with a small dollop of aioli. Serve immediately. Makes 12 oysters.

ele

Back at the mill the next morning, I sat with Erin at a table in the sunlight, drinking coffee.

"I love that you have an all-female crew," I said.

She laughed. "We call ourselves the Estrogen Café. In our medicine chest there's Aleve, tampons, and vitamin B-twelve. We all get our periods at the same time."

"I saw one guy here last night," I said.

"That's our dishwasher. He changed his name from something normal to Dirt. He's the most gentle, peaceful guy. I feel so bad when diners overhear us going, 'Hey, Dirt, can you do this?' Like a room full of women are abusing him." We both laughed.

We talked about how she is entirely self-taught and, despite working in catering for many years, never went to culinary school.

"You'll find no fancy sauces, smoking guns, or sous vide here," she said. "I'm not Noma! You should recognize every word on my menus." And indeed, her instinctively pure palate comes through in her unfussy, astonishingly delicious cooking, her minimal, beautiful presentations. Her dishes are rooted in tradition; many of her recipes came from her mother and grandmother, which she then elevated and made her own. Her menus are unpretentious but sophisticated, using as few ingredients as possible in combinations both exciting and viscerally satisfying.

For Erin, the magic is all in the ingredients. "They're the stars," she said. "I get the best produce. My friend will text me a photo of a cauliflower in her field and I'll say, 'bring me twelve of those.' Later, she serves them herself."

"So your staff are farmers?"

"They farm by day and cook here at night. They're my best friends. They love to get away from their husbands and kids. They teach me about food and pick out stuff for me, like bolted cilantro, which they know I love. We're curating each other's businesses. And they get to plate the salads made from the greens they grow."

"So you're as farm-to-table as it gets," I said. "And as local."

"My mother even works here," she said. "She's the front-of-house meet-and-greeter."

Then she told me that she'd even made the tables herself, in classic Maine DIY fashion, out of barn boards and plumbing fixtures.

"They're spaced far apart because I want it to feel comfortable, like you're eating dinner in my house," she said. "I want that homey feeling."

I confess I fell a little in love with her at that moment.

ele

Erin was born and raised in Freedom. By the time she was fourteen, she was flipping burgers on the line in her parents' diner, the Ridge Top, only a mile from the old mill. After college at Northeastern in Boston, she moved to California to become a doctor.

"Then I came home for Christmas, and there was my old highschool sweetheart . . . one night with him, I got pregnant. I moved back home to live with my parents at twenty-one. My ex-boyfriend wasn't at all interested in being a father at that point because our lives were going in totally different directions, so he's never been a part of my son's life at all, and I've always been fine with that."

She smiled. "My mom was my Lamaze partner! I named my son Jaim for the French, 'I love,' *j'aime*." She pronounced it *Jaym*, like James without the "s."

"As a single mother, I got to pick the name; I didn't have to consult with anyone else. After Jaim was born, I started baking at home, as a single mom. I delivered cakes and cookies."

Erin got married at twenty-four and moved with her new husband to an apartment in an old bank building in Belfast.

"I worked for a local catering company for years and years. I started thinking, What am I doing? I had to create something. Turning thirty was a crisis for me. I struggled with that birthday. I needed direction, a stake in something creative. I didn't have the money for culinary school. Why would I go into debt to learn a trade that would never make enough money to pay it off? I did the math: I couldn't afford to move somewhere else, so I got creative and scrappy."

In December 2010, she started an underground supper club out of the apartment in Belfast she shared with her husband, calling it the Lost Kitchen.

"Legally it was a fine line," she said. "It was in my house, one dinner a week, BYOB; people made donations for ingredients instead of paying. I taught myself to cook on a four-burner 1987 GE stove. No recipes, no rules. I was obsessive about reading cookbooks and experimenting, and my customers were my guinea pigs. I'd serve a five-course meal once a week."

This rigorous culinary autodidacticism paid off.

"By November, dinners were selling out in two minutes, every time I sent out an e-mail, with fifty people on the wait list. I'd look outside and not see a single person I knew. We'd turn on a light, like a brothel. People would ring the doorbell. As they came in, I checked their names off the list until they were all there. Then we turned off the light, locked the doors, and served dinner. They sat at four communal tables, family-style. It was so exciting, a real confidence boost. For all the years I'd been catering, I had to adhere strictly to preset recipes, proportions multiplied out to feed a hundred. It was so freeing to just cook. So exciting. But my hope was always to open a restaurant."

In May 2011, she and her then-husband bought their Belfast building, an old bank. After a five-month renovation and build-out, Erin opened the Lost Kitchen as a bona fide restaurant downstairs.

"I put my heart and soul into that place and had crazy success," she said. "I had a following. My career was taking off. Then I lost the place."

"What happened?" I asked.

"My husband got it in the divorce," she said. "He was so angry when I left, but I had to. I felt like he was threatened by my growing success. I wanted to grow and develop, and he didn't want that; he wanted his pretty little trophy wife. He's twenty years older than I am, and I was his second wife; he has grown kids not much younger than me. I married him at twenty-four, a single mother. He legally adopted Jaim a couple of years later. In the divorce, he tried to get full custody and was awarded half. He changed the locks when I moved out. I took only what could fit in a suitcase. I lost my grandmother's china . . . so many things. But they're just things. I had to let go, to move on."

Broke, homeless, and heartbroken, she moved back to Freedom with Jaim, in with her parents again ("Thank God for them!" she said). For a time, while Jaim stayed with her ex-husband, she lived in a cabin with no electricity or running water.

"I used a chamber pot, I was so broke. The funny thing was, I *did* have a pot to piss in! It made me realize that I hadn't lost quite everything."

Erin's friends helped her raise the money to buy a 1965 Airstream. She gutted it with a sledgehammer, then built a kitchen in it and turned it into a mobile supper club, taking it to farms and destinations for pop-up dinners all over Maine.

"I knew that it takes a good eight months to a year to open a restaurant, to get all the licenses, etc., so this felt like a quick and dirty way to keep moving forward. I served a couple of meals at Eliot Coleman's Four Season Farm—dinners in the greenhouse, under the apple tree. I roasted pork chops over an open fire, served burgers and beer in barns. Every weekend, a different location. I'd go a day early to scout and forage local ingredients. It felt like I was going toward the cause."

Then one of Erin's friends in Freedom, a farmer whose chickens are now served at the Lost Kitchen, told her to check out the town's old mill, which her father-in-law, Tony Grassi, was restoring.

The Mill at Freedom Falls was in operation for 133 years, from the time it was built as a gristmill in 1834. In 1894, it was converted to a woodturning mill, which ceased operations in 1967. From then on, the enormous old wood-frame mill on Sandy Stream, formerly the dominant feature of the community, sat dormant and abandoned and falling down. Tony Grassi's renovation took eighteen months. The massive project resulted in a revitalized, meticulously restored building, bright and airy, refitted with clean, true boards and sturdy underpinnings. And in turn, the community of Freedom was itself revitalized. Grassi's daughter opened a school in the mill, and then Erin French opened the Lost Kitchen. Freedom's farmers and their children have now become the old mill's lifeblood, instead of the other way around, as it used to be in the olden days.

"Food and kids," said Erin. "If you want life in a place, those are the things to bring to it."

The first time she walked into the newly renovated mill's empty first story, still with sawdust on the floor, and saw the view, the raw wood, the possibilities, her jaw dropped. "I thought, this is it," she said.

She presented a business plan to potential investors, mostly friends and family, used money her grandfather left to her family as collateral to get a bank loan, and signed a lease. Over the next few months, she built out a simple open kitchen behind a polished concrete island. Much of her old crew from Belfast came with her.

"I decided to have a regular menu with changes every night. Local, seasonal, all about this place: This is what's available now."

With symbolic aptness, the Lost Kitchen opened on Independence Day of 2014. Less than six months later, Erin's cooking had become renowned far beyond Maine for its inventive, instinctive sublimity. Her old fans from her first restaurant as well as many new ones came every night from miles away.

That winter, she was planning to close the Lost Kitchen in order to write a cookbook for a major New York publisher. And she'd fallen in love again. She and her new beau had recently bought a 160-year-old farmhouse together, a mile from the Lost Kitchen.

"It was a real rebirth, coming home," she said. "This is all a result of hard work. I give everything, every day; I have not an ounce left.

But I've never been healthier or happier. Every time I cross that bridge I'm grateful. And it feels so good to touch people—to give them memories, sustenance, community; it's the most wonderful thing in the world to be doing. I've come full circle." She added, "As an homage to where I came from, there's always a burger on my menu."

After we finished talking, I thanked her and hugged her good-bye and drove back to Belfast. As I drove, thinking back over our conversation, I was struck by the difference between Erin's delicate, petite blonde prettiness and her tough-minded moxie and grit. She's the physical embodiment of her food: lovely and sophisticated on the outside, authentic and down-to-earth on the inside.

At our hotel, I collected Brendan and Dingo and our luggage. On our way out of town, hungry again, we stopped for brunch at Erin's former restaurant, which is right in downtown Belfast, on a busy corner. Erin had told me that after she left, her ex-husband brought in Matthew Kenney, a nationally known restaurateur, to help him get the place back on its feet. Renamed the Gothic, the place was almost empty; the only customers were one other couple, who sat in the bar, and us. We had the dining room to ourselves. The two young chefs who'd been recently hired to revitalize the place cooked us a prix fixe, four-course vegetarian brunch.

After we had eaten, they came to our table to ask how everything was. I asked them where they were from; one was a transplant from Philly, the other from one of Kenney's other restaurants in Miami. They'd both been here only a few months.

"We're trying to get people to come back," they told us. "The Gothic's reputation has suffered a blow in the past couple of years."

I looked around at the sunny, spacious room. Our meal had been expertly made and nicely presented, but it was food you might find in Venice Beach or Miami Beach, not Maine: a smoothie, a quinoa and tofu scramble, gluten-free quinoa bread with a poached egg and meatlike slab of mushroom, and for dessert, bananas Foster. The food was expert, but not exciting, especially in light of our dinner the night before, but beyond that, there was something off about it all, something wrong. This urbanely crafted vegetarian and vegan fare didn't feel organic to Maine, the way Erin's food had. It felt grafted on, overthought, more conceptual than delicious.

We left the Gothic crew a good tip and drove away, back down the coast, wishing we could go back to the Lost Kitchen for dinner that night. Of course, it was closed on Sundays, but we vowed to return as soon as we could, and as often.

Chapter Six

Literary Lobster
and Clam Condoms

Naturally, as new residents of Portland, we were constantly struck by the fact that this town was teeming with lobsters: pulled-in-for-the-winter stacks of lobster pots reeking in the late autumn air along Casco Bay, lobsters on license plates, lobster-shaped beer openers and lobster refrigerator magnets and stuffed lobsters in gift shops, guys sweltering in fuzzy red lobster suits down on Commercial Street all through tourist season, plush antennae bobbing. In fact, due to its ubiquity in Maine life, the lobster, rather than the moose, could easily be the state animal.

Before the settlers came, according to the Gulf of Maine Research Institute's website, lobsters were so common and plentiful that the Native Americans waded along the shore and caught them bare-handed and fertilized their fields with them. They also used lobster meat as bait on their fishhooks to attract "better" catch.

Despite the abundance of lobster, though, it seems the Wabanaki didn't actually eat them. As the website of the Acadia National Park

Service informs us, "Archaeological evidence shows that Wabanaki families on Mount Desert Island one thousand years ago hunted and harvested a variety of land and sea animals. People ate seals, porpoises, white-tailed deer, moose, beaver, and many varieties of birds. They fished for sculpin and flounder at high tide on mudflats and gathered sea urchins, clams, and blue mussels, which were steamed open to reveal the delicate meat. However, Wabanaki people avoided one particular Maine 'delicacy'—lobster. Only one lobster claw has been discovered in twenty years of excavating Maine coastal sites."

Europeans, however, had been eating lobster since Greek and Roman times; the British, who prized them, brought this knowledge of lobsters' edibility with them to the New World, although the colonists quickly came to disparage them, maybe because they were so huge and plentiful. In colonial times, lobsters were harvested from tidal pools.

According to James M. Acheson in *The Lobster Gangs of Maine*, "The English settlers who came to the Popham Colony off the mouth of the Kennebec River in 1607 reported that they gaffed fifty lobsters for food within an hour. Captain John Smith of Virginia, who visited Monhegan and Midcoast Maine in the early 1600s, enthusiastically described the plenitude of lobsters that could be taken in any bay. The lobsters were said to be of enormous size, some measuring up to five feet long."

Likely because of this surfeit and ease of catching, as well as their weird insectlike appearance and the brutish preparation and awkwardly messy consumption (there really is no graceful or refined way to eat a whole boiled lobster), lobsters were considered "poverty food" and fed to children and prisoners, as well as the indentured servants who'd exchanged their passage to America for seven years of service to their sponsors.

(Apocryphal stories have it that the servants evidently considered lobster roughly on par with bread and water; according to their contracts, they weren't supposed to be forced to eat it more than three times a week, and when some employers failed to abide by this, their servants rebelled. This story is also, interchangeably, told about prisoners. Although no one can pinpoint the exact source, and its veracity is dubious, it does make an instructive point.)

In 1622, Governor William Bradford of the Plymouth Plantation apologized to a new arrival of settlers that the only dish he "could presente their friends with was a lobster . . . without bread or anything else but a cupp of fair water."

Nonetheless, by the nineteenth century, lobsters had regained their former European culinary prestige here in the New World. According to *America's Founding Food: The Story of New England Cooking*, by Keith Stavely and Kathleen Fitzgerald, lobsters in New England were cooked "in sauces for other fish, or as accompaniments to roasts . . . When not potting lobsters, baking them in pies or using them in sauces, eighteenth- and nineteenth-century New England cooks were apt to stew or fricassee them . . . Boiled lobsters were served cold with dressing, not hot and 'in the rough,' as we are most likely to encounter them today."

Until the early 1800s, lobsters were caught by hand along the shoreline in shallow water and eaten locally. Large-scale lobster trapping, using boats equipped with seawater tanks in their holds, called smacks, didn't come into existence in Maine until the mid-nineteenth century, when demand for lobsters in Boston and New York turned north after the Cape Cod stocks had been overfished out of existence.

Shortly afterwards, to meet the growing demand in other places too far to reach by boat, since live lobsters don't travel well and their meat doesn't preserve well, canneries sprang up in Maine; the first was in Eastport in 1843. An enormous amount of lobster meat was canned and shipped around the world in those days . The canneries also canned and shipped fish, corn, shellfish, and clams. By 1880, there were twenty-three lobster canneries operating on the Maine coast. Canned lobster meat quickly became so popular that by the second half of the nineteenth century, its value outstripped that of fresh.

At first, there were so many lobsters in the Gulf of Maine that anything smaller than five pounds was considered piddling. But the fishermen and canneries became so enthusiastic about the profitability of this new commercial enterprise, they colluded in stripping the Gulf of its bounty as fast as they could, so a mere twenty years later, they were happily canning lobsters as small as half a pound, called "snappers." The lobsters were so overfished by this point, the whole fishing-and-canning operation moved north again, to Nova Scotia.

In 1872, in response to the sudden dearth of this once-plentiful resource, the lobster industry in Maine was regulated to prohibit the catch of females bearing eggs and any lobster smaller than ten and a half inches long overall. The fishery was closed seasonally, between August 1 and October 15. Suddenly, canning's profits fell off steeply, and by 1895, lobster canning had ceased in Maine altogether, and the canneries had either closed or moved on to other products.

On our daily walks along the Eastern Prom, toward the end of the paved path, we often notice the appetizing scent of baked beans wafting over the bay from the B&M factory at the edge of the water, toward Yarmouth. (This smell of molasses and vinegar is unfortunately often superseded by the smells from the sewage-treatment plant at the end of the Prom, but on some days when the winds are favorable, it triumphs.) I had assumed that the Burnham & Morrill Company had always been in the bean business, but in fact, originally, they were lobster canners who shipped lobster meat around the world. When the lobster industry became regulated, they were forced to switch to beans to stay in business.

This strict, universally observed regulation of the wild lobster stock did save the fishing end of things, and the lobster industry has boomed to an all-new high in recent years, thanks to warming waters in the Gulf of Maine, whose once-teeming, plentiful fish—cod, pollock, hake, and haddock, and the fishing canneries they supported—have been just about wiped out. The absence of fish means no predators for the lobsters, which has also helped their numbers increase. Now, lobster is pretty much the only game left. It's the single sustaining catch of the state's economy, representing 80 percent of the value of Maine's fisheries. This lobster monoculture supports not only the fishermen, but also the boatbuilders, mechanics, bait sellers, and, of course, the tourist industry.

And so, in a strange twist of global-warming luck, increased temperatures have led to an all-time high in the lobster population. After a decades-long average of 20 million pounds per year of lobsters, 2013 saw a staggeringly huge total catch of 125 million pounds. However, despite this bonanza, according to *A Cruising Guide to the Maine Coast*, "The lobsterman himself hasn't changed much. Still fiercely independent, he goes out when he wants and wrests a living from the sea in winter and summer. He takes great pride in his boat, his self-reliance, and his ability to feed his family. He complains about the price of lobsters at the co-op, and the cost of fuel. He worries about overfishing and declining lobster stocks, and too many part-timers getting lobster licenses. He sees seals as lobster thieves. He gets angry about mussel-draggers and scallopers spoiling good lobster grounds. He doesn't much like all the regulations and the 'Gummint Fishcrats,' as Captain Perc Sane calls them. But he hopes it will work out all right, and keeps on doing what he's best at—pulling lobsters from the bottom."

Unfortunately, it probably won't work out all right. For now, the temperatures in the Gulf of Maine are in a "sweet spot" for lobsters, but as the heat increases—and it is increasing now, warming faster than any other body of water on earth—the thriving Maine lobster population will most likely collapse. Further south, in Long Island

Sound, as well as Connecticut and Rhode Island, the lobster industries collapsed in 1999, when their waters reached all-time high temperatures, compromising the lobsters' immune systems and causing them to die off, massively, of shell disease, a bacterial infection. Fifteen years later, those lobster stocks further south have not recovered, and it's likely they never will.

In an article called "The Lobster Bubble" published in August 2013 on ThinkProgress.com, Joanna M. Foster wrote, "If this leads to a crash in the Maine lobster industry, experts agree it would almost inevitably lead to irreversible gentrification of Maine's coast. While the going has been good, lobstermen have invested in bigger boats and more equipment to take advantage of the record lobster numbers. Much of this gear is owned by the bank. It's a bit like the housing bubble, and if the lobsters go, lobstermen won't be able to make their payments and the bank will have a glut of lobster boats."

Foster continues: "The irony of the situation in Maine is that the lobster fishery is one of the best-managed fisheries in the country. Because the communities are so dependent on the resource, and by law all lobstermen are owner/operators in Maine, everyone out on the water abides by laws prohibiting the capture of egg-bearing females, large breeding lobsters, and small juveniles. If not for climate change, the lobster fishery could be extremely sustainable, a shining success story of a well-managed fishery."

Oh, well. Damn it. Climate change sucks.

Farming lobsters, unfortunately, is tricky, due to lobsters' complex life cycles: They require expensive live feed in the larval stage, and they're cannibalistic when they get older, which is problematic on a whole other level. Meanwhile, other fishermen, many of them the sons and daughters of lobstermen, are looking into aquaculture of oysters and mussels. In 2009, a lobster fisherman named Adam Campbell, along with his sons, started an oyster farm on the island of North

Haven, in order to supplement the income from his lobster catch, and eventually, replace it. By 2013, oysters represented 60 percent of his income.

Foster quotes Campbell, saying, with the classic die-hard Maine attitude: "It takes about four years to get anything from a new oyster farm. When I was getting started, I was out on the lobster boat all day, and in the bay with a headlamp all night, getting eaten alive by mosquitoes. I know that growing oysters will never earn me the kind of status that bringing in a boatload of lobsters will around here, but I know that lobstering won't be this good forever, and this island is my home, where I met my wife and raised my kids. I'm not going to be pushed out."

ele

Fragile and provisional though their existence may be, for the time being, lobsters are still abundant around here. The lobster roll is easily the most popular dish in the state: chunks of tender, sweet lobster meat lightly tossed with mayonnaise, a bit of chopped celery, parsley, lemon juice, salt, and pepper, piled on a toasted, buttered soft roll and served with coleslaw on a wax-paper boat plate. Every local market has a bubbling, algae-smeared lobster tank filled with squirming, armor-plated little warrior-like sci-fi insects, claws banded to keep them from killing and eating one another, antennae waving with anthropomorphized indignation and panic.

Lobster is easy to cook at home: Toss the live, writhing, banded fighters into a huge pot of boiling salt water and clap the lid on for ten or fifteen minutes, depending on the size; some people claim they don't suffer as much if they're hypnotized beforehand by stroking their backs until they stand on their heads, but I'm more inclined to believe those who swear by sticking them in the refrigerator beforehand to numb them, just long enough so they're still alive.

Haul them out of the boiling water when they're bright red, let them cool a little, and have at them with picks and nutcrackers, fingers and forks, dipping everything into melted butter and sucking out each leg and joint, and the head. The roe, a bright red-orange, dense, spongelike mass called coral, is slightly fishy-tasting, sweet, and delicious; the weird green stuff, called tomalley, which is the liver and digestive system, is prized by some, but not by me, although I love the rest of the beast.

However, despite my love for them, for some reason, during our first year and a half in Portland, our adventures with lobsters were few and far between. In fact, we only had whole lobsters once in all that time.

J's Oyster is a small, low-ceilinged, warm little shack in the Old Port, perched on the end of a wharf, with plate-glass windows looking out at the harbor and bay. The first time we went, the sailboats parked in the slip had a foot of snow on their roofs and the water was dark blue. We went in and sat at the crowded bar. We ordered glasses of rough red wine and were handed paper plates of free Happy Hour oysters. The oysters at J's are working-class mollusks, no-nonsense, nothing fancy, to put it mildly—unlike Maine oysters, which are uniformly excellent and pristine, these blokes come from the Chesapeake Bay and have dirty, knobby shells.

To go with them, we ordered a bucket of steamers. They arrived hot and tender, with bowls of hot steaming liquid and little cups of melted butter.

As we learned from the waitress, who demonstrated for us, this is the most basic way to eat a large Maine steamer: pluck its hot chewy body straight from the shell, take off the black "condom" from its neck, swish it in a little bowl of hot cooking water to wash off the grit, dip it in melted butter, and slurp it down. Steamers are so meaty, so muscular and chewy and tender and sweet, they remind me of a good steak.

On the day after Thanksgiving after our first year in town, we took our friend Rosie to J's Oyster to meet pals of hers, fellow eaters and drinkers and appreciators of mollusks and bivalves. The five of us crowded around a little table in the back corner. I ordered a double rye on the rocks. Rosie and I sat shoulder to shoulder with our little paper cups of melted butter and feasted on steamers and the big, knobby Chesapeake oysters.

Then our lobsters arrived, small and lurid red, ringed with coleslaw and boiled ears of corn. When we opened them up, we discovered, to our dismay and curiosity, that their body cavities were filled with black goo.

"What's this?" we asked our waitress.

"Oh, that's just their eggs," she told us, laughing. Clearly, we were not the first diners to wonder. "They just haven't moved down to the tail yet. You can eat 'em."

"Okay," we said, and then we devoured our dinners without a second thought. She could have told us anything, really; it would have been hard to spoil our pleasure in those lobsters. They were just the slightest bit overcooked but incredibly sweet, fresh, and delicious. We dismantled them with nutcrackers, picking every fleck of meat from their body cavities, sucking and slurping and digging meat out with our fingertips.

When I finished, melted butter was running down my chin, my hands were covered in lobster juice, and I felt feral. Rosie looked exactly the same way. We grinned at each other. I had poppy seeds in my teeth from the coleslaw, and I didn't care.

$\ell\ell\ell$

Like lobsters, clams are plentiful in Maine. And also like lobsters, they're eaten with gusto, and they're very versatile. You can bake them in the oven, or more traditionally, under seaweed and wet canvas on a beach, with lobsters, potatoes, chourico (Portuguese sausage), and corn.

I first became aware of the existence of clambakes as a sophomore at Mingus Union High School in Cottonwood, Arizona, in 1977, when I played Julie Jordan in the drama club's spring production of *Carousel*, a Rodgers and Hammerstein musical that's set in Maine. One of the crowd numbers begins, "This was a real nice clambake, we're mighty glad we came," and goes on, "Remember when we ate those red-hot lobsters out of a driftwood fire . . ." and continues, "Then at last come the clams, steamed under rockweed and poppin' from their shells . . ." The song always made me hungry, although I had no idea, really, what it was about. I'd never eaten clams or lobster before, but suddenly, I wanted to.

I still have never been to a clambake, but I've learned a little more about them since I've moved up here, and I'm just as interested now as I was at fifteen in experiencing one. Although many people, even Mainers, evidently assume that the clambake originated with the Natives, according to the book *Clambake: A History and Celebration of an American Tradition* by Kathy Neustadt, there is no archaeological evidence to support this supposition. Although Native Americans did roast clams, the clambake as we know it is a purely Yankee invention, and not a colonial one either, since the Puritans regarded such leisurely, decadent outdoor feasts as frivolity.

It wasn't until 1769, at the Old Colony Club in Plymouth, that the humble clam assumed a place in New England festival tradition. That year was the first annual Forefathers' Dinner, a feast commemorating the *Mayflower* pilgrims, and attended by the Club members, *Mayflower* descendants who were primarily Harvard-educated gentlemen and their families. In addition to clams, this first-ever feast had on its menu "a large baked Indian whortleberry pudding," "a bowl of sauquetash" (likely an old spelling of "succotash"), oysters, codfish, a haunch of venison, sea-fowl (which I hope was not seagull), frost-fish and eels, apple pie, cranberry tarts, and cheese.

No mention is made of how these clams were cooked, but, according to Neustadt, "this meal, while hardly a clambake itself, established for clam-eating in general a symbolic context and core of meaning that would deepen and intensify in the years that followed."

The date of the first official modern Yankee clambake is unknown, or at least, not pinpointable, but one possibility is the year 1825, when a Rhode Island schoolteacher named Otis Storrs took a group of children out on a sloop to Rocky Point. He discovered when dinnertime came that they had no provisions, and so he "invented the clambake on the spot." Within a decade, clambakes had become as regionally popular as socials, dances, fairs, circuses, and picnics. Small private clambakes soon gave way to commercial enterprises.

"Today," writes Neustadt, "it is possible to argue that every aspect of the clambake—its organization, the food preparation, building the fire, and serving the meal—carries a wealth of symbols." A clambake combines the four elements, earth, air, fire, and water. It often occurs at the end of the summer, commemorating the harvest of the fruits of "the physical and the social world—drawing all that is alive and lively together—before the world grows cold, dark, and barren."

A communal activity from start to finish, it takes a group of people both to execute and to consume a clambake. First, you dig a fire pit and gather seaweed, along with buckets of seawater to keep the rockweed wet, and a bunch of good-size rocks. Then, once the pit is lined with rocks, you build a wood fire and let it burn until the rocks are glowing hot. It's important to let it burn out completely just as the rocks reach optimal temperature; timing is essential. Then you rake the ashes to make a "bed" to insulate the pit. Over that goes a layer of seaweed, and then the seafood: mussels, steamers, lobsters, quahogs. Alternating layers of wet seaweed and food are piled in: linguica or chourico sausages, corn, potatoes, carrots, onions. A large canvas, thoroughly soaked in seawater (or sometimes beer), is wrapped over the whole caboodle, and then, while the food steams and bakes, everyone hangs out on the beach, talking and drinking beer and relaxing, for several hours, until it's time to uncover it all and eat.

The chorus of the clambake song in *Carousel* ends: "Our hearts are warm, our bellies are full, and we are feeling prime. This was a real nice clambake, and we all had a real good time!" Apparently, when he wrote the lyrics, Hammerstein had never been to one himself, so he researched the matter and, in so doing, created a visceral paean that evokes a sense of sunburned, happy Mainers on a beach at summer's end in 1873, gorging on the fruits of the sea and land.

And thus a New York Jew inspired a romantic yen for clams in the heart of a teenage Arizona girl who eventually, finally, moved to Maine.

ℓℓ

Newcomer's Clam Chowder

As a New Yorker, I loved those tomato-based, celery-heavy Manhattan deli chowders with hot grease floating on top. And I also used to love thick, roux-based New England chowders with oyster crackers—until I learned I could not eat gluten. So I tinkered with these classic recipes to make a thin-yet-rich broth with a savory, chunky soup. This chowder is cheap and easy to make, and takes only an hour or so. It's also very good, if I do say so myself.

First, set out a board of cheese, crackers, and homemade spicy rhubarb pickles—if you happen to have any on hand—to keep your dining companion (note the singular—you won't want to share this with more than one person) occupied while you cook. Make sure to pour him or her a glass of cold dry white wine (or whiskey) and another for yourself.

In a big covered soup pot with an inch or so of water, steam 24 littlenecks or cherrystones or 12 quahogs. If they don't all open right away, remove the ones that do, rearrange the closed ones for maximum space, cover again, and give them another go-round. When they've all declared themselves, discard the holdouts. Strain and reserve the steaming liquid, about 2 1/2 cups. Coarsely chop the clam meat.

Meanwhile, sauté 1/4 lb. of chopped bacon or pancetta, the fattier the better, in a large cast-iron soup pot over medium flame until it renders its fat and starts to curl up and get crisp. Add 1 yellow onion, minced, and 1 minced garlic clove, and cook for about 8 minutes, stirring every so often.

Add to the pot 1 large diced Yukon Gold potato and 2 ears' worth of fresh corn kernels with the reserved clam liquor (it should be just enough to cover), 2 bay leaves, and black pepper to taste. You won't need salt; the clam liquor and pancetta provide the ideal amount. Simmer, lid on, for 10 to 15 minutes.

When the potatoes are soft, turn off the flame. Add 2 cups of very hot whole milk and the chopped clams and stir well. Cover again, and let sit for 5 to 10 minutes to let the flavors marry, as they used to say.

Serve in 2 big bowls. Eat it all. For dessert, serve fresh berries with cream, and more cold wine.

ele

One late-summer morning, I woke up with a to-do list as long as my arm. Lying there, waking up, I felt no desire to do anything productive at all, all day. In fact, I felt rebellious and lazy. I got dressed and walked Dingo along the sidewalk in the sparkling, lush, sweet Maine summer morning.

"I don't want to work," I said when I got home. "I don't want to run errands."

"Let's go to the beach," said Brendan, who was clearly in the same mood. "Let's have a picnic."

Less than four minutes later, we were in the car, bathing suits on under our clothes, wearing our straw beach hats, headed for Cape Elizabeth. Dingo rode in back along with the beach towels.

On the way, we stopped at the lobster shack we call the Mail-Order Bride's because of the busty, artfully made-up Russian woman we assume is married to the owner; she sits behind the counter and rings everything up with a fatally bored, disdainful expression that says, "For this I leave Russia? To work in lobster store and be married to Maine man?"

They have excellent lobster salad at the Mail-Order Bride's: mounds of fresh, tender, perfectly cooked meat bound lightly with good mayonnaise, served on crunchy iceberg with thinly sliced ripe tomato, nothing else. We also got a big bag of sea salt and cracked pepper potato chips, a bottle of chilled rosé, and two bottles of water, mainly for Dingo.

And then we headed for Ferry Beach, forgetting in our excitement that they have a strict no-dogs rule in the summertime between nine and five. When we got there, the parking lot was full, so it was moot. We were out of luck. We drove a bit aimlessly around the back roads, wondering how to sneak onto a beach somewhere. No luck there, either.

"I know," said Brendan. "The Inn by the Sea. They take dogs. We can use their beach."

A minute later, there it was, the place where I'd taken Brendan for his thirtieth birthday on a weirdly hot March day in 2012; Dingo had come along too, and he got to dine with us in the lobby restaurant alongside all the other dogs. From the dog menu (yes, they have a dog menu), we ordered the "Meat Roaf" for him. A big bowl of rice, ground beef, minced carrots, peas, and green beans was set down next to his smaller bowl of ice water. Dingo stared at the waiter as if he might be an angel from heaven, then stuck his nose into the bowl and didn't look up again until it was empty. And he stayed with us in our room, where the staff had provided him with a soft dog bed and treats.

Now we parked in their lot and walked Dingo down their wooden boardwalk to the beach, where we saw the no-dogs signs. So we set up camp at a picnic table in the shade by the beach and ate our lobster salad and potato chips and drank our wine. The air was sweet and fresh and cool; the sunlight filtered through the branches of the trees to dapple the ground.

After lunch, we walked Dingo back and left him in the car, under a tree in the shade, snoozing in the backseat with all the windows rolled down, a cool sea breeze keeping him comfortable. Then we came back to the beach, unrolled our towels, and lay in the sun in our bathing suits until we were baking hot. We walked into the green, clear, cold, lapping waves of the north Atlantic and paddled around. Back on our towels in the sun, we dozed, tingly and zinging and euphoric from lobster and wine and seawater. We awoke at the same time and smiled into each other's eyes.

"We live in Maine," I announced, as I liked to do occasionally, enjoying the happy oddness of it. Neither of us had ever expected to live here, not by a long shot, and yet, now that we did, it felt inevitable.

"We live in Maine," Brendan agreed.

ele

Until I decided to make Lobster Thermidor, Brendan and I hadn't been truly baptized into Maine life, if only because we hadn't cooked a single lobster in our own kitchen. It was so much easier to order lobster in restaurants.

Not surprisingly, there was no Lobster Thermidor to be found on any current menus in Portland—it's too labor-intensive, rich, and anachronistic. But with my fiftieth birthday approaching, I was beginning to feel anachronistic as well. Scenes from my past were starting to float up into the present, and I started taking stock of my life, examining this half-century I had lived from the perspective of my newfound contentment with Brendan in Maine.

Certain echoing remnants of my old passion for New York started resounding in my inner ear. I was visited by a ghostly nostalgia for that city I'd loved so much and for so long—not a wish to go back, but an appreciation of that two-decade-long love I'd had for it, and for the food there. Not only the actual food, but also, and somehow even more resonantly, the literary, legendary, romantic food of the golden age of hotel bars and jazz clubs and Broadway pre-theater seatings that served fancy dishes whose names consisted of an expensive main ingredient followed by a glamorous sounding name: Beef Wellington, Oysters Rockefeller, Clams Casino, Steak Diane, and, most of all, Lobster Thermidor.

This decadent-sounding concoction of lobster in cream sauce conjured up old New York's hotel restaurants, the glamour and fizz of a long-ago, long-lost city I'd never known, except in books: cigarette holders, highballs, men's hats, swing bands, and proper literary feuds that ended in fisticuffs at the Algonquin, where it was, of course, on the menu.

Until recently, I had never eaten Lobster Thermidor, let alone cooked it. My romance with the idea of it was fueled solely by books, mostly novels, set in Manhattan in the early to mid-twentieth century.

As with most literarily spawned romances, I suspected that it was probably best left to the imagination, just like the most swoon-worthy literary romantic heroes: Who would want a real-life Heathcliff, so crazy and obsessive and terrifyingly brutal? Or a Mr. Darcy in the flesh—a condescending, aloof snob?

Likewise, I always harbored a suspicion that Lobster Thermidor, despite its wonderful name, would probably turn out to be a few overcooked chunks of subpar shellfish in a depressing, gummy sauce, nary a cigarette holder nor highball in sight.

The time had finally come for me to cook lobster (albeit in its most decadent form) and join the rest of Maine. And I wanted to connect it symbolically, to knit together past, present, and literary past pluperfect. Thus, I'd finally learn what Lobster Thermidor tasted like.

ello

Thermidor was the name of a French play about the overthrow of Robespierre and the Reign of Terror that took place in the late-summer month of Thermidor, the eleventh month in the French Republican calendar. For the play's 1894 opening at the Comédie-Française, a chef at Marie, a nearby theater-district restaurant, invented, in its honor, a dish of lobster meat in a sauce of cream, mustard, egg yolks, and cognac, sherry, or brandy, topped with melted Gruyère. Because Lobster Thermidor was complicated to make and involved expensive ingredients, it became known as a dish for special occasions.

For my own Thermidorian special occasion, I researched, sifted through methods, and finally found a 1940s *Gourmet* magazine recipe from a chef named Louis P. De Gouy that struck me as just right—simple, classic, and elegant, streamlined even, with a minimum of ingredients and a clearly laid out series of steps. I adjusted it a little, adding back in the traditional mustard and Gruyère, as well as shallots, and a cup of lobster liquor (strained lobster-steaming water), to thin and flavor the sauce. I made an ingredients list, and then we were off to shop.

We bought a lobster pot down on Commercial Street at the kitchen supply store, then headed to Fishermen's Net, the seafood market on Forest Avenue, for our lobsters. We picked out a couple of live two-pounders, because we needed shells big enough to stuff. They were active and full of protestations, despite their banded claws, but we were undeterred.

Back at home, we washed our new, huge galvanized-steel pot with its stencil of—what else—a lobster on the side, and then we filled it with salted water. When it boiled, we, meaning Brendan, held each of the healthy, feisty pair while I removed the claw bands, then in they went headfirst. We clapped the cover on and left them to it. After ten minutes, we hauled them out and put them in a colander and sat at the counter contemplating them while we drank some wine and ate a dozen very fresh Damariscotta oysters, briny, plump, and small, with mignonette. The lobsters were bright red, enormous. Their limp claws and antennae dangled over the colander's edge. I pulled an endive apart and dressed the paired leaves with Humboldt Fog goat's milk cheese, chopped caper berries, and minced shallot, and we ate that, too.

And then the lobsters were cool. We put on some music—a decadent Italian crooner named Paolo Conte—and turned it up loud and poured more wine and got to work. We cracked the claws and snipped the tails and stripped the lobsters of their meat, and (in the case of the female of the pair) roe, set it aside, then washed the shells. (This all took a while, and was painstaking work, as always.) Then I made the sauce while Brendan made the custard. This also took a long time, but, unlike picking the meat from the shells, it seemed to go very fast. We danced around each other at the stove, not speaking, concentrating hard.

In a double boiler, Brendan whisked two egg yolks with sherry and hot cream until it thickened. I softened mushrooms and shallots in butter, added the cup of lobster liquor with the strained roe and cooked it down, then added all of the lobster meat, plus more cream and sherry, a teaspoon of mustard powder, cayenne, salt to taste, and black pepper. It cooked into a glossy sauce, not too thick. At the end, we added the custard.

Since our former six-burner Vulcan stove, which came with the kitchen and has since been replaced, had no broiler, we had borrowed a blowtorch from our upstairs tenant, a welder. When everything was done, we packed the sauced lobster with a slotted spoon into the clean shells, which we'd arranged in a baking dish. We sprinkled on a layer of grated Gruyère, and then, with a nod to Julia Child—it was the week of her hundredth birthday, after all—we turned on the blowtorch until the cheese was bubbling and beginning to brown.

Afterwards, neither of us could recall ever having had more fun cooking in our lives.

With a second bottle of ice-cold Pouilly-Fuissé, we ate the creamy-lobstery-cheesy-spicy Thermidor on top of a mound of saffron Jasmati rice, with the rest of the sauce alongside in a pitcher to use as needed. (Because the recipe served four people, we had plenty left over for the next night.) It turned out to be a sexy, wonderful dish. The chunks of lobster were meltingly tender. The browned cheese (with a slight whiff of propane) added its nutty tanginess to the cream-and-mustard richness.

As I ate the Lobster Thermidor, I savored the dish's romantic name on my internal palate along with the actual, literal dish itself on my tongue. I felt a sudden swooping uplift as my old excitement about literary New York hotel bars returned, my joy at the idea of a glamorous woman in pearls and gloves being helped out of a taxi by a doorman with an umbrella, ushered beneath an awning into a hotel lobby to join her smoking, highball-swilling, witty, opinionated literary friends . . .

When my plate was empty, there I was, in Portland, Maine, exactly where I wanted to be. Rather than feeling nostalgia, either for my own New York or for the imagined, lost one, I experienced a simple happiness at my ability to re-create any of it, whenever I wanted, in food.

After a plain, light salad of butter lettuce with shallot vinaigrette, we ate cold slices of cantaloupe, and then two chocolate truffles. There were no cigarette holders or literary fisticuffs to be seen, and our kitchen bore no resemblance to the old Algonquin (or even the new one), but it was a feast to remember, a Thermidorian triumph, and proof that reality can trump fantasy, every now and then.

ℓℓℓ

Lobster Thermidor (adapted from Louis P. De Gouy, *Gourmet* magazine, 1941)

2 (2 lb.) live lobsters
1/2 stick (1/4 cup) unsalted butter
1/4 lb. mushrooms, trimmed and thinly sliced
2 large or 4 small shallots, minced
1/2 tsp paprika
1/8 tsp salt
1/4 tsp black pepper
1 tsp mustard powder
4 T medium-dry sherry
1 cup heavy cream, scalded
1 cup lobster liquor (liquid from the shells, reserved)
2 large egg yolks
1/3 cup plus 1/2 cup grated Gruyère

Plunge lobsters headfirst into an 8-quart pot of boiling salted water. Loosely cover pot and cook lobsters over moderately high heat, 10 minutes from the time they enter the water, then transfer with tongs to sink to cool.

When lobsters are cool enough to handle, twist off claws and crack them, then remove meat and roe. Halve lobsters lengthwise with kitchen shears, beginning from tail end, then remove tail meat, reserving shells. Cut all lobster meat into 1/4-inch pieces. Discard any remaining lobster innards, then rinse and dry shells.

Heat butter in a 2-quart heavy saucepan over moderate heat until foam subsides, then cook shallots and mushrooms, stirring, until liquid that mushrooms give off is evaporated and they begin to brown, about 5 minutes. Add roe, lobster meat, paprika, mustard, salt, and pepper and reduce heat to low. Cook, shaking pan gently, 1 minute. Add 2 T sherry, 1/2 cup hot cream, 1/3 cup Gruyère, and the lobster liquor, and simmer 5 minutes.

Meanwhile, whisk together yolks and remaining 2 T sherry in a small bowl or the top of a double boiler. Slowly pour remaining 1/2 cup hot cream into yolks, whisking constantly, and, over simmering water, cook the custard, still whisking constantly, until it is slightly thickened and registers 160 degrees F on an instant-read thermometer. Add custard to lobster mixture, stirring gently.

Preheat broiler. (If you don't have a broiler, use a blowtorch.)

Arrange lobster shells, cut sides up, in a shallow baking pan and divide lobster with some of the sauce into shells. Cover with 1/2 cup grated Gruyère, divided. Broil lobsters 6 inches from heat until golden brown, 4 to 5 minutes. Serve remaining sauce on the side, with wedges of lemon. Serves 4.

ell

Chapter Seven

Maple, Mutton,
and Moose Muffles

One day, on our way from Portland to the farmhouse, we stopped at the Earle Family Farm on Brownfield Road, just across the border from Maine and just before the turnoff onto our dirt road. This farm is full of life and bursting with activity: weeding, harvesting, moving flats, tending the stand. It's a 130-acre biodynamic farm. Their hand-built greenhouse is filled with flowers and herbs. Next to it is a garden; another, larger one is in the field just above, and their sheep are pastured higher still on the slope of Dundee Mountain. The little store in the barn has a cash box stuffed with change, and it runs on the honor system. Prices are on a chalkboard next to an old hanging scale. Packaged meat and eggs and perishable produce are kept in two old fridges and a freezer. There's an enormous basket of yarn for sale, too, hand-dyed hand-spun skeins from their sheep.

We bought a pound or two each of their just-picked late-summer tomatoes and squashes and cucumbers and peppers, plus eggs from their chickens. We waved to Tom Earle, driving by on his tractor, as we walked back to say hello to Danny, the new ram. He was markedly obese, and his balls must have weighed twenty pounds, collectively. They hung between his hind legs like giant soft durian-size bobbles, swaying and undulating and almost touching the ground.

"Damn, that boy is hung," said Brendan.

I laughed.

The fat, fluffy ewe in the barn with him looked exhausted. Ruth, Tom's wife, told us that she'd had to separate them with chicken wire.

The Earles had no frozen lamb that year; the previous spring, Ruth told us, many of their lambs died of something mysterious, a wasting disease. This year, all the sheep were obese, also mysteriously, something to do with the rain and grass and temperature, Ruth guessed, but she didn't know for sure.

"So, no lamb—not now," she said. "We're butchering chickens in mid-November, though. You want stewing chickens? Yeah, they said they'd do the older hens when they do the turkeys. Nice that it's at the same time. I could do it myself—I know how to do the whole thing, start to finish—but it's better to have someone else do it if you're the only one who can. It's not a job I can do by myself. You eat organ meat?"

"Sure, we do," I said. I'd happily eat anything at all from their farm.

"Well, I'll keep that in mind when we butcher the pigs. Oh, and I'm running a pickling workshop tonight. I think I'll see what happens if I throw some lemon cucumbers in my pickling mix. Have you ever had one? Here, taste; just brush off those prickly things. Want to come to the workshop?"

I did, in fact, want very much to go, but I had a lot of work to do, and wanted to get to it. I asked if I could come another time.

Ruth sent us home with some sweet, rich mutton sausage made from their ewes that she had in her freezer, refusing to accept any money for it.

Ruth and Tom Earle seem to know how to do everything, in the nineteenth-century style of farming. They are always working, all day, somewhere on their farm. When I was young, in high school and in the years following, I attended and then worked at three different Waldorf schools in anthroposophical communities, so called because they were formed around the teachings of the early-twentieth-century Austrian mystic and clairvoyant, Rudolf Steiner. He gave his over-arching philosophy the rather ambitious name of *anthroposophy*, which means "the knowledge of the nature of man." His theories gave rise, in a practical sense, to revolutionary new forms of education, farming, and medicine.

There were biodynamic farms attached to the communities where I lived—in Spring Valley, New York, and then Chateau de La Mhotte in the Allier district of France, and finally, Harlemville, in Upstate New York—so I couldn't help overhearing a thing or two about its basic concepts, along with discussions of the etheric and astral bodies, Ahri-man and Lucifer, Findhorn, and homeopathic medicine. But all I learned, really, about biodynamic farming is that things are done organically, according to the phases of the moon, and it's deeply spiritual, arcane even—not the first adjectives I would use to describe the Earles.

Tom is slight, lanky, handsome in a rawboned way, taciturn, sweet-natured, and warmly practical. Ruth is talkative, energetic, bright-eyed, small and round and strong, with long gray hair and a soft, round face. They look, in fact, like a quintessential nineteenth-century New England farming couple. They do not exude one whiff of mysticism, but evidently intricate beliefs and practices are at least partially the reasons for the abundant, beautiful produce they grow in fields of granite-strewn, thin soil, the unbelievably delicious meats and chickens and eggs from the animals they raise and pasture.

We drove away from the farm discussing their mutton sausage—how good it was the last time we'd gotten some. In the house, we unloaded the bags of food and put things away. We drank tequila on ice with limes while I made a quick semi-succotash of the Earles' pattypan squash and green-and-orange, knobby, lumpy, richly ripe heirloom tomatoes, chopped and sautéed in olive oil with smoked paprika, Worcestershire sauce, and the tiny bit of old dried thyme left in the glass jar. While it bubbled, I fried four of the eggs we'd just bought. They were so fresh, their yolks were orangey-gold and their whites puffed up a little in the hot oil. I slid them on top of the vegetable stew, two per plate, and we tucked in. The still-runny egg yolks melded into the savory gravy, the whites were crisply browned, and the whole thing was delicious.

ele

The following winter, as we were heading out to take our walk one morning, Tom Earle came up the icy path across the yard to our front door, asking to tap the maple trees that line the driveway by the barn. We tagged along with him over to the barn, where his pickup truck was parked. He scrambled up into his truck bed to gather stacks of galvanized-steel buckets.

"Apparently now galvanized steel is no good for eating," he said, "but I don't know."

From the cab, he fetched a ball-peen hammer, a battery-powered drill, a small metal tap, and a plastic spout.

He approached the nearest maple tree. We followed him, clambering over the hard icy packed snowdrift. They're old, the trees here, with silvered, hoary bark, tall and shaggy.

He told us that this was a good time to collect sap now, cold nights and warmer days, when the sap, frozen in the roots all winter, thaws in the sun and rises hydraulically up the trunk and into the branches to feed the tree.

"They have vacuum pumps now, the modern sugarers, and even with the new machinery, they only get about seven percent more than with these old methods. And that's only ten, twenty percent of the tree's sap. Some of them are planting maple trees a few feet apart and when they get high enough, they go through and whack off the tops and take out the sap that way."

He shook his head and laughed.

"Kind of like mountaintop removal mining," I said, cringing a little as Dingo took a shit right by the front right wheel of Tom's truck.

Tom politely ignored Dingo and considered the lower trunk. This one already had a hole in it.

"The hole always leaves a little bruise," he said. "You don't want to use an old hole."

He walked around the trunk and stopped. "The sap is everywhere right now, but a good spot is usually under a branch."

He drilled a shallow hole a foot below the biggest low branch, then gently pocked in the metal tap with the hammer.

"You can hear the sound change when it hits the sap," he said, setting the bucket's handle into the hook in the tap so it was wedged securely just below it. A clear, thin drop welled and pinged into the bottom of the bucket. "The first drop," he said, attaching the spout.

"I wonder who first thought to tap maple trees," I said.

"The Indians didn't have buckets, so they hollowed out tree trunks and set them under the spouts to collect sap," he said. "And to sugar it off, because they didn't have pots, they would drop hot rocks into the tree hollows. It's forty to one, the ratio of sap to syrup. It takes two days in a pot with a good fire going. Imagine how long it took with hot rocks."

"I wonder if animals like maple sap," I said.

He laughed.

"Everyone knows sugar," he said. "I've got a terrible sweet tooth, myself, but we'll have enough maple syrup left over to sell." He invited us to visit his sugar hut later on, an invitation we accepted, and then off we went for our walk in the sudden springlike warmth. The dirt road had melted in rivulets and ice shards. The air temperature was less than 30 degrees, but the sun warmed everything up.

By the time we got back, less than an hour later, Tom had moved off to tap another copse of maples, and the trees lining the drive each had two buckets attached to their lower trunks.

ele

Maple Oatmeal

We eat this for breakfast on icebound winter mornings. It warms the inside of the rib cage and keeps us full for hours.

In a saucepan, stir 1/2 cup organic steel-cut oats into 1 cup of water with a pinch of salt. Add 1 T or more of maple syrup and 1/2 tsp of cinnamon. Simmer, covered, according to the oatmeal directions. Stir a few times while it cooks, adding more water as necessary. When the oats are almost done, add 3/4 cup fresh or frozen wild low-bush blueberries and stir well. Let simmer a few more minutes. Serves 2.

ele

Maple syrup is native to North America. The Indians made incisions in trees during the spring thaw and tapped them with reeds and collected the sap either in birch buckets or hollowed-out trees; they produced syrup either the way Tom Earle described, with hot rocks, or by letting the sap freeze overnight and skimming off the water ice that rose to the top in the mornings, leaving the sugars below.

When the first colonists arrived, the Natives taught them to collect sap; instead of making incisions, they drilled holes into the trees and extracted it with spouts. Maple syrup and maple sugar were the primary sources of sweetness in early New England cuisine, since cane sugar had to be imported from the West Indies.

Maple syrup is more nutritious than either cane sugar or honey, containing manganese and zinc, as well as small amounts of potassium and calcium and trace amounts of amino acids. It's also delicious.

When I was little, we ate Aunt Jemima or Log Cabin imitation maple syrup in our family, or, when money was especially tight, Caro corn syrup heated and mixed with imitation maple flavoring. When I read about sugaring in the *Little House on the Prairie* books, I instinctively craved the maple candy Ma made by pouring hot maple syrup into the snow. We used to get maple candy from our grandmother, who often summered in Maine, and I loved it madly. It was a rare and treasured treat. I couldn't believe how good it was, how light, how full of flavor. It melted on the tongue into a memory of pure sweetness, a clean taste, unlike the usual chemical candy we ate, Jolly Ranchers and Sweet Tarts, Pop Rocks and Hot Tamales.

My first taste of real maple syrup was another such happy shock. It was so different from Aunt Jemima, which was thick and sweet and simple-tasting. I don't remember when this happened, exactly, but I do remember the puzzled excitement I felt: Real maple syrup had a complex, rich flavor, mixed caramel and vanilla and plant life, a vegetal, fresh taste with some of the dark earthiness of mushrooms, as well as the tang of applesauce. It was amazing stuff, I knew right away.

ℓℓℓ

Tom had asked us to keep an eye on the buckets, to make sure the tops stayed on in the wind and that they didn't overflow. We peered into several of them over the next few days, but nothing much seemed to be happening with regard to output.

We watched Tom come by and empty the buckets periodically. He told us that this particular spring was turning out to be a bad one for maple sugaring, even though the nights were nice and cold, since the days didn't warm up enough to make the sap rise. He was disappointed, he said, but next year would probably be better. I told him I looked forward to watching him tap the trees again next spring and boil down the sap in his sugarhouse.

It was (and is) amazing to me—a former New Yorker who spent my entire post-school life in the city before I first came up here—to live in such close proximity to people who know how to do stuff—who've learned, and who practice, the old traditional ways.

When my ex-husband and I renovated our nineteenth-century row house in Greenpoint, Brooklyn, we did most of the work ourselves, in part because there was no one to hire. He had worked for about fifteen years after college as a building contractor, but when his joints gave out and he left that business, there was no one to hand it on to. All the young kids were now in IT and media.

Up here, that's not the case. The contractors who renovated our Portland house were our tenants' best friends; finding them was the easiest thing in the world. Likewise, I had just been wanting to watch someone tap a maple tree, and Tom Earle came walking up to our front door one warmish late-winter morning.

Sometimes I feel like all I have to do is ask, and I meet someone who has what I want.

One winter in Portland, at the first meeting of our newly formed Scotch Club, which is exactly what it sounds like, I idly expressed a yearning to cook moose. It turned out that one member, who lives two blocks away from us, had a freezer full that she wasn't sure what to do with (her girlfriend's father is a hunter).

"I'll make you a deal," I said. "If you give me some of that moose, I'll cook it for the next Scotch Club meeting."

When I went to her house to collect it, she handed me three packages of frozen meat marked BACKSTRAP, NEW YORK SIRLOIN, and STEW MEAT. I was so excited I could hardly contain myself. I took them straight home and thawed the packages in a pot of hot water. The meat was a deep ruby-purple, with no fat on it. It smelled mineral-fresh, not gamey at all. I reserved all the liquid that pooled in the bags from thawing.

I had decided to bourguignon the hell out of the moose, so I used Ina Garten's recipe, substituting moose for beef. I used plenty of thyme, butter, lardons, cognac, and an entire bottle of dry red wine. I set the cognac aflame, too, which was exciting.

That night's Scotch Club meeting began in the living room with cheese, crackers, and a tasting of the night's first single malt, Glenfiddich, which we all pronounced smooth and tasty. Then we thronged into the kitchen and filled our plates with fresh buttered gluten-free fettuccine topped with moose bourguignon and buttered peas, and alongside, a salad of herb mix and fennel with a strong vinaigrette. The moose meat was tender and savory and stalwart enough to sop up all the rest of the single malts that followed that night.

ℓℓ

Moose Bourguignon (adapted from Ina Garten)

2 T rendered duck fat
8 ounces dry-cured, center-cut, applewood-smoked bacon, diced
2 1/2 lbs. moose meat cut into 1-inch cubes
Kosher salt

Freshly ground black pepper
1 lb. carrots, sliced diagonally into 1-inch chunks
2 yellow onions, sliced
2 tsp chopped garlic (2 cloves)
1/2 cup cognac
1 (750 ml) bottle good dry red wine, such as Cotes du Rhone or Pinot
Noir
1 can (2 cups) beef broth
1 T tomato paste
1 tsp fresh thyme leaves (1/2 tsp dried)
4 T unsalted butter at room temperature, divided
3 T fine-milled Acadian buckwheat flour (I used Bouchard)
1 lb. frozen pearl onions
1 lb. fresh mushrooms, stems discarded, caps thickly sliced

For serving:

2 lbs. gluten-free fettuccine, boiled according to directions and tossed
with salt to taste and 4 T butter
1/2 cup chopped fresh parsley

Preheat the oven to 250 degrees F. Heat the duck fat in a large
Dutch oven. Add the bacon and cook over medium heat for 10
minutes, stirring occasionally, until the bacon is lightly browned.
Remove the bacon with a slotted spoon to a large plate.

Dry the moose meat with paper towels and then sprinkle with salt
and pepper.

In batches in single layers, sear the moose in the hot fat for 3 to 5
minutes, turning to brown on all sides. Remove the seared cubes
to the plate with the bacon and continue searing until all the
moose is browned. Set aside.

Toss the carrots, and onions, 1 T of salt and 2 tsp of pepper in the
fat in the pan and cook for 10 to 15 minutes, stirring occasionally,
until the onions are lightly browned. Add the garlic and cook for 1

more minute. Add the cognac, stand back, and ignite with a match to burn off the alcohol. (This part is a lot of fun, and very dramatic.)

Put the meat and bacon back into the pot with the juices. Add the bottle of wine plus enough beef broth to almost cover the meat. Add the tomato paste and thyme. Bring to a simmer, cover the pot with a tight-fitting lid, and place it in the oven for about 1 1/4 hours, or until the meat and vegetables are very tender when pierced with a fork.

Combine 2 T of butter and the buckwheat flour with a fork and stir into the stew. Add the frozen onions. Sauté the mushrooms in 2 T of butter for 10 minutes, until lightly browned, and then add to the stew. Bring the stew to a boil on top of the stove, then lower the heat and simmer for 15 minutes. Season to taste. Serve over buttered fettuccine. Sprinkle each plate with parsley. Serves 6 to 8.

ℓℓℓ

Moose are delicious, there's no doubt about that. Humans have hunted and enjoyed their meat for thousands of years. The Native Americans, in addition to enjoying the fresh meat, made pemmican, a portable, concentrated dried jerky made of game meat, fat, and wild berries that kept indefinitely. The Europeans adapted the pemmican recipe for their own uses, which included long ocean voyages and dog-sled trips into the wilderness. Moose can generally be incorporated into regular recipes calling for any type of red meat; my bourguignon was the perfect case in point.

Since that particular moose was already dead, its meat already butchered and frozen in neat packets, it was easy to remove myself from the idea of an actual moose, as I cooked and ate it—easy to separate this meat from the fantastical beast I'd seen on that dirt road by the lake in New Hampshire almost four years before. Of course, when an animal's body has been dressed and prepared for cooking offstage, it's been turned into food and is no longer strictly the flesh of a once-living thing. Language helps with the larger, more problematically sentient-seeming mammals: Cows become beef; pigs, pork; sheep, mutton. Deer, when eaten, are called venison, as are all members of the deer family, including moose.

But it's complicated at its core, the idea of eating (and cooking) a moose. They're lovely wild animals, and they seem to be dying out.

Moose are loners, except during mating season. Like all members of the deer family, they are herbivores; the word *moose* comes from an Algonquin word for *twig eater*. They browse through the woods, eating leaves, twigs, and buds off trees, long grasses, and shrubs, and they also love to wade into ponds and marshes and eat aquatic plants. In winter, they forage for pinecones and lichen, scraping the snow with their wide, flat hooves, which also function as snowshoes. They can run up to thirty-five miles an hour for short bursts, and they're excellent, fast swimmers.

As a sort of interesting aside, after mating season is over, the moose's antlers fall off and are eaten by rodents, who crave the calcium in them.

Because moose are shy and solitary, as well as increasingly rare, it's not especially surprising that I have so far only had one encounter with the official state animal of Maine. Along with so many other species, moose are now endangered in most parts of the United States, their numbers thinned by climate change. Warmer winters mean more ticks, and ticks love moose; too many of them on one animal can kill it. They're especially pernicious in New Hampshire due to longer autumns and shorter winters. Sometimes a single moose carries as many as 150,000 of the little bloodsuckers; they bleed out, literally, until they're little more than ribs, antlers, and loose skin.

Moose also die of overheating in the increasingly warm winters. They pack so much fat on their torsos, they have trouble cooling themselves when the weather isn't cold enough, as it increasingly isn't. In Minnesota, the average winter temperatures have risen 11 degrees since the mid-twentieth century. And if the heat and ticks don't get them, brain worms might. Which is why in New Hampshire (as well as out in Minnesota and Montana) the once-plentiful moose populations are dwindling fast.

But right next door in Maine, whose borders go much farther north, the current number of moose was estimated to be as high as 76,000 in 2012, which is a robust population; but this year, in 2014, they've fallen closer to 65,000, so it's happening here too, although moose hunting in Maine is still a going thing. This year, moose-hunting permits will be issued to only 3,095 lottery winners in Maine (it was 4,110 last year) out of about 50,000 applicants, only 10 percent of whom can be nonresidents.

Reputedly, moose are far more difficult to hunt than deer because of their elusiveness. And because they like to wade in shallow water, nibbling on the aquatic plants they find there, many hunters have reported shooting and killing their game, only to have to drag it from a pond or lake, an enormous, ungainly, soaking-wet carcass, before they can even begin to address the subsequent work of skinning, gutting, and butchering it. Moose hunting is therefore not for the weak of heart or body or mind. It is challenging enough to find the moose, let alone get it out of the woods.

The increasing endangerment of moose begs the question: Should we cook a moose at all? Or rather, should we hunt it? Many animal-rights groups would ban the practice. Moose are threatened, after all. But there are also some compelling traditional arguments in favor of hunting moose, the first one being economics: One butchered and properly stored moose can provide up to four hundred pounds of meat, which will feed a family for a very long time, with meat to spare to give away. As long as the population sustains itself, hunting moose controls overpopulation and allows those that remain to have additional resources. Moose hunting also reduces moose-car collisions, which are almost always fatal to both moose and driver.

Even so, few issues seem to polarize Mainers as much as the hunting question, which pits "flatlanders," typecast as bleeding-heart liberal urban-dwellers, against northern Mainers, people who learned to hunt from their parents, who learned from theirs, and so on, back to the seventeenth century. Hunting is a way of life up here. Many families depend on it. Hunting lodges' economies do, too. It's an ongoing dance between practical necessity, tradition, and beloved and formative cultural activities on the one hand, and progressive, protective, ecological concerns on the other. The recent anti-bear-baiting referendum on the Maine ballot brought a record number of voters to the polls in a state known for very high voter turnout; it was defeated by a wide margin, proving that for now, the die-hard traditionalists outnumber the progressives in Maine.

Although moose hunting in Maine is legal (if declining) for now, who knows how long the moose population will last in this rapidly warming climate? Like the lobster, that other iconic (and delicious) animal of Maine, we may find ourselves mourning their local absence in our lifetimes. The lobster is already gone from waters south of Maine; the moose is almost gone from states west. At the moment, Maine exists in a fragile and likely temporary state of grace.

Although I count myself among the tender-hearted and ecologically concerned progressives, I have (possibly hypocritically) vowed to eat moose every chance I get, anytime I come across a generous hunter willing to share. It's already dead; I don't want it to go to waste (and yes, this is the same argument that allows animal lovers to buy secondhand fur coats).

Moose is as delicious as lobster, and as versatile and easy to prepare. Moose venison, being lean, high in protein and minerals, tender, and flavorful, can be eaten with minimal preparation. There's a long tradition of eating moose in the northeast corner, and a long history of appreciating its fundamental ease of preparation. It seems that the most common Native American moose recipe, besides pemmican, was simply "moose steaks." In addition to being roasted or grilled over an open flame and dried and preserved with fat and berries in pemmican, moose meat was also traditionally cooked in stews with onions, carrots, and potatoes, or hung and smoked, then sliced and eaten.

The tongue was the part of the moose most highly prized by many Native American tribes. In times of plenty, hunters snared their moose, killed it, and then discarded the entire carcass after cutting out the tongue. In leaner times, of course, the entire animal was put to use, from snout to hoof to liver to hide.

One old Alaskan homesteader recipe, called Jellied Moose Nose, calls for a "moose jawbone," pickling spices, and onion and garlic. The directions are short and to the point, labor-intensive and a bit grisly, but also oddly poetic:

ello

Jellied Moose Nose

Cut upper jawbone of moose just below the eyes.

Put in large kettle of scalding water and parboil 45 minutes.

Remove and cool in cold water.

Remove hair and wash thoroughly.

Put in fresh water with onion, a little garlic, and pickling spices.

Boil gently until tender.

Cool overnight in same juice.

Remove bone and cartilage.

Slice thinly and pack in cans or jars; cover with juice.

Chill; slice and serve cold.

ℓℓℓ

It turns out that moose nose is an old delicacy. In his 1916 compendium of all things moose, aptly named *The Moose Book*, Samuel Merrill gives what might be the definitive treatise on how to cook a moose, including his own views on "moose muffle," or rather, the "fibrous flesh of the cheek, and the gelatinous prehensile upper lip." He compares the elegant, luxurious taste of "stewed muffle" to turtle soup, and pronounces it far better than pigs' feet. He quotes an early-eighteenth-century monograph on the moose by a gentleman he calls Judge Dudley, who was a son and grandson of governors of the Massachusetts Bay Colony: " 'The moufflon, which forms the upper lip, is very rich, juicy, and gelatinous. This is cleaned and dressed in the manner of a calves' head.' "

To forestall the inevitable shock and revulsion on the part of the uninitiated, Merrill proffers the following eloquent, if slightly baffling, defense of muffle-eating: "The moose's muffle is not merely an olfactory organ: it is a member which is used as deftly as a man would use his hand in picking off twigs of considerable size from trees, the moose often reaching high in the air and breaking down the tops of saplings by this means. Like the beaver's tail it is a useful substitute for a hand, and like the beaver's tail it is the choicest tidbit which the animal can furnish for the table."

The Reverend Joshua Fraser, a military chaplain, describes a dish of muffle after a dinner at an Indian camp on the upper Ottawa thus: "The crowning dish was that grandest of all dishes, moose muffle. This is the immense upper lip and nostrils of the animal, and I have no hesitation in pronouncing it one of the most toothsome and savory of all the dishes within the range of the gastronomic art. It is white and tender as spring chicken, yet firm and substantial as fresh beef, with a flavor combining the excellencies of both."

The Moose Book also advocates spreading raw or roasted moose marrow on bread or using it to thicken stew, extols the deliciousness of moose feet, liver, and tongue, and compares the crisp, rich flesh of a moose's roasted, well-basted upper lip to the "crackling" of roast young pig. Merrill adds that moose meat is the only type of venison suitable for pickling in brine. Evidently, pickled moose meat is as tender and flavorful as the best corned beef.

However, "the fat is indigestible and unpalatable," he writes, "and should be trimmed off and thrown away, its place being supplied by pork or butter." Moose steaks should be thick-cut and served hot and rare, seasoned only after cooking. "If a piece of meat has hung a day or two too long to suit an over-fastidious taste," he suggests helpfully, "the gamy flavor may be corrected by adding a little jelly—any kind which is not sweet—and a dash of port or sherry."

Merrill's recipe for moose stew is the most direct and unfussy one I've found:

"Saw the marrow bones in pieces two inches in length; cut the meat in medium-sized pieces; add three slices of pork cut in quarter-inch squares, and three or four onions sliced; add pepper and salt, and a piece of butter as large as an egg. Boil three hours. Add three or four potatoes, quartered or sliced, in time to cook. When done add two or three tablespoonfuls of flour in a pint of water, stirring till it boils. For dumplings, use batter as for cream of tartar biscuit, put into the stew five or ten minutes before serving, according to size."

He adds, "Small pieces of tender meat, too small for the broiler, may be utilized in pies—made as chicken pies are made—or in Hamburg steak." He provides a recipe for Moose Steak in Chafing Dish that involves another egg-size piece of butter, melted, a seasoned steak, seared and then cooked, covered, for ten minutes, and then a tablespoon of port or sherry and a little currant jelly for each person.

All these recipes sound delectable, especially the ones involving an egg-size piece of butter, but nothing sounds more strangely weird/ sublime than moose muffle. Someday, if I ever manage to accompany a moose hunter into the woods, and we further manage to kill a moose, I will claim the jawbone, bring it home, and discover for myself what all the fuss is about. Moose muffle strikes me as the most economical of foods; it puts into literal practice the old French animal-husbandry technique now popularly known as "snout to tail." Eating the moose's snout, which nine times out of ten is discarded by hunters in the woods and left for wild carnivorous animals to scavenge, seems to me to confer on the animal the highest respect. I remember the moose I saw several years ago on the dirt road in the woods by the lake; its upper lip was distinguished by its size, its length. It was a finely wrought, useful upper lip, muscular and hardworking and prehensile, as Merrill pointed out.

When I look at it that way, eating moose muffle is not disgusting at all. It's beautiful. The snout is the most important part of a moose, the part that enables it to forage for food and stay alive, the part that comes into direct contact with the world, that most clearly communicates its will to live.

ele

Maple syrup and venison, including moose meat, go hand in hand in native northeastern American cuisine. Both are available in the wild, and moose are hunted in the spring, the season when maple trees are tapped. Both demand skill and prowess as well as knowledge of the woods to obtain.

Venison cooked in maple syrup was considered by the indigenous tribes as a dish fit for the chief. An Algonquin legend has it that a chief's wife, needing water for that night's venison stew, accidentally grabbed a bucket that had been left by a maple tree, into which sap had dripped all day, after her husband had made a gash in the tree earlier with his tomahawk. The resulting stew was so delicious, he requested it thereafter.

Maple syrup was a mainstay of Wabanaki cuisine, much as salt was for the British. The Wabanaki legend about maple syrup is equally telling: Glooskap, their benign, caretaking, heroic trickster god, whose name has many variants, decided that the original abundance of sweet syrup oozing year-round from the broken branches of maple trees was making the people too lazy, and too fat, which was destroying their civilization. So he watered it down in the trees, one measure for each day between moons (creating the present-day ratio of sap to syrup), and made it harder to get and available only for a brief time each year. Then the Indians had to make buckets to catch it, collect wood for the fires, and heat rocks to boil it down. Thereafter, the Wabanaki tribes held an annual festival during the maple-sap season, honoring their Creator, who provided them with this precious sweet fluid.

Glooskap's mythological lesson—an appreciation of nature's bounty is necessary for survival, as well as a practical work ethic and generationally shared know-how—is reflected exactly in the values I see everywhere in Maine today, whether these skills are used for present-day sap gathering or moose hunting.

Most of the native Indians of Maine died out tragically, brutally fast, during a three-year period called "The Great Dying," from 1613 to 1619, of smallpox and other European diseases against which they had no antibodies, no chance of recovery. Successive plagues in ensuing years killed most of the rest of them; by the end of the eighteenth century, the few Wabanaki who had survived had fled to Canada.

But before they were wiped out, they generously taught the newcomers many of their secrets, which live on here, still.

Chapter Eight

The Essential Blueberry
and the Wild Mushroom

Like the moose and the maple, mushrooms and blueberries exist in the wild up here and are there for the taking to anyone intrepid enough to come and get them. Unlike the moose and the maple, though, they require no special skill to collect or hunt, beyond knowing where the blueberry patch is and which mushrooms are edible and where to find them. This turns out to be astonishingly easy. Throughout Maine and the White Mountains, there is a bounty of these edible plants; in fact, in the growing months, the northeast corner is a cornucopia of delicious, healthful, literally organic food, a free lunch just growing there, to be taken away by anyone lucky enough to find it. Foraging up here is easier than in places further south; it turns out that having a real, harsh winter causes plants to look the way they ought to once they finally grow again in the warmer months. (This strikes me as yet another reason to love the winters up here.)

ele

I arrived here a city-slicker ignoramus about so many things. Amazingly, the only time I'd ever picked blueberries was back in August of 1969, the month I turned seven, the year before we moved from Berkeley to Tempe, when my mother and sisters and I spent the summer with my grandparents in their rented farmhouse in Midcoast Maine. It was near a beach whose name I don't remember; we called it Blue Boat Beach because of an upside-down dinghy that was always there. That summer, we picked wild blueberries that grew in a meadow near our house. They were warm and sweet and bursting with juice. We were West Coast kids, and had never had blueberries before. My sisters and I gorged on them as fast as we could pick them.

My scant lessons in foraging continued in 1980, when I lived in the Allier, the rural center of France, the year after high school. There, I picked up basketfuls of sweet, meaty chestnuts in the forest. We roasted them in the fireplace around Christmastime. Peeling them hurt our fingers, but the meat was so sweet and rich, it was worth it. In the spring, I gathered the peppery, bright-green watercress that grew in a large, stream-fed stone pool, and put it into salads with lamb's ear lettuce. It was a thrill to go outside and find food growing naturally.

A few years later, when I was in college, I spent summers on an island off Nantucket called Tuckernuck, where my mother's then husband's family had a house. The small island had no paved roads, electricity, or stores, nothing but twenty or so old shingled cottages scattered through grassy moors and scrubby woods. We went surf fishing at dawn for striped bass and bluefish, casting out into the waves, standing waist-deep in the water. When I reeled in a fish, I clonked it on the head to kill it, then slit its belly open with a sharp knife and reached in and pulled out its entrails, feeling as macho as Hemingway. Later, on the breezeway of our house, I attached it by the tail to a big, rough clipboard and scaled it. We baked these fish with herbs and potatoes. They always tasted better than any other fish I'd ever eaten, because we'd caught them ourselves earlier that same day, straight out of the ocean.

We also took quahog rakes and a bucket out in the dory at low tide to pull huge, knobby clams from just under the sand on the shallow seafloor. A bucketful of them yielded a big pot of chowder, with some effort and time, and it was always worth it. Just as with the wild blueberries in Maine and the chestnuts and watercress in France, it was even more exciting to eat the food we'd found or caught than it was to eat lettuce, tomatoes, and cucumbers from the little kitchen garden. Gardening takes a lot of ongoing work, whereas foraging in any form feels romantically primitive and elemental and is instantly rewarding. The taste of the wild is seductive. Those blueberries I ate as a little kid have stayed with me like a visceral, instructive taste-memory: The act of eating food straight from its source, raw, unprocessed, still warm from the sun or briny from the ocean, is possibly the best eating experience there is.

Blueberries are so easy to find and identify, a seven-year-old can do it. But hunting mushrooms always struck me as a scary process best left to the experts. Never having hunted them, I imagined mushrooming as something like an Easter egg hunt—you prowl around the woods until a glowing white or pearlescent orb leaps at your eye. Of course, as a novice, I planned to invest in guidebooks and exercise extreme, obsessive caution, but what I was really gunning for was to tag along with a local experienced guide, someone to teach me the difference between edible and toxic fungi: morels and "false morels," chanterelles and jack o'lanterns, chicken of the woods and the intriguingly (and no doubt accurately) named sulphur shelf.

Fresh mushrooms are amazing, sautéed very briefly in olive oil with garlic, thyme, lemon juice and zest, tossed with hot linguine and topped with parsley and Parmesan cheese, but they're not worth dying for, or even spending a night doubled up in acute gastrological pain for. Very few things are.

ꙮ

Even though they're associated with Maine, the first time I picked wild blueberries after I moved up here was in New Hampshire, on Foss Mountain.

It was late August, and I had spent that whole summer learning to drive. I took my test three days before my fifty-second birthday; I had never gotten my driver's license before. No one taught me as a teenager, and once I got into my twenties, I developed some sort of phobia about it: I didn't want to learn. I was irrationally convinced I'd crash and die if I got behind the wheel. My college boyfriend taught me, but I never took the driver's test, and then, after I moved to New York, it was moot, because I took subways or walked everywhere, or my husband drove.

But now that I lived up here, it seemed ridiculous that I couldn't drive myself to the grocery store, couldn't take Dingo to the Eastern Prom when Brendan was out of town. Everyone—even cretins and nincompoops—had driver's licenses. Why not me? So I learned, which is to say, Brendan taught me, all over again. I parallel-parked around the Western Prom, angle-parked in the mall parking lot, and tootled us around town and back and forth, to and from the farmhouse, all summer long.

Although Brendan was an excellent and thorough teacher, and I had been the principal driver of the family for three months, I hardly slept the night before my driver's test. I lay awake, going over parallel parking in my mind: cut hard to the right, reverse, gradually straighten it out to back in at a diagonal, cut hard to the left, ease it in, straighten it out . . . all night long. In my mind's ear, I heard my hard-ass driving instructor saying, "What are you DOING?!" and "You have to pay attention!" and "NOOOO!!"

We got up the next morning at six o'clock, which for us is pre–crack of dawn. I showered, then fed and walked a sleepy and perplexed Dingo while Brendan made coffee. There was a sepulchral silence in the kitchen as we ate our toast. Shaky from insomnia and nerves, I drove us the hour and a half from Portland to the DMV in Tamworth, New Hampshire. I made so many uncharacteristically nerve-wracked mistakes on the way that if it had been my driving test, I would have failed several times over.

"I'm going to flunk," I wailed.

Dingo, his head in the rearview mirror, ears at half-mast, seemed to concur, if his consternated expression was anything to go by.

"I'll probably hit a tree on my test."

"You'll be fine," said my instructor. "You know what you're doing. Just relax. I promise, you will pass."

He later told me that he knew exactly what the test would entail; this was the same DMV where he had gotten his driver's license, sixteen years before.

My examiner was a taciturn, portly man with a short white Afro who had me drive for fifteen minutes on gently rolling country roads. Remembering to signal, stop, check my mirrors, and obey the speed limits, I took a right, another right, a left, then a right, and another right. Then came the hard part: He asked me to back the car into a spot in an empty church parking lot. I couldn't see the white lines I was supposed to park between and had no other cars to guide me, so I fucked it up not once, but twice; I'd asked for a do-over. After all that anxiety, he hadn't had me parallel-park at all; unfortunately, I'd practiced reverse parking exactly twice.

I drove out of the parking lot in disgrace, took a left turn onto the sleepy road, a right turn onto the two-lane route I'd started on, and suddenly, there we were, back at the DMV. It was over.

"I took some points off for your parking," said the examiner. "Because frankly, that was"—he paused, as if searching for the correct word—"terrible."

With a dour expression, he handed me the score sheet. And then I saw that he had checked the box next to PASS.

I leapt from the car, giddy with joy, threw my arms around my strict, demanding, handsome driving instructor, who was waiting there with Dingo, and waltzed inside. As she took my beaming photo, the DMV lady told me, "Oh, honey, no one can park; we all park like crap. I practically hit my own garage every night."

After that ordeal, the rest of the day was ours. I drove us to the farmhouse, where Brendan's parents made us a beautiful lunch: fresh pesto with linguine (they made gluten-free pasta for me, because they are sweethearts), cantaloupe with prosciutto, and a caprese salad with ripe farm-stand tomatoes. Sitting outside at the table in the grass, looking at the mountains, we drank the bottle of champagne I'd brought to celebrate.

Then, for an hour or so, I fell into a near coma on the couch in the summer barn. Dingo, as worn-out as I was, burrowed into a spot behind the couch and conked out, too. Later, after we woke up, Brendan and his mother and I (and Dingo) went up Foss Mountain to pick blueberries.

ele

By now, having lived up here for a number of years, I'd learned a thing or two about blueberries. The blueberry plant was among the first to appear in the barren wasteland left behind when the gigantic glacier finally receded, fourteen thousand years ago. This hardy, ground-hugging survivor grew on granite crags, in crevices, near the coast, in the mountains. Wherever there was soil, they grew, and they didn't need much of it. They held on through hot summers, fogs and rains, and long, cold winters. In fact, to produce fruit, they needed the cold winters, and the extremely acidic soil of Maine was likewise hospitable to them. They increased their strength through the years with a system of underground rhizomes, establishing their hold on the northern wilderness. Their tiny bell-shaped flowers matured into fruit; adapting to a range of environments, the blueberry divided into many varieties and tastes from tangy to sweet, known collectively as "the greatest taste on earth."

The Wabanaki tended the blueberry barrens and gathered the fruit one thousand years ago. They dried the berries and used them in venison jerky, or pemmican, and made little dried cakes out of them, which they stored in birch containers. They made blueberry tea, juice, and syrup, which was used medicinally, for coughs. They used them as dye in basket-making. In all, they considered blueberries magical gifts from the gods in times of starvation, as did the birds and beasts, which have always depended on them for winter survival.

Blueberries are truly a magical gift of nature, unique, versatile, and delicious eaten straight from the plant, as well as high in antibacterial properties and antioxidants. They're rich in vitamins and have healing properties for the eyes and heart. The Natives cared for and cultivated the wild blueberry barrens by burning them periodically to ward off insects and pests and to encourage new bushes to grow. When the Europeans arrived, the Indians taught them their methods of managing the wild blueberries. Colonial cookbooks are full of blueberries in recipes with names like Grunt, Buckle, Fool, and Slump.

There are two basic types of blueberry: highbush and lowbush. Lowbush berries grow wild and are smaller and native only to the northeast corner, whereas highbush berries are larger, hybridized, commercial, more plentiful, blander, and are cultivated anywhere you can grow them. The general opinion seems to be that lowbush berries are scarcer and harder to get, but they taste much better.

The ubiquity of blueberries in the American diet is a relatively recent phenomenon. Highbush berries didn't even exist until the daughter of a New Jersey cranberry farmer named Elizabeth Coleman White dreamed them up in 1911, wanting to augment the profit of her seasonal cranberries. She worked with a botanist named Frederick V. Colville to develop a larger, easier-to-harvest blueberry with a longer growing season. Now, highbush berries account for about 40 million tons per year of commercially sold blueberries, whereas only 75 million pounds of lowbush berries are harvested and sold out of state, I suspect because the natives choose to keep most of them for themselves . . .

Although they were plentiful and easily preserved, wild blueberries stayed strictly local until the Civil War and the building of the railroads, when they were shipped down to soldiers (Maine sent the highest proportion of men of any Northern state to fight in that war); since then, they've been a mainstay of Maine's economy as well as its culture. The "blueberry rake" is passed down in families, and blueberry picking is a seasonal tradition that brings people back to Maine from wherever they've strayed to join relatives in picking and preserving and enjoying that feeling of sweet warm indigo juice running down your chin on a rare and divine summer day.

ele

We settled into a patch on the flank of the ridge, hot in the sun, and picked handful after handful of the perfectly ripe little lowbush berries, which fell off the stems into our hands. Dingo wallowed happily in a shady leftover rain puddle.

"FUCKER!" Brendan suddenly yelled at the wasp that'd stung his hand, dropping his box of berries and leaping about. As his hand swelled into a monstrous lobster claw, we decided the fun was over. We quickly consolidated all the remaining berries in the basket we'd brought and hiked back to the car, which lurched down the steep, mud-rutted dirt road.

As the sun set, back at home, we all sat outside and drank cold Frascati, watching hundreds of dragonflies trolling through the air for little gnats and midges and, we hoped, some of the wasps who'd taken up residence that summer in every available crevice of the house's exterior.

Then, at the long table with candles lit in the summer barn, we feasted on steamed lobsters and lemon butter, corn on the cob, and asparagus. Dessert was maple-walnut ice cream from a local creamery with, of course, blueberries.

Since I don't make or eat dessert or sweets, I asked my friend Millicent Souris, a baker, chef, and cookbook author who lives in Brooklyn but comes to Maine as often as she can, for her favorite way to cook blueberries. She sent me the following delectable-looking recipe. It goes well with shortbread or any other buttery cookie.

Blueberries with Lemon Curd à la Millicent

I love blueberries. You don't have to peel them, pit them, or cut them. Check them for stems and duds and move on. Blueberry pie is a classic, and also seemingly my nemesis, as it's a juicy mess that rarely has time to set up. My attitude toward fruit is, less is more. I grew up with cornstarch-filled diner pies and syrupy canned fruit. I am fully aware that this past has influenced my hands-off approach with fruit desserts. I want to taste the sunshine. Please, when it comes to berries, give me summer.

Lemon Curd (yields 2 cups)

juice and zest of 3 lemons
8 T (1 stick) unsalted butter
1 cup granulated sugar
3 large eggs, lightly beaten
pinch of kosher salt

Fill a medium-size saucepan about one-third full with water, and heat on medium. Use a bowl that will fit on top of the pot, or nestle down a bit, but will not touch the water. Cut the butter into small chunks and toss in the bowl with the sugar. Place the bowl on the pot so the butter starts to melt as you zest the lemons (keep the zest separate to add at the end). Whisk the melting butter and sugar together and add the lemon juice, continuing to whisk until blended.

Lift the bowl. If the water is rapidly boiling—anything over a gentle simmer, really—turn it down and let some of the heat escape to bring the temperature down.

In a separate bowl, continue to beat the eggs together well, until they are fluffy and full of bubbles, and the whites and yolks are integrated. Add the beaten eggs to the other ingredients in the bowl on the stove, whisking everything together. Once this mixture is combined, use a rubber spatula to continuously scrape the bowl around the sides—especially the bottom—so the mixture cooks evenly.

The point of using the double-boiler method is to gently cook your eggs with everything. If the heat is too high, it will scramble the eggs before they become a curd. The mixture will thicken over the next 7 to 10 minutes and become more cohesive and firm along the edges of the bowl. The curd is done when you can lift the spatula, run your finger through the curd on it, and it's thick and satiny, like pudding.

Add the zest and salt. Mix. Turn into another bowl and cover with cling wrap; otherwise, it will form a weird skin. Refrigerate for at least 30 minutes.

Blueberries

1 pint blueberries, picked through for stems and duds
1/4 cup raw sugar
juice and zest of 1 lemon
pinch of sea salt
a few sprigs of tarragon, mint, or chervil, chopped
1 tsp vanilla, or a scraped vanilla pod

Pick the leaves off the herbs and chop. Bruise the herb stems by crushing them in your hand for a few seconds and then toss with the blueberries; there's a lot of flavor and fragrance in the stems. Toss the blueberries with sugar, salt, and vanilla. Add the lemon juice and zest. Let the fruit mixture sit for at 30 minutes. Serve with the lemon curd.

ele

Mushrooms proved to be slightly trickier than blueberries to find and collect and eat. We started hypothetically.

One fall morning, after a breakfast of toast with scrambled eggs, Brendan, Dingo, and I set out on the "circle walk," a four- or five-mile loop that's the alternative route to our usual daily walk to the main road. We'd always seen a lot of mushrooms in the summer and fall, so this time, on a lark, we decided to bring a covered straw basket, not unlike the one Red Riding Hood might have carried to her grandmother's house.

With Dingo trotting just ahead of us, sniffing and peeing and eating grass and trundling along, looking nothing like the big bad wolf, we found a patch of trumpetlike mushrooms by the old graveyard. From then on, we were on the scent, occasionally heading off the road into the woods, on the trail of something neon-yellow or otherwise intriguingly colored or shaped, scrambling over rocks and roots, distracted, then heading back to the road and resuming our walk until something else caught our eye. We weren't after edible mushrooms; we were just collecting for the fun of it.

"There's another beer can," I said. "There's another one. Another one. There are as many cans as there are mushrooms. Oh my God, another one. Next time we should collect Bud Light cans. Who the hell are these people?"

I had a clear, uncharitable image of a bunch of backwoods yahoos driving their old pickup trucks along the road, throwing empties out their windows and hooting into the quiet air.

"Hey," said Brendan, heading for a clump of mushrooms. "Look at those."

We tried to take only one example of everything we found, but couldn't restrain ourselves if something looked particularly worthy. Walking takes on an entirely new dimension when you're focused on picking things up from the ground.

Back at home, I unpacked the basket and arranged our haul on the granite steps just outside the kitchen door, and then we stood and admired them for a while. We'd found orange horns that looked like tiny Victrola speakers with gills underneath, dead-white, penislike, obviously toxic deaths' caps, bright yellow and soft brown clumps of waving fronds that could have come from a coral reef, a bouquet of conjoined, delicate little oyster-colored coins, long slender stems with big flat caps of pale green, pale beige, muted red, gentle yellow, and dirty white, a hobbitlike shaggy "old man of the woods," and other wonders and curiosities.

We couldn't eat any of them, because we had no real idea what the hell any of them were, but we did feel a certain proprietary satisfaction.

ele

Then, a year later, right after I passed my driver's test and got excited again about foraging when we went to Foss for blueberries, we ran into our neighbor, Dorcas, a lively and smart seventy-four-year-old, semiretired estate lawyer, well-read dynamo, and amateur mycologist. She lives down the dirt road from us with her husband of over fifty years, and we often see them out with their sweet old golden retriever in all seasons, walking on the road by the lake, or snowshoeing or cross-country skiing through the meadows. Often, in the coldest months, the four of us are the only people along the road. We always stop and say hello and exchange news like a bunch of happy hermits, comparing notes.

This day, however, I was on a mission: I was hell-bent on convincing her to take me mushrooming. Luckily, she didn't put up much of a fight, and a few days later, she picked Dingo and me up in her Prius after breakfast and whisked us off to her secret spot, a spot I swore never to reveal to anyone, especially not in print. Mushroomers are jealous and possessive, and with very good reason.

It was a hot, muggy, early-September day. The three of us set off through the woods on a well-kept path strewn with pine needles, soft and springy underfoot. It was cooler in the trees. A breeze lifted the hemlock and pine branches with soft whooshing sounds.

"Be careful where you walk," she said. "It's very hard to see them, and easy to step on them by accident."

I immediately slowed down and paid attention to the ground.

"Shoot," she said after we'd walked for a while without finding anything, "maybe we're too late; maybe they're already all gone."

Black trumpets are also known as black chanterelles, trumpets of death, and horns of plenty. They're funnel-shaped, and when they dry, they're inky black. Apparently, they're one of the hardest mushrooms to find, and also one of the most delicious, which explains why Dorcas is so careful about revealing her source.

We walked along slowly, intently scanning the ground and chattering away. She told me about her experiences on the board of directors of the Nature Conservancy, where scientists frequently give talks about various aspects of conservation and nature, of course; it's one of three local boards she sits on. She walked along as easily as I did, nimble and athletic, while she told me about the foremost mycologist in our area, who taught her to hunt black trumpets and chanterelles and got her started in mushrooming. I noticed that she never stopped scanning the ground right at our feet.

"Hey," I called out helpfully every time I saw a mushroom or other fungus, no matter what kind, scalloped dun-colored fungi covering a fallen log, a dead-white toadstool with a neon-orange underbelly. "There's a mushroom. It looks fresh. Maybe we're not too late."

"The brighter the color, the more poisonous the mushroom," Dorcas said. "They're easier to find, but they're no good to eat."

We continued on, slowly, searching every inch of pine needles, fallen branches, dried leaves, and earth.

"There, a whole patch!" she said. "More dried ones; shoot, we might be too late. The season may be over already. We got two big bags of them in August."

I didn't see them at first, and then I did: small black shriveled things against the dark ground, almost invisible, spreading for several feet along the path. They looked not even remotely edible, like bits of crumpled tarpaper or lumps of volcanic rock.

"They grow along the path," she said. "I think they like a bit of sunlight."

And then, at last, we found a patch of edible, fresh black trumpet mushrooms in a boggy depression in the path, beautiful little horns on slender stalks with a chalky gloss to the dark color. We picked a couple of handfuls excitedly; it had been a treasure hunt, and now we had been rewarded for our patience.

"I can see why people love mushrooming," I said. "You kind of get hooked. Now I just want to find more. How do you cook them?"

"I sauté the black trumpets in butter and pour it all over steak, or I cut them up into a beef stew."

"I'm suddenly starving."

We went on, deeper into the woods.

"What's that blue barrel?" Dorcas said, pointing.

"I don't know," I said.

We set off to investigate and found a plastic blue cylinder with a hole cut in its side and branches arranged around it and inside it.

"I know what this is," said Dorcas. "It's a bear-baiting trap. Look, the hunter loads it up with donuts and sits up there and waits for the bear to come and then he shoots it. There's even a rest for his rifle."

Beyond the bear-baiting trap was a blind in a tree, a lookout made of lightweight steel with a ladder driven into the trunk and a wooden permit dangling from the underside of the perch.

Dorcas made an impatient huffing sound and closed up the trap with the circle of blue plastic; for whatever good it would do, we agreed, it was better than nothing.

I had just heard of bear-baiting for the first time, because there was a referendum to ban it on the ballot for the upcoming election, and I'd been getting a lot of phone calls from activists, hoping to convince me to vote to support the ban. Being an animal lover, albeit a carnivorous one, I had decided without thinking too much about it that bear-baiting must be bad if so many people in my part of the world were fighting so hard to outlaw it. The trap looked unsportsmanlike and unfair to me, too. "Shooting fish in a barrel" came to mind. I felt sorry for any poor bear that came wandering along innocently, looking for his lunch, thinking he was just enjoying a free donut, and then, *boom*.

On our way back to the car, Dorcas mentioned that her husband was at home that morning, picking the ripe tomatoes from their garden, and when she got back, they would put them up in sterilized jars.

"How much of your own vegetables do you grow?" I asked.

"All we need in the summer, of course. It's so nice to go out to the garden and see what's ready, and that's how we decide what to have for dinner. Our favorite thing to make is fresh tomatoes sautéed with whatever's ripe and served over pasta—eggplant, zucchini, peppers, and garlic, of course. We love garlic."

"How much of your own produce do you freeze and can and put up for the wintertime?"

"Oh, I make lots of pesto from our basil and freeze that, along with peas, green beans. Our grandchildren love to help shell peas. And we grow our own onions, and they keep nicely. We have a huge freezer. We also have a yearly share in half a cow, a lamb, and a pig, from three different local farms who butcher them for us, and of course we share the meat with our family because it's so much, and we get our chickens at Sherman Farm Stand, because they come from a farm in Maine that lets them run around, pecking in the sunlight."

"God," I said enviously, admiringly. "How great. I have never had a garden, I've never grown anything, but I would love to try to start one next year."

We came to the car and all hopped in, twelve-year-old Dingo leapt into the backseat as easily as Dorcas had walked over the forest path. It made me glad for the thousandth time that I'd brought him here, away from the city's exhaust and grime, noise and stress.

"Well," said Dorcas, "what do you want to plant?"

"I think I'd better start with things that are easy to grow so I feel rewarded and encouraged to keep doing it."

By the time we got back to our dirt road, Dorcas had advised me to start with a ten-by-ten-foot plot, measure it out before winter and cover it with nonporous black plastic to minimize weeds next year, and to start with cucumber, zucchini, tomatoes, green beans, basil, lettuce, and tomatoes. We talked about compost and seasonal plantings. The more we talked about my future garden, the more excited I became. If I could learn to hunt mushrooms, I could learn to garden. Everyone else in this part of the world seemed to know how to do these things already, but to me, it was all still arcane, mysterious, and magical. Learning these things, even imagining learning these things, felt to me like a triumph, a challenge. It made me feel like a slightly different person: a better one.

When Dorcas pulled into the barn driveway, two hours after we'd set out, she handed me the bag of mushrooms.

"I'm not taking your mushrooms!" I said. "No way!"

But she insisted. I knew how kind this was; such generosity does not come along very often. I accepted with thanks and took my treasures inside.

I cleaned the mushrooms by tearing them gently in half and shaking out the pine needles and bits of earth from their crevices. They are very thin-skinned and delicate and velvety, and they come apart in long strips. Also known as the "poor man's truffle," they have an earthy perfume. Brendan and I admired them all afternoon there on the cutting board as we went about our day.

After we came back from a cooling swim in the lake, when the shadows got long over the meadows and the day began to wane, we opened some white wine and I embarked on dinner, excited to cook these beautiful things.

℮℮

Black Trumpet Mushrooms
with Chicken Thighs and Mustard Sauce

In a large, shallow skillet, sauté 2 minced shallots and several minced garlic cloves in lots of butter and olive oil. When they are soft, push them to the side and brown four skinless, boneless chicken thighs well; while they brown, dust them with sea salt, black pepper, paprika, and Old Bay seasoning. Remove them from the pan and add the cleaned strips of mushrooms and cook them for a minute or two, then put the thighs back in and pour in a whisked-together sauce of 1/3 cup each half-and-half and chicken broth, plus 1 tsp of Dijon mustard. Cover the skillet and let simmer for 10 minutes.

Serve over wild rice with a side of steamed, garlicky baby spinach. The mushrooms taste clean, faintly smoky, and very rich, and their texture is delicate and meaty. They are the best I've ever eaten. Serves 2.

℮℮

While we ate, a ferocious rainstorm blew in and washed away the heavy heat and was gone in twenty minutes; afterwards, the air was golden and almost chilly. Fall had come, just like that.

When we woke up the next morning, the milkweed was growing tall again in the mown meadows, and the air was tinged with autumn. After breakfast, Brendan and I set off into the woods behind our house and, on a wooded path that will remain secret forevermore, we found our own patch of black trumpets. Brendan spotted them. They were dried and black, like most of the ones Dorcas and I had found, but the fruiting body is there, and we'll watch it for fresh ones.

On the way home, Brendan stopped to look at an enormous scalloped fungus growing at the base of a tree.

"I think this is a hen of the woods," he said.

I examined it. It looked exactly like a gigantic maitake mushroom, otherwise known as a hen of the woods, also known as the dancing mushroom, because people do a dance when they find it. I recognized it from seeing them for sale in supermarkets, neatly packaged, for around $20 a pound.

"I think you're right," I said, excited. "You found a hen of the woods! A huge one! You're so good at this."

"Beginner's luck," he said.

I handed him the plastic bag I'd brought in my pocket just in case, and together, we gently harvested it and carried it away with us. We guessed from hefting it that it weighed about three pounds. When we got home, we identified it easily; there are no known toxic lookalikes, and it looks identical to its photographs.

A little while later, we dropped that big, fresh, beautiful hen of the woods off at Dorcas's, our first-ever mushroom find, with a note thanking her for showing us the way—a tribute to our mycology guru, and a sign of honor among thieves.

And now we have our own mushroom patches, two kinds, to guard jealously and possessively and secretively.

Chapter Nine

The Great Disappearing Codfish
and the Perfect Oyster

One early summer afternoon in Portland, in the gold liquid sunlight and fresh, barely warm air, we took Dingo on a hike along a bluff. We passed a ruined stone villa in a copse, crumbled forts and batteries, and Portland Head Light, the oldest lighthouse in Maine. We watched small birds ride the swells where the waves crashed into the seaweedy rocky shore, stopped to sit on a stone wall so Dingo could loll in a patch of tender young dandelions like an odalisque, prompting us to call him Dingolion and Dandelingo because we were loopy with the beauty of it all—high on it, in fact. Across the bay, old summer houses sat cozily on an island in green scrub atop rocky cliffs. A solitary, blue, trim, old-style fishing trawler with a short mast chugged past the islands to the mouth of the harbor, beyond the lighthouse, out to sea, to catch . . . what? Smelts? What's left out there now, we wondered?

When we got home, I took things out of the fridge to make a sort of New England bouillabaisse, a savory fish stew with carrots, Old Bay, and smoked paprika instead of fennel, orange, and saffron.

I'd bought the cod and shrimp at Whole Foods. The guy at the seafood counter had assured me the cod had been wild-caught in Scandinavia, and the shrimp had been "responsibly" farmed, which I took to mean that it wasn't laden with dangerous bacteria, antibiotics, or shrimp food made of GMO corn and soy by-products.

Neither fish nor shrimp had come from the Gulf of Maine, as there are hardly any left in there anymore. Wild fish are so locally endangered, Whole Foods won't sell them (few people will; and if they do, it's mostly haddock and hake), and they're proud of that fact. It struck me as ironic that the store feels virtuous about importing fish from thousands of miles away; honestly, neither option—selling endangered fish nor selling fish that took a lot of petroleum to transport—seems like a good choice. In spite of my better instincts, being only human, I bought a pound of cod anyway.

As the pot of imported Scandinavian fish soup simmered away, smelling of New England no matter where the fish had come from, I thought of the old legend that the Gulf of Maine was once so full of enormous codfish, some of them weighing up to 700 pounds, you could walk across their backs on the surface of the water. Captain John Smith described the Gulf of Maine as laced with "silvered streams" of fish.

Because cod has almost no fat, unlike herring and other cold-water fish, it's easily cured and stored. In the early colonial days in New England, cod was a booming trade that involved enormous fishing boats and beachfront processing operations that would squeeze oil from cod livers; gut and dry the hundred-plus-pound behemoths caught by the hundreds every day by each boat; and then smoke them or preserve them in salt. This preserved cod was transported in 300- to 900-ton ships all over the world, including the Deep South, where it was traded for cotton or rum, which was in turn shipped to England and traded for salt, which was brought back to preserve even more cod. This was called the "triangular fish trade"; along with felled lumber and quarried granite, as well as blocks of winter ice that were cut, stored in enormous warehouses, and shipped to the South and all over the world, codfish were the foundation of Maine's economy for hundreds of years.

By the late 1800s, the Gulf of Maine had all but been fished to extinction. Maine's economy started to collapse. Refrigeration made the ice trade moot, and railroads enabled lumber and granite and other goods to be transported more cheaply and efficiently from other places, rather than in the holds of Maine ships.

The Civil War also disrupted the trade routes between the North and South. Lumbermen, fishermen, and granite quarry workers went off to fight—73,000 Mainers in all, the highest proportion of the population of any Northern state. And while the war raged on, 18,000 other Maine men left the coast to take lower-paying, harder jobs in huge offshore fishing industries; even more moved away to farm the rich land in the Midwest, whose soil was deeper and more fertile.

"But," writes Colin Woodward in *The Lobster Coast*, "a great number of them decided to stick it out on the rockbound coast. Building their own small boats, they set about fishing whatever would provide a living on their own terms. Few would have guessed that the American lobster, that ungainly crawler who infested the bottoms of the coves and harbors outside their bedroom windows, would prove their lasting salvation."

And it still does—at least these days, at least for now. And when the lobsters are gone, the hardy, scrappy Maine fishermen will find another way to wrest a living from the sea: possibly by cultivating oysters, and possibly by harvesting or farming highly nutritious and ubiquitous seaweed, which is even more humble than lobsters ever were.

Meanwhile, the Maine cod, haddock, and halibut populations have never recovered from all those feverish decades of systematic decimation and profit, and it's likely they never will. But even so, there is still nothing that tastes more purely and traditionally of this wild maritime region to me than fish soup.

ℓℓℓ

New England Fish Soup

Mince 1 large onion, 3 medium carrots, 2 celery ribs, and 7 or so garlic cloves. In a big sturdy soup pot, heat a good dollop of oil. When it's hot, add the vegetables with a dash of Old Bay seasoning, a teaspoon or two, and another of smoked paprika, and stir well.

Thinly slice 2 or 3 spicy pork sausages, ideally chorizo, and throw them in. Add a dash of salt and another of black pepper. Turn the heat down low and let it all simmer, stirring often, for about half an hour, till everything is soft and melded into an aromatic wad of flavor.

Small-dice 4 small red potatoes. Add them to the pot and stir well. Pour in half a bottle of easygoing, dry white wine (Pinot Grigio works well). Turn up the heat till it bubbles, then turn down and let it simmer a while until the alcohol has cooked off and it's reduced a bit.

Add 2 cups of fire-roasted tomatoes or very good tomato sauce, and an 8-oz. jar of clam juice. Add enough broth—vegetable, fish, or chicken—to cover the solids, just over an inch. Bring to a boil and turn down and let simmer. Taste, adjust the seasonings, adding more broth as required.

Chop 1 lb. of cod, haddock, or other firm, white sea fish into bite-size pieces. Peel and likewise chop 3/4 lb. of shrimp. Finely chop a bunch of flat-leaf parsley. When it feels like a nearly finished soup, everything tender and the flavors just right, add the seafood and parsley to the pot and let it simmer, stirring a few times, for 10 more minutes.

Mince 3 to 4 cloves of garlic. Add them to a bowl with a dollop of good-quality mayonnaise and another of olive oil. Mix this quick aioli together and spread on 2 to 4 pieces of hot toast and cut them into triangles. Serve with big bowls of soup. Serves 4.

ᘉ

One fall day a couple of years ago, a USPS Flat Rate Priority box of two dozen oysters in ice packs arrived in the mail from Cape Cod. Beau, a college acquaintance turned Facebook friend, and a fellow food lover, had gathered them himself near Wellfleet, where he lives. When he'd posted a general offer to send oysters for bartered items, I pounced on it within seconds, trying to come up with something to swap.

The postmistress joked with us that we were lucky she hadn't eaten the oysters herself and pretended they'd never arrived. We certainly felt lucky. They were some of the freshest, sweetest oysters either of us had ever eaten. The instant we got home from the post office, Brendan put them on ice and got out the shucker while I made a shallot-vinegar sauce and a ketchup-horseradish-Tabasco-Worcester-shire sauce mixture. We poured ourselves some cold white wine and stood at the counter and downed all twenty-four of those oysters with wild gusto. When they were gone, we grinned with dazed, chops-licking glee at each other.

Oysters in this country have a rich and fascinating history. According to *The Oxford Encyclopedia of Food and Drink in America*:

The changing role that oysters played in American cuisine, from the wigwams of the Wampanoags to the famous New York City oyster saloons and gradually to the dining rooms from Boston to San Francisco, is a saga that progressed from sheer necessity to serendipity. The Indians taught the colonists to harvest and cook oysters in a stew that staved off hunger, and in 1610 food shortages in Jamestown, Virginia, led settlers to travel to the mouth of the James River, where oysters sustained them. Two centuries later, a feature of the American diet became a between-meal snack at a vendor's stand, and a dozen or two half shells became a prelude to a more substantial oyster pie or, on the West Coast, an oyster omelet known as Hangtown Fry. By 1840, annual shipments of oysters from the Chesapeake Bay to Philadelphia had reached four thousand tons. By 1859, residents in New York City spent more on oysters than on butchers' meat.

I've always had trouble writing about my passion for eating raw oysters. It's akin to writing a good sex scene: both are purely sensual pleasures, immediate and universal at the same time. Putting the particulars into words can feel a little silly and potentially over-the-top if the words aren't absolutely and unswervingly wed to a visceral truth. And there are only so many ways you can describe either experience.

No one has written better about this magical, sensual creature than the great, late M. F. K. Fisher. Her fourth book, *Consider the Oyster*, is the definitive book about oysters. It's short enough to read in one sitting, and it demands, like a poem, to be reread immediately on finishing it. It's filled with recipes so direct and concrete you can taste them as you read, along with arresting images—a chilly, delicate gray body sliding down a red throat.

Fisher wrote *Consider the Oyster* in 1941, while her second husband, the love of her life, Dillwyn Parrish, was suffering from Buerger's disease, a rare autoimmune response to smoking; the phantom pain from his amputated leg become so bad that he eventually shot himself. That she chose to write about the oyster—aphrodisiac, mysterious, a source of pleasure and strength—during the darkest time of her life suggests that the book was intended at least in part as a source of comfort. But not one word is self-pitying or elegiac; the tone is joyful, playful, and succinctly optimistic.

It opens with a witty overview of the "dreadful but exciting" life of an oyster, followed by mouthwatering descriptions and recipes for certain ways oysters can and should be eaten—either raw, in their shells, with various condiments and buttered brown bread, or cooked in buttery, milky stews and soups and all manner of other delicacies. Fisher is typically democratic and broad-minded but firmly opinionated at every turn; on the question of which alcohol goes best with oysters, she runs through the possibilities and concludes that just about anything will do.

The book ends with nostalgic memories, her own and others': her mother's schoolgirl treat of baked oyster loaf, a San Francisco bohemian's passion for the Hangtown Fry, the story of a virginal young man's wishful and fruitless overindulgence, and a fleeting, poetic trespass on a Chesapeake Bay oyster bed at dawn. This book packs a wallop in a small amount of space, satisfies without satiating, and goes down easily, pithy and nutritious and sweetly briny.

Oysters are perfect, eaten raw. But they're also good when they're cooked, and different: meatier, richer, plumper. Cooking them brings out their essential sweetness and briny purity, so they combine beautifully with starch and aromatics, herbs and fats, in a warm indulgence of pure pleasure. Here's a recipe I created for what's essentially an oyster casserole, inspired by others, including Fisher.

ele

Classic New England Oyster Dressing or Stuffing

7 cups day-old cornbread, crumbled
1 lb. raw oysters (about 30)
8 oz. pancetta or thick-cut bacon, chopped
1 stick salted butter
1 cup minced celery
2 cups minced onions
1/3 cup minced parsley
1 T each minced sage and thyme
3/4 tsp each salt and black pepper
1/4 tsp nutmeg
1/2 tsp ground clove
1 cup oyster liquor or chicken stock
1/4 cup madeira or port
1 large beaten egg

Toast the cornbread crumbs on a cookie sheet in a 400-degree oven for 10 to 12 minutes. Put into a large bowl.

Melt butter till it foams in a large skillet, add pancetta or bacon, and cook till crisp. Add celery and onion and cook for 7 minutes, till they soften. Turn off the heat and stir in the herbs and spices. Add this mixture to the oysters and the cornbread crumbs. Toss and moisten with oyster liquor or stock, madeira or port, and egg.

You can fill the cavity of a turkey with this stuffing and bake it that way. But I prefer it on its own, as a dressing, baked separately in a buttered dish for 30 minutes at 350 degrees.

ele

One summer a few years ago, we stayed in Brittany for three days with friends of Brendan's family. Jean-Louis and his wife, Marie, and their son live in an old stone house in a small, insanely picturesque village called Saint-Briac-sur-Mer.

Jean-Louis is a real cook, whereas Marie, by her own admission, can't boil an egg. They're both French, but Marie is also Russian, which gives her personality a tragic depth. She has olive skin, wide blue eyes, and short, curly hair, and is a few years younger than I am. Jean-Louis is an energetic, handsome man twenty-five years older than she is, which beats Brendan's and my age difference by five years. As a foursome, we all seemed to be about the same age, which proves something, maybe.

Jean-Louis cooked up a storm for us, to put it mildly. On our first night in Saint-Briac-sur-Mer, he made a *filet de bar* (broiled sea bass), with a fennel salad and chickpeas in olive oil. The next morning, before lunch, he sauntered out in his espadrilles to the village market, which camps outside their front door once a week (it's like a movie set, missing only an accordion player and Audrey Tautou), and bought a dozen oysters for everyone but Marie, an animal-lover and vegetarian who ate leftover chickpeas instead. He opened a bottle of cold Pouilly-Fuissé, and we tucked in.

The oysters were plump and robust and salty, even coppery, flinty-tasting, extremely intense. Their deep, shaggy shells were filled with brine and rested on a bed of fresh wet seaweed and had hats on, the flat tops of their shells, which contained nuggets of oyster meat we chewed off before emptying each shell down our gullets, brine and all. With these, we ate bread and butter, even gluten-intolerant me, because fuck it, that was the best lunch of my whole life.

Afterwards, we staggered off for afternoon naps. I slept so deeply I had no idea where I was when I woke up. I think those oysters had a narcotic quality, like the poppies in *The Wizard of Oz*.

It turns out, amazingly, that these Belon oysters also live in Maine, where they're more accurately called the "European flat oyster," since only true "Belons" come from the Belon River estuary. Call them what you will, Belons were transplanted to Maine decades ago.

The Browne Trading Company—a Portland seafood purveyor down on Commercial Street that sells top-quality seafood, wine, caviar, and cheese—also carries fresh, raw Belon oysters. On their website, they give the history of this rare creature in Maine: "While local legend has it that they came from Europe in the bilge of ships and took root here long before we were a country, in truth they were deliberate transplants by scientists to the Boothbay Region in the 1950s. Here they were able to adapt to survive in Maine's cold waters and were able to reproduce and establish various beds throughout the Maine coast."

The French transplants went feral, and then oyster farmers began to cultivate them. Now they're established here, both wild and farmed; they flourish on "harder, rocky bottoms in rivers such as the Damariscotta where they are actually harvested by divers—who have limited access once the rivers and inlets freeze over. . . . With so few harvested a year (estimated at no more than 5,000), the Maine 'Belon' is among the rarest oyster available anywhere."

One night at a writer friend's cocktail party, I met a young oyster farmer named Abigail Carroll. She began cultivating oysters a few years ago in a nature conservancy in the Scarborough River around Nonesuch Point, just south of Portland. Her oyster farm, Nonesuch, is now among the most famous and successful in Maine; Scarborough River scores an A for cleanliness, and her oysters are described as "bright, fresh, salty-sweet, with delicate grassy undertones."

I cornered her by the fireplace and got her to talk about oysters.

"I never meant to be an oyster farmer," she told me. "I'm a native Mainer, but I wasn't going to live here. I was always going to travel and live abroad. I studied languages at Barnard, French and Spanish, then got a master's in international affairs from Columbia. I lived in Paris for a decade, working in start-ups and writing and learning about food and wine."

"And now you're a Maine oyster farmer," I said.

"That was accidental! It's the result of a consulting project gone awry. Very awry. When I agreed to write a business plan for this guy, I declared, 'But I'm not getting on the water!' Famous last words! I wound up owning the farm and being the farmer."

"Do you raise Belon oysters?" I asked.

"Ah, the European Flats," she said. "While they are considered a rare delicacy, and you get a premium for them, it's rare to find someone who actually likes them!" She laughed. "One oyster grower likened the taste of a Belon to licking an aluminum pail."

"I love them," I said. "But I can see that they'd be an acquired taste. They're very metallic and briny, it's true."

She laughed again. "Here's a Belon story: I visited a French oyster grower, Anne Guelt, who laughed when I told her that we had to put rubber bands around our Belons to keep them closed. The adductor muscle on the Belon is quite loose, so for better storage, you need to actually fasten the shells closed. Anne said that was very old-fashioned, and in France, they actually 'train' the oysters to stay closed. She says they take the oysters out of the water for an hour or so, then put them back in the water, then back on land for a longer period of time, and then back in the water. They do this 'training' until the oyster can predictably stay closed when it's out of the water, and have a decent shelf life. She told me that she had trained one oyster so well that she left him out for twenty-three days in the living room before he let his adductor muscle go and opened up and died! I love the idea that Anne had a pet oyster."

"A champion pet oyster," I said, laughing.

"We had a funny experience with a Belon as well. We mistakenly harvested one when we were trying to harvest just regular *virginica* oysters. So we had to drive the Belon back out to the farm. It opened its shell, and as I reached out to touch it and close it shut, it snapped shut before I could reach it. This little game went on, with my team laughing hysterically, for the whole trip back to the farm."

"How do they fare here, in these foreign waters?" I asked.

"Belons do really well in Maine. They're notoriously difficult to raise and susceptible to disease—French and temperamental!" We both laughed. "But they seem to do well here. I wish we could find a reliable source of Belon seed. They are a whole lot of fun! Wild Belons live in our estuary, but I'm a farmer, and I believe very much that we should reap what we sow and not steal the spoils that naturally exist in the water. As it is, we don't have enough oysters."

This is true: Maine's oyster supply can't keep up with demand.

In a 2011 *Press Herald* story by Ann S. Kim about Abigail Carroll's Nonesuch Oysters and another young oyster farmer named Nate Perry, Kim said, "The strength of Maine's brand is based not just on the state's reputation as a pristine area. There's a biological basis as well . . . Water temperatures in Maine are relatively cold, which means that oysters here generally do not spawn. When oysters direct their energies toward reproduction, their glycogen content falls, making them less sweet and plump. . . . Maine oyster farmers cannot grow enough to satisfy demand, and it's not uncommon for growers to have to ration the number they provide to each account."

To which Abigail added, "There aren't enough Maine oysters for the world."

I completely agree.

ℓℓ

Last spring, on our way up the coast to visit our friend Madeleine, a doctor who lives in Camden, Brendan and I stopped for lunch at a pub in the town of Damariscotta. We ordered a dozen local Glidden Point oysters and two glasses of Muscadet to start. The oysters arrived with a small bowl of shallot vinaigrette and lemon slices; we doused them in lemon, poured a little mignonette into one each, and ate them. Our eyes widened. These oysters were cleanly tangy, on the small side, with a complex flavor that opened out the longer we rolled them around our mouths. We chewed them gently, swallowed happily, and sipped some wine.

"These are amazing," I said.

We ordered another dozen. After that day, we began to make occasional pilgrimages, taking the hour-long drive up to Damariscotta on the theory that oysters should be enjoyed as close to their source as possible.

As it turns out, I'm not the first person to have figured this out. Native Americans and early settlers of the Maine coast once feasted on wild oysters from the Damariscotta River, leaving behind heaps of shells, charcoal, bones, and artifacts known as *middens*, piled high on the banks of the upper estuary. As Peter Smith writes in the *Smithsonian*, "the Damariscotta River has long been the epicenter of oyster shucking. Shell heaps rise on both its banks—towering middens of flaky, bleached white shells discarded between 2,200 and 1,000 years ago when American oysters flourished in the warm, brackish waters.

"[But] the early abundance didn't last, probably due to predatory snails brought on by a rise in sea level, rather than overharvesting, and neither has the subsequent introduction, in 1949, of European flat oysters. Today, though, hundreds of thousands of native oysters are once again being cultivated by oyster farmers."

ele

Oysters are named according to geography, defined by their location, the distilled essence of wherever they live: They are the briny, slippery, concentrated essence of the ocean. They constantly filter seawater through their gills—as much as fifty gallons a day—for plankton and other nutrients, and because they're stationary, wherever they are is how they taste.

Call me biased and locally chauvinistic, but in my opinion, Maine oysters from the Damariscotta River are, along with those oysters from the Belon River estuary of Brittany, the best in the world, even better than the famous Malpeques from Prince Edward Island. I do not know why, but maybe it's as simple as the fact that those waters just taste better to me.

I find oysters from the West Coast too creamy and less interesting on the whole; the Pacific Ocean tastes blander to me, not as complex as the North Atlantic. Oysters from New England waters south of Maine are likewise less potent and tangy than their northern cousins; those waters have warmed in recent decades, and due to overfishing and pollution, the once famously productive Chesapeake Bay oyster beds have been decimated; meanwhile, New York, Connecticut, and Massachusetts oysters are delicious enough, but not as good as Glidden Points by a long shot.

Gulf oysters, from Louisiana and Texas, are brackish, sexy things, enormous and full of intriguing flavor; the warmer southern Atlantic waters confer an easy taste, as well as enough toxins to knock out an elephant, so there's an added element of danger to eating them. At one oyster bar in New Orleans recently, I downed a dozen and then another dozen, dousing each behemoth in Tabasco, horseradish mixed with ketchup, and lemon, tipping each knobby shell into my mouth and slurping the half-dollar-size creature onto my tongue and letting it linger there.

I always chew oysters. I savor each one. As I swallow, I taste the length of its body down the entire length of my tongue. It is, quite frankly, the most sexual culinary experience in the world. The closest second I can think of is eating a rare and juicy steak, or a ripe mango, or sashimi so fresh it's still quivering. But these are, in fact, closer to eating than sex.

There's a good reason oysters are famously reputed to be aphrodisiacs; in addition to their inherent sexiness, they have a potent nutritive value—they contain zinc, selenium, calcium, vitamins A and B12, protein, and other energy- and life-giving elements, but they're very low in calories, about 100 per dozen, so they never make you feel stuffed or overfull, and they go down like pure nuggets of seawater and energy.

Oysters are by turns male and female, and are capable of fertilizing their own eggs. And they're more sexually productive than bunnies. In the female stage, an oyster can release up to 100 million eggs a year. A baby oyster reaches sexual maturity as a male when it's about a year old, releasing sperm into the water. A group of spawning oysters clouds the water with sperm and eggs: liquid sex.

Speaking of which, oysters are a tradition for Brendan and me on Valentine's Day, when we eat and drink and make merry all day long in a shameless pursuit of pleasure even more concentrated than our everyday decadence. After our traditional breakfast of blini with salmon roe and blood orange mimosas, we take a long walk through the woods, out onto the frozen lake, and back up the long hill. When we come home, warm and breathless, I build a fire and Brendan shucks a dozen or two very fresh raw Maine oysters, which we eat on ice by the fire with two sauces, minced shallots in champagne vinegar, plus a mixture of lemon juice, ketchup, Worcestershire sauce, Tabasco, and horseradish.

The oysters are followed by crisp endive leaves festooned with capers, crème fraîche, and dill, leftover blini with mild, tangy sheep cheese, then steamed clams with melted butter, then steamed asparagus with a dipping sauce, and finally, to end this day of simple and light but luxurious and self-indulgent eating, strawberries dipped in dark chocolate.

It's all delicious, of course, but the oysters are the high point, *the* point, the thing that tells us it's Valentine's Day, the thing that propels us to shuck off our clothes and feast again.

Chapter Ten

Holy Donuts, Wholesome
Potatoes, and Bean Holes

I walked into the Holy Donut's Exchange Street shop in Portland at ten o'clock on a Wednesday morning. In a nice touch of life-soundtrack serendipity, Al Green's "Love and Happiness" was playing on the speakers. I got in line, and when it was my turn, I asked for the last gluten-free, dark-chocolate and sea-salt donut in the rack, which was in a covered case separate from the regular donuts, and an iced coffee. The friendly tattooed counterman gave me my order with easy-going dispatch. As I added cream and simple syrup to my iced coffee, I told him, "I'm here to talk to Leigh. She's expecting me."

The Holy Donut is, quite simply, one of the best things about my new life in Portland. Since I gave up gluten in 2002, at the very top of my list of the food items I most desperately missed were donuts.

During the many years I lived in Brooklyn, way, way back in those happy days before I realized I couldn't eat them, I would hike over to Peter Pan Donuts on Manhattan Avenue in Greenpoint whenever I needed a fix. I'd order a chocolate honey-dipped and a cruller and a cup of their not-bad coffee and sit at the counter and indulge myself.

I don't have much of a sweet tooth. I could live happily ever after without brownies, cupcakes, cake, ice cream, pie, cookies. But donuts—or doughnuts, as they were once spelled—are another thing entirely. They're not baked; they're deep-fried—crisp and just greasy enough and, at their best, not too sweet. They're nuggety bombs of decadent toothsome animal deliciousness; they stick to your ribs and give you a zingy kick and don't make you crash. Other sweets seem like a waste of stomach space to me. Donuts give you the ultimate bang for your buck. They were my Paradise Lost of pleasure eating for many, many years.

ℓℓℓ

Several months after I moved to Portland, the first Holy Donut opened on Park Avenue. I don't remember how I first heard about Leigh Kellis's gluten-free Maine potato donuts, but shortly after the amazing news of their existence reached my ears, I was standing in line at the counter, waiting for a fresh hot cinnamon-sugar donut just out of the fat. I ate it immediately, standing next to the counter, holding it in its wax-paper lining, letting it melt on my tongue, swooning at my first donut in about ten years.

This was the real thing: shaped by hand, with that genuine old-fashioned homemade feeling; light, nutty, cakey on the inside and crisp on the outside, with the sandy crunch of cinnamon sugar between my teeth. I finished it and bought another one and ate that one more slowly, licking cinnamon sugar off my fingers.

In the next months, Leigh added more flavors and glazes to her gluten-free choices: dark-chocolate sea-salt; pomegranate with chai glaze; lemon that tasted bright, fresh, zesty; Maine blueberry; coconut milk–glazed dark-chocolate . . .

While I waited for Leigh, I looked around her new, second location, appreciating its brightness and airy coziness. The Old Port is tourism central, a maze of crooked cobblestone streets and gift boutiques, well-preserved historic buildings and gelato shops. Cruise ships regularly dock on the pier on Commercial Street and disgorge hundreds of passengers at a time, who walk slowly through the streets in crowds. The Old Port is different from the rest of the city, in that it's geared to visitors, not locals.

But the new Holy Donut felt like an unpretentious neighborhood joint, just like the original. It has homey decor—a scuffed tile floor, exposed-brick wall, couches and a big potted ficus in one window, tables in the other. Ceiling fans whir overhead; good music plays, not too loudly, on the sound system.

I sat at the only empty table and bit into my donut. I was starving because I'd been up since seven-thirty and hadn't eaten breakfast; I'd been saving my appetite for this, and it was worth it. The dark chocolate had melded with the riced potato in the batter to form a velvety-textured wall of flavor that dissolved on my tongue. Then came the bright crunch of sea salt on the satiating outer layer of clean, delectable oil. I took another bite. My eyes fluttered with joy.

As I sipped some iced coffee (a rich, roasty special blend from Coffee By Design), I saw Leigh heading toward my table. She's a slender brunette in her late thirties with sparkling green eyes and chiseled cheekbones. She's as gorgeous as a movie star, but she doesn't play it up; she was wearing a plain sleeveless shirt and jeans, her hair up in a ponytail, dangly earrings her only concession to glamour.

"I'm Leigh," she said, shaking my hand. "I'm sorry to keep you waiting; I'm just trying to finish up back there."

"Take your time, no rush," I said. "I'm having a great time with my donut and iced coffee."

While I waited, I noticed that the line at the counter kept expanding, then shrinking, then expanding again. The place was consistently full, mid-morning on a weekday, with families, businessmen, writer types, tourists, but it felt neither crowded nor precious, and not overly loud. The high ceiling absorbed the ambient noise, and the spaciousness gave a sense of calm.

Several minutes later, Leigh sat down across from me.

"There are three guys working behind the counter," she said, "but I'm the only one who notices details, so I have to constantly be on it."

"You're the owner," I said. "That makes sense. By the way, this iced coffee is amazing."

"We use coffee ice cubes," she said with pride. "So it doesn't get watered down."

I looked into my cup: yup, coffee ice cubes. No wonder. I took another sip.

ele

Leigh was born and raised in Portland, Maine. She attended Deering High School. After graduation, she worked in "every restaurant in town. I can't walk a foot down the street without seeing someone I know. Every single aisle in the grocery store."

Three years ago, she was a single, recently divorced mother, living in her parents' attic with her young daughter and working as a bartender while she worked toward a degree that would enable her to be a Spanish teacher.

"In those days, right after I left my ex-husband," she told me, "I just wanted pleasure." She paused and smiled. "After we split up, I went on a pleasure-seeking kick: food, wine, decadence, freedom. And I was obsessed with donuts."

"I'm obsessed with donuts, too," I said, smiling back at her.

"I was dating the guy who owned the place where I was bartending," she said. "He loosened me up, encouraged me to drink, eat, have fun. We traveled, and everywhere we went, I had to find the donut shop. Because we didn't have that here. This town had a total lack of good donuts. And more than anything else for me, donuts represented decadence, pushed that button for me. They are the ultimate pleasure food. Life is short, it's full of drudgery; we need pleasure!"

I ate the last bite of my own donut, nodding in total agreement.

"One night, my then-boyfriend and I were having dinner. And out of the blue, he looked at me and said, 'You know what you should do? You should open a donut shop here in Portland.' Straight out of nowhere. I said, 'That's a weird idea. I have no business skills, no baking skills, and I'm a single mother with no money.' I went home and slept on it, and when I woke up, I know it sounds corny, but I knew he was right; I knew that this was my life's calling."

Shortly after he provided her with the inspiration for her life's work, they broke up.

"He was the angel, the muse behind this place," she said. "He gave me the idea. And the rest of it was one hundred percent me."

That next day, Leigh went to the nearest Borders and looked through cookbooks she couldn't afford to buy, writing down all the potato donut recipes she could find.

"I made donuts starting at the crack of dawn when the babysitter arrived, five days a week, for the next three months," she said. "I was a madwoman in the kitchen, like I was on a mission from God. They were awful. The recipes were wrong. But if I didn't make donuts for one day, I felt like that day was wasted."

She eventually hit on the *Joy of Cooking* recipe; it was perfect.

"The potatoes are peeled, then boiled, then put through a ricer, not mashed. It makes the donuts velvety."

She brought samples of her now-excellent donuts around to coffee shops and other businesses. Orders quickly started coming in and growing, from two or three dozen a day to twelve, forty, and then one hundred dozen a week. Her father, recently retired, helped her fill orders.

After only seven months from the day she'd made her first donut, Leigh left her bartending job, moved out of her parents' attic, and opened the first Holy Donut shop in a former market. Her father came along as her business partner.

"We use all fresh ingredients—organic sugar, Vermont flour, local eggs. And local berries, lemons and limes zested by hand, and the best chocolate, Callebaut super-dark chocolate and Bensdorp cocoa powder. It's a strange way to make donuts, it's so labor-intensive; it takes seventeen people from start to finish, mixing the dough, hand-shaping each donut, frying them, glazing them. It's not the most profitable way, but I don't take any shortcuts."

While Leigh talked, she had not missed a single thing that had happened in the place. Now she turned around and then quickly got up.

"Empty racks. Do you mind if I get up and refill them?"

I watched her bring in trays of fresh donuts, including one of the gluten-free dark-chocolate sea-salt. With difficulty, I resisted the temptation to eat another one.

"How did you hit on the idea to make gluten-free donuts?" I asked her when she came back.

"It was sort of a fluke," she said. "I found I had the time and energy to experiment again. The science of gluten-free is beyond me, but again, I got lucky. I use a combination of Arrowhead Mills and Bob's Red Mill gluten-free flour blends. Other blends are inedible, like cement, but these two together are perfect."

"And they're really gluten-free," I said. "I've watched them make them at the Park Avenue place. They use separate fryers."

"And a separate room to mix the dough and glaze them, separate glazes and ingredients," she said.

"I've eaten many of them, and I've never once had a bad reaction," I said. "And I've heard from people who've eaten both kinds that your gluten-free donuts are even better than the regular ones."

"They're more dense, more cakelike," she said. "Maybe they are better. Every now and then I eat a dark-chocolate sea-salt one and go, 'Holy shit, these are magnificent.' "

♊

According to the old joke, a Maine farmer who's asked what he's growing answers "Rocks." But the truth is that Maine, although it's the most wooded state in the country, with a short growing season and long, harsh winters, is a very good place for farming, thanks to Maine farmers' tried-and-true techniques and scrappy know-how.

In the *Portland Press Herald*'s Source section's inaugural issue, in their essay tracing the history of Maine farming, Mary Pols and Meredith Goad wrote,

> "Ezekiel Holmes, an 1824 graduate of the Medical School of Maine at Bowdoin College, [. . .] was essential to opening Aroostook County to farming, visiting in 1838 and authoring a report that spoke glowingly of the enticements of the potential farmland there. He urged men, 'just starting in life' with strong arms and good courage to 'Go to the Aroostook.'

> "And the men—along with some women—did just that, beginning in earnest in 1842 and making their way along a new road built during the 1838–39 Aroostook War. By 1860 there were 22,000 people in Aroostook County. By 1870, it had 3,209 farms and 133,024 acres of improved land."

The conditions turned out to be ideal for these "rocks," as were the cool nights and warm days of summer, precipitating a cycle of May planting and September harvesting. In the mid-twentieth century, Maine produced more potatoes than any other state—even Idaho. Over the centuries, the quiet, humble potato has been as important a contribution to the state's economy as the iconic lobster; it could be called the state vegetable.

"In the early 1800s," said Jim Gerritsen, an organic potato farmer, in a 2006 speech to the members of MOFGA, or the Maine Organic Farmers and Gardener's Association,

> "the first white settlers to Aroostook County started carving fields out of the forest and immediately began planting potatoes. What they found was that unlike the marginal soils covering most of New England, the geologically distinct, well-drained, fertile loam soils of Aroostook along with the cool northern climate were perfect for growing potatoes. Over the next hundred years, farmers made steady and massive efforts to clear the trees from hundreds of thousands of acres in order to grow potatoes."

Gerritsen went on to explain how Maine's Potato Empire was created in Aroostook County. The marriage of good soil and annual precipitation, along with the arrival of the railroad, meant that by the early 1950s an annual crop of almost a quarter million acres anointed Maine as the leader in United States potato production.

This is no longer the case. A switch to heavily publicized Idaho russets, as well as an increasingly industrialized food industry and subsidizations of Western farms, and low prices, have caused the Maine potato to lose its national sovereignty in the market; it's now a quarter of what it was at its peak. But Maine's potato-farming culture is still closely knit and cohesive, largely unchanged in 150 years.

> "Going back many generations," said Gerritsen, "everyone in Aroostook has worked in the fields, picking potatoes. We are one of the last areas in the United States where schools are still closed

for Harvest Break so that kids can help farmers get their crop in. Often the teenagers that we hire are taught potato-picking technique by their parents and grandparents who, they themselves, learned when they were young pickers."

ℓℓℓ

"We used to get our potatoes from Fryeburg," Leigh told me. "We peeled and boiled and riced them by hand. But we outgrew that. Now we sell one-point-two million donuts a year—"

"Over a million," I repeated, amazed.

"—so we don't have time to process the potatoes ourselves. Five hundred pounds a week! We buy them already peeled and parboiled from a number of Aroostook County farms."

I looked around. The line of people waiting to buy donuts had stretched to the door again, but the place still felt peaceful, comfortable, quiet.

"Do you ever think of franchising?" I asked.

"I'm scared of losing the soul of the place," she said. "This country is so full of retail chains. I want a family business, where you walk in and feel that it's local Portland people, trying to hold our own here. I'm disenchanted with corporate crap. I feel it the minute I walk in the door if it's a chain; it makes me feel flat. I'm passionate about being local, supporting local."

"I can tell," I said. "You feel it in this place. But what about creating the same feeling in donut shops in other cities, that same sense of homeyness? Could it be done?"

She thought about this.

"My father and brother-in-law are on board; they're psyched about the idea of growing the business. But I don't think more stores would equal more happiness. I could go insane; I'm already close. I'd have to oversee the design of each shop, and then make sure everything was done right."

"It does seem like a lot of headaches," I said.

"I just want to stay the course. We serve two things: donuts and coffee. People say I should expand my products, sell pies, sandwiches, smoothies, merchandise . . . but I want to keep it simple, stay true to what we do really well. I want a strong business, but I want my original vision to be reflected in the experience. It would be easy to lose that. Having two shops is exciting; I feel very proud and so lucky. I mean, three years ago, I was bartending, I was dirt-poor. Thank God for my parents' attic! But I thought I would be stuck there forever."

"I'm still wrapping my mind around more than a million donuts a year," I said. "That is amazing."

"I am profoundly grateful," she said. "I love being self-sufficient. I expected a one-woman operation, clearing maybe two hundred dollars a week, enough to pay the bills, a little college fund. When you're down-and-out, you have to be resourceful. I had family support, a college degree, and creative passion. Luck is ninety-nine percent hard work. This town needed a donut shop and I was the conduit. It makes people happy. It's a nostalgia thing; it smells and tastes like Grandma's cooking. I want coming in here to be a nice experience. I was craving that, deeply craving a place that makes you feel good about life."

"Is that how do you feel when you walk in here every morning?"

"No, I feel anxious!"

We both laughed.

"I have twenty-eight employees. Every morning I think, Okay, what is the issue du jour? Today, thank God, we had no major issues other than that we're understaffed. But yesterday, they forgot to put the potatoes in the dough. Four batches had to be thrown out. We make them all by hand. They're not perfect; we're not a factory. I have no control over human error, humidity, the variations in the potatoes. Every batch is slightly different."

She pointed to the opposite wall.

"That's the Holy Donut mascot over there, the goddess of compassion, Quan Yin. I also think of her as the goddess of allowing yourself pleasure, to eat what you want. I attribute the success of this place to the gods of pleasure, to that original feeling I had right after my divorce. I was on a kick, a pleasure kick, and this is where it led me."

A few minutes later, I said good-bye to Leigh and walked home through the golden, sweet Maine summer morning, my stomach happily satiated, "Love and Happiness" playing in my inner ear.

ele

The next night, in a potato-celebrating mood, I threw together a Maine niçoise. While Brendan fed Dingo and opened a bottle of cold Orvieto, I washed four large Aroostook County potatoes and put them on to boil and trimmed a bunch of asparagus and put it on to steam, feeding a few of the ends to Dingo, who considers them delicacies on a par with anything in the world. I chopped the quarter head of radicchio and the endive that were in the fridge and put them into a big salad bowl with a handful each of pea shoots and arugula, then tossed this crisp salad in a mustard vinaigrette.

When the asparagus was just steamed, I cut it coarsely into bite-size pieces and let them cool on the cutting board. When the potatoes were just tender, I quartered them lengthwise and tossed them in a bath of equal parts apple cider vinegar and white wine vinegar and let them marinate and cool in the fridge for fifteen minutes. Then I made the sauce: two generous tablespoons of Hain mayonnaise plus the juice of one juicy lemon, a big handful of minced chives, three garlic cloves, minced, white wine vinegar, olive oil, and a lot of black pepper.

I divided the asparagus between two plates, then opened a can of wild Alaskan pink salmon and divided it likewise, then drizzled the fish and the asparagus in some of the chive-lemon-garlic-mayonnaise dressing. I drained the vinegar-soaked, cooled potatoes and tossed them in the rest of the mayonnaise dressing with two minced celery stalks and dished it out, threw a handful of capers over the potatoes and the fish, dusted the potato salad with smoked paprika, then put the dressed salad alongside everything else.

We sat at the counter, a little sunburned, relaxed from the long walk we'd taken earlier in the fresh clean air. We listened to Edith Piaf and ate every scrap of everything while we sipped the crisp, barely fruity wine, all the tastes still lingering on my tongue—garlic and fish and asparagus and potato and capers—Dingo sprawled at our feet, too sacked out to beg.

Strangely, given that we were in the middle of what passes for a heat wave up here, this meal kicked off a week of steady potato-eating. The next night, we made a pilgrimage to the steak frites at our local bistro; their fries are addictive—crisp, thin, and drizzled with aioli. The sliced steak is tender and savory and cooked to perfection, charred outside, pink inside. It's a dangerous addiction to tempt, a splurge we can only afford every so often, so whenever we do, we enjoy the hell out of it and eat every scrap.

The next night, I made a clam chowder with two dozen littlenecks, onion, pancetta, two cobs' worth of corn, and a large diced Yukon Gold that turned tender and mealy in the clam-liquor broth and soaked up the brininess. Clams and potatoes and pork are an unbeatable combination, especially with corn and onion, especially in a savory soup.

The night after that, to continue our impromptu potato festival, I served boiled new red potatoes and steamed asparagus alongside thick, fresh organic pork chops marinated in orange and lemon juices, olive oil, ginger, garlic, Worcestershire sauce, smoked coriander, and rosemary.

Then, the next night, to cap off this decadent, gluttonous, gourmandesque Potato Week, we made thick, juicy, lean, flavorful burgers, ground bison mixed with chopped onion and Worcestershire sauce and fried in butter in a cast-iron skillet, on toasted gluten-free buns. And, of course, we made oven fries: thin-wedge-sliced Yukon Golds and matchstick sweet potatoes baked in peanut oil in a hot oven, well salted. We dredged them in a ketchup-mayonnaise dipping sauce. Alongside, we made a salad of tomato, red onion, and avocado. As we ate this meal, or rather, shoved it into our mouths, we asked ourselves how it was possible to drool and eat at the same time.

Potato, potahto, potato, potahto! They're so good in hot weather, any way you slice, dice, bake, or boil them. They have a cooling property in the summer, although they're equally warming in winter. They're magical that way, like a Thermos.

ele

Around the winter solstice, when the days are short and dark, I can't stop sleeping. I seem to have been infected by a seasonal parasite, a sleep tapeworm or zombie virus that awakens at dark and renders me unconscious so it can wreak its insidious takeover of my person while I'm zonked out. Every day, I try not to give in, but I'm unable to resist. I start to nod off when the sun goes down, in mid-afternoon, no matter how much sleep I've had the night before (sometimes, in that season, ten hours). I have no choice but to stop what I'm doing, get into bed, and conk out, sometimes for an hour, sometimes two. It doesn't matter what deadline is looming before me or how long my to-do list is. The parasite doesn't care about my life at all beyond its wish to take it over.

When I return gradually to wakefulness from my dream-filled nap, at five o'clock or thereabouts, it's pitch-dark night already, and I've accomplished exactly nothing since I fell asleep. I shake myself awake, stagger back to my desk, sit down, and try to pick up where I left off, to reconstruct whatever it was I was doing before I blacked out. As I start typing again, my brain slowly coming back up to speed, I can feel the parasite curling into its lair somewhere in my skull, sated for now with whatever part of my brain it feeds on while I'm out.

Eventually, it's time to cook dinner.

Down in the kitchen, I foggily survey the contents of the fridge and cupboards. There are polenta, pine nuts, Savoy cabbage, a package of chicken breasts, red peppers, leeks . . . I yawn and blink, lose my train of thought. I know I'll be asleep again by ten p.m., but it feels so far away.

"What do you feel like eating?" I ask Brendan, who blinks at me from his computer, where he's been fighting his own sleep parasite all afternoon, working away.

"I'll cook," he says. "What do you want?"

"I don't know," I say. "What would you make?"

"I don't know," says Brendan, who as usual seems to be in the same mood I'm in. "What do you feel like?"

The truth is that there's really nothing I actively feel like eating. I can't even think about cooking or eating anything enterprising or challenging or surprising or difficult. My stomach wants carbohydrates. My palate craves nursery food. My soul wants warmth and quiet.

"How about baked potatoes?" I say.

"Perfect," says Brendan.

During sleep season, there is nothing, nothing at all, like a baked potato for dinner, or lunch, or even—in theory, anyway—breakfast. It's the easiest thing in the world to make, for one thing: wash a potato, prick it, cover it in oil and salt if you prefer, or not, and stick it into a hot oven for fifty minutes or so till the skin is crackling and the inside is soft. You can put anything you like on top: sour cream and chopped chives, or a fried or scrambled or poached egg with steamed chopped spinach if you want something green, or nothing at all but a little butter, salt, and pepper. A baked potato is starchy and hearty but not too big. It's nourishing and comforting, but not filling or heavy. And it's cheap.

Russets are traditionally the best for baking, but I'm partial to Yukon Golds. Their skin doesn't give chewily between the teeth like russets', but their buttery-yellow insides taste richly of the essence of potato and are denser, whereas russets' innards are white, fluffy, a little bland. And a Yukon Gold can stand up to baking; its skin is thinner, but it crackles.

One bleak, frigid day, I reached into the cheese case at the supermarket and yanked out a small brick of something called "bacon cheddar" and put it into the basket without even thinking about it. Its ingredients were unfathomably decadent: the usual full-fat cheese stuff, plus bacon and hickory smoke. I had never bought or eaten or even noticed its existence before, but I neither resisted nor questioned the sudden urge to possess it.

At home, near lunchtime, without consulting Brendan, I stuck two scrubbed, pricked large Yukon Gold potatoes into the oven. While they baked, I sautéed a large minced yellow onion in olive oil and plenty of Worcestershire sauce, slowly, on low heat, so the onion softened and started to brown and caramelize but didn't burn.

When the potatoes were done, I cut them in half, slid them onto a cookie sheet, and smothered them in grated bacon cheddar. I stuck them back in to broil until the cheese was melted and bubbling and the whole kitchen was fragrant with fake smoke flavor, along with the smell of browned onions.

I pulled them out and covered them in the onions and served them with a small bowl of kosher salt and the pepper grinder. We sat at the table and ate our lunch without speaking. The sun was already beginning to set. I could feel the zombie virus awakening in my head, turning sinuously with sinister velvet lullaby rhythms. The baked potato felt like an amulet, an antidote that would protect me while I slept.

∾

Potato Salad

There are approximately 18,987,998 recipes for potato salad in this country, and many more in other countries, especially Germany. But mine, I say without humility, is a good one, maybe even better than average.

Feel free to adjust all the amounts; they're only guidelines, and everyone has favorite proportions that may differ from mine.

Boil 2 lbs. of new red potatoes till the flesh is still firm and their skins just begin to split; be careful not to overcook them. Drain them, cut them in halves or quarters while they're still hot, put them in a bowl, douse them in apple cider vinegar, salt and pepper them, and chill them, covered.

When they're cold, add to them 3 minced celery ribs, 3 chopped hard-boiled eggs, 1 minced medium red onion, and, if you like, some capers, fresh dill, and anchovies. Some people love apple in their potato salad; I am not one of them. But go ahead if you must.

Make a dressing of 1/2 cup mayonnaise, 2 T of mustard, 1 tsp paprika, and 2 minced garlic cloves.

Mix everything together and eat right away, or chill and eat later. Very good with hot fried chicken, barbecued chicken, or cold left-over chicken of any kind. Serves 6 as a side dish.

ﻚ

Arguably, the other essential vegetable of Maine is also a starchy one, which seems appropriate, given the length of the winters up here and the fact that both can be stored well throughout the cold season and eaten till the first asparagus pokes its head up in early spring. It's that dried, nutritious staple of larders and cupboards and jars in every kitchen, the humble bean.

It strikes me, from what I've heard and read, that almost nothing says Maine more than "bean hole."

During the months when they left the coast and its rich and teeming sea life and migrated inland for the short growing season in Maine and the White Mountains, the Wabanaki farmed. They did this long before the European settlers arrived, but their methods have been preserved and practiced for centuries afterwards.

Corn, squash, and beans, that holy trinity of symbiosis and nutrition, were their primary crops. Like all Native farmers from Nova Scotia to Mesoamerica, they interplanted them in the same mounds. The three plants nourished the soil and provided support for one another in a variety of ingenious ways. The cornstalks allowed the bean vines to climb; the vines stabilized the stalks in strong winds; the beans fixed the nitrogen in the soil for the next year's crop of corn;

and the shallow-rooted squash vines covered the base of the mound, living mulch that kept the soil from drying out and prevented weeds from growing. The spiny squash plants also repelled predators from the corn and beans. Every season, the plant matter left over from the harvest was mixed back into the ground as fertilizer and compost. And these "three sisters" in combination were nutritional perfection: The corn gave carbohydrates, the dried beans supplied protein, and the squash contained vitamins and minerals, and their seeds could be made into oil.

The Wabanaki made a traditional bean-and-corn dish called "hull corn soup." Dried white corn kernels were boiled for half an hour in hardwood ashes and water, a weak lye solution that "cleaned" them; white corn kernels are larger than yellow, not nearly as sweet, and they're encased in an inedible, tough outer hull. Afterwards, the now-blackened skins had to be removed, a time-consuming process they made go faster by kibitzing as they hand-rubbed each kernel. These hulled kernels were added to dried yellow-eye beans, with salt pork or venison when meat was available, and plenty of water. The Wabanaki also baked yellow-eye beans with maple syrup and bear fat in ceramic pots in the ground.

The European-descended newcomers to New England adapted their own versions of both the corn soup, which they called succotash, and the baked beans, but both recipes originated with the Wabanaki. According to the University of Maine's excellent Maine Folklife Center website, "the most unique cooking process for beans in Maine developed in the Maine logging camps. Pork and beans, baked in a bean hole, remains the logger's main dish. The slow, long cooking makes the bean very digestible as well as tender and delicious. In the logging camps, beans were served at every meal."

They go on to describe the bean hole as "a stone-lined pit in which a fire is built until a good bed of coals forms. A cast-iron bean pot (holds about eleven pounds of dried beans) is lowered into the pit, covered over with dirt, and allowed to cook, usually overnight. Several bean pits could keep beans cooking at all times."

According to lore, the loggers learned to make bean-hole beans from the Native Americans, and then other Mainers learned from the loggers. The tradition was so popular among Mainers that it continued after the logging camps were abandoned. Even now, bean holes can be found at family camps throughout Maine. There's evidently something about ritualistic underground slow-cooking that appeals deeply to Mainers, whether it's a clambake or a bean hole.

ele

Beans are nutritious, no doubt about it. They're full of calcium and iron and protein, as well as fiber and the "good" kind of carbohydrates that keep you full for a long time. The expression "full of beans" says it all. And they're delicious, adaptable, easy to grow, harvest, and store, and relatively cheap. Like the potato, probably because of their richness in starch, beans are cooling in hot weather and warming in cold. They'll do any dance with any partner, as long as you treat them with patience and respect.

Of course, there are plenty of jokes about beans, beans, the musical fruit, and we've all made them and heard them and we all know why they're so funny, but if dried beans are properly soaked and rinsed and prepared, they aren't as likely to upset anyone's digestive system (or their family members' olfactory delicacy). Although I've never tried this, I've heard that if you stick a piece of kombu, or kelp, in the cooking water, its enzymes will break down the raffinose sugars in beans, the culprits that produce those offensive gases.

A pot of baked beans in an oven, simmering away for hours on a cold winter afternoon, is one of the most comforting smells I know of.

Baked beans are so easy to make, and so rewarding when they emerge from their long slow hot bath: rich and deep, porky and molasses-y, salty and sweet, soft and dense. And the beans retain their shape and integrity through it all, whether you use Jacob's Cattle beans from Fryeburg or Midcoast yellow-eyes.

In Arizona, chili was always on our school lunch menus in the early 1970s, and I was an instant fan. The Arizona version of chili had both beans and meat, as well as peppers and tomatoes and corn. In college in Portland, Oregon, I taught myself how to make it from scratch. When I moved to New Hampshire, and then Maine, I developed a version using local ingredients that's cheap, easy, and fun to make. It's a warming, hearty supper on a crisp October night when the chilly wind is blowing the dry leaves against the windows and the sun sets unexpectedly early and you suddenly know in your bones that winter is coming, again.

∼

Arizona Native's Yankee Farm Stand Chili

I have mixed feelings about some of the farm stands up here. On the one hand, they can seem like a bit of a scam—much of their fresh produce is trucked from Vermont, or even farther, the same exact stuff I find at Hannaford, but more expensive and not as consistently fresh or organic. On the other hand, their frozen meats—especially their poultry, but also the lamb and pork, is the best and most flavorful available. And they have bins of heirloom dried beans. In Fryeburg, I find Jacob's Cattle and soldier beans, which are grown in Western Maine; yellow-eye beans are more popular on the coast. They also have local maple syrup and beautiful, varied, heaping piles of locally grown gourds, squashes, and pumpkins in the fall.

One day, at Sherman Farm Stand over in Fryeburg, Maine, a few miles from the farmhouse, I got a wild hair of inspiration and pulled together

the ingredients for this chili. I've made it a few times, and I would confi-
dently enter it into a Yankee Farm Stand Chili contest, if one existed . . .

When you wake up in the morning, add 2 cups of dry Jacob's Cattle or soldier beans to at least 12 cups of boiling water. Turn off the
flame and soak for a few hours, covered. At noon or so, rinse
them well, put them back into the pot, and add just enough fresh
water to cover them plus an inch or two. Bring to a boil again and
simmer them, covered, until they're soft.

In a big soup pot or Dutch oven, heat 1/2 cup peanut or canola
oil. Add 2 chopped yellow onions, 8 chopped garlic cloves, and 3
chopped jalapeno peppers. Stir and add 4 T chili powder, 1 tsp
oregano, 1 tsp cumin, 1 T paprika, a dash of cayenne pepper, 2 to
4 tsp salt, 1 tsp black pepper, and 2 medium bay leaves. Stir well
and sauté on low. When onions soften, add 1 lb. ground turkey.
Stir and sauté on low heat for 6 to 7 minutes.

Add 3 ears' worth of fresh raw corn, removed from cob, and 4
chopped large ripe tomatoes. Stir well. Add 1 chopped red pepper,
1 chopped yellow pepper, and 1 chopped orange pepper. Stir well
again. After a few minutes, add the drained, cooked beans, 1
24-oz. can of diced fire-roasted tomatoes, and 2 cups chicken
broth. Bring just to a boil, then turn down. Let sit, simmering and
uncovered, for 1 1/2 hours. Add more chicken broth as needed.
Taste and adjust seasonings. Serve with bowls of minced red
onions, chopped avocado, sour cream, and chopped cilantro.
Serves 2 people for several meals and gets better every day.

ᘮᘮ

The summer I turned fourteen, in 1976, I went to Agawamuck
wilderness camp in Upstate New York, above the tiny hamlet of Harlemville. There, we campers learned how to make brown bread
steamed in a coffee can in a trivet in a kettle alongside baked beans in

a cast-iron pot, over an open fire. Outdoor cooking was part of our wilderness training; I'm certain we also learned to make other things, but camp-cooked baked beans and brown bread are what I remember most about our al fresco culinary education. We also slept in tents on platforms in the woods, went on four-day canoe trips, took twenty-mile hikes, did "balance" courses, and collected and drew leaves and insects for purposes of identification.

Someone at the camp, some counselor, must have been a Mainer. The brown bread, made with whole-wheat flour, rye flour, cornmeal, and molasses, leavened with baking soda, was cylindrical and dense and damp and sweet with raisins; the circular thick slices were addictive, slathered with butter, hot from the coffee can where the bread had steamed for a couple of hours next to the bean pot. The bean pot itself was a crusty old thing, impossible to get entirely clean in our outdoor sink with its cold-water pump, but we tried.

We were twelve campers in all, six boys and six girls between twelve and fourteen years old. Naturally, various dramatic, intense, unforgettable romances and alliances formed between us in the eight weeks of camp. While our hearts broke and swelled and fell in love and broke again, we also became physically strong and quick and hardy, we budding teenagers who might otherwise have spent the summer lounging in front of the TV eating potato chips, tanning at the local pool, and mooching around the mall, or at slumber parties, making crank calls and eating sugar cereal and flirting with call-in radio deejays and playing "Light as a Feather" and summoning ghosts with the Ouija board.

Instead, we woke up early, gathered around the dining table for camp-made granola and milk from the farm below, spent our days in the woods and on the rivers, and spent our evenings after dinner in the assembly tent, a huge tepee on a platform in the woods; there, we sang and told stories until bedtime, miles from any mall, far from the nearest TV set. If we wanted to swim, we jumped into the pond in the meadow just down the mountain.

We got our milk, eggs, and vegetables from the biodynamic farm down in the valley below us, where my little sisters were campers at the Hawthorne Valley Farm Camp. Once a week, the counselors made a shopping run to the nearest supermarket, which for all I know was in Hudson, and brought back bags of oats, dried beans, molasses, whole-wheat flour, spices, rice, lentils, canned goods, and other basic staples.

That summer, sadly, was the closest I've ever come to living the way people lived in the Maine lumber camps and the game wardens' cabins up in the Allagash. I've read every book I can get my mitts on about that way of life; by all accounts, it was a hell of a lot of fun. The most famous of these is, of course, *We Took to the Woods* by Louise Dickinson Rich, but there are others: *Nine Mile Bridge* by Helen Hamlin and *My Life in the Maine Woods* by Annette Jackson are two of my favorites. These women—and men, too, in some cases—all write about the sheer joy of living in the far northern wilderness of lakes and rivers and woods and almost no roads, year-round, in almost total isolation. I love the vicarious sense of adventure I get, reading about their unforgettable experiences in the thrilling scenery, the sense of peace and self-sufficiency, the deep satisfaction of hard work, all the canoeing and snowshoeing and skiing and fishing and hunting, the cutting of wood and planting of gardens. These are some of the most purely joyful books I've ever read.

Louise Dickinson Rich described the Pond-in-the-River dam on a day when the river drivers opened the gates to let the pulpwood go downstream: "It's lovely on the dam on a bright spring morning, with the wind blowing down across the boom and filling the air with the sharp smell of resin, so strong and fresh that you can taste it. The planks tremble under your feet, and the roar of the river and the thumping of the wood fill the ears. The river is deep blue and crisping white, and the cut ends of the pulp are like raw gold in the sun. All the senses come alive, even that rare sense that tells you, half a dozen times between birth and death—if you are lucky—that right now, right in this spot, you have fallen into the pattern of the universe."

Dickinson Rich also wrote with almost as much happy exuberance about their every-Saturday-night meal in their cabin on the Andro-scoggin River: "Baked beans can be terrible or they can be swell . . . baked beans have to be baked. That sounds like a gratuitous restate-ment of the obvious, but it isn't. Some misguided souls boil beans all day and call the lily-livered result baked beans. I refrain from com-ment."

She gives her recipe as follows, and I'd trust it over just about any other one, if only because she writes with such authority and certainty on the matter, and she isn't someone I'd care to contradict or cross: I'd rather hang out with her in the North Woods for a while, going along happily and trustingly on any adventure she cared to propose, eating any meal she cooked.

We use either New York State or Michigan white beans, because we like them best, although yellow-eyes are very popular, too. I take two generous cups of dry beans, soak overnight and put them on to boil early in the morning. When the skins curl off when you blow on them, they've boiled long enough. Then I put in the bottom of the bean pot, or iron kettle with a tight-fitting cover, a six-by-eight square of salt pork, with the rind slashed every quarter of an inch, a quarter of a cup of sugar, half a cup of molasses, a large onion chopped fairly fine, and a heaping teaspoonful of dry mustard. This amount of sugar and molasses may be increased or cut, depending on whether you like your beans sweeter or not so sweet. This is a matter every man has to decide for himself. The beans are dumped in on top of this conglomerate and enough hot water is added to cover, but only cover. The baking pot should be large enough so there's at least an inch of free-board above the water. Otherwise they'll boil over and smell to high heaven. Cover tightly and put into a medium oven—about 350 is right. They should be in the oven by half past nine in the morning at the latest, and they should stay there till suppertime, which in our family is at six.

She goes on to say that "there is no trick" to making good baked beans besides baking them correctly—the right amount of water, proper tending, and even oven temperature. And you have to be willing to stay right by those beans all day and not go anywhere else. But it's worth it: "My beans are brown and mealy, and they swim in a thick brown juice. They're good. I always serve them with corn bread, ketchup and pickles."

ℓℓℓ

Camp Agawamuck's session was only eight weeks long, and I was there almost forty years ago, but even though it was nothing compared to Dickinson Rich's transcendent joy, I remember my time there as totally absorbing, happy, and challenging in the best way. And I remember, too, the smell of a pot of beans cooking over a camp-fire, how good they tasted, and the complete satiation they gave me after a long day spent hiking and paddling and swimming outside. When you're truly hungry, there is nothing better than a bowl full of warm beans with brown bread and butter. I slept deeply afterwards in my sleeping bag, tucked in my aluminum-and-canvas cot with a full stomach, piney air blowing in the screened tent window, and the sound of boughs overhead in the wind.

At the end of the summer, I arrived back home in Arizona in time to begin high school. I was clear-eyed (because of severe allergies, I hadn't been able to wear my contact lenses all summer; highly myopic,

I'd managed wilderness camp without them, learned to gauge distances and depths, to identify trees, to hike and rock-climb in an increasingly familiar blur until I forgot all about them and started to "see" things in my own half-blind way). I was brown and strong, and my head was full of the smells and sounds and sights of the woods and memories of campfire suppers. I was, in fact, "full of beans."

ℓℓℓ

In Maine, Saturday or Sunday beans seem to be traditional fare just about everywhere, going back to the Pilgrims, who cooked baked beans and brown bread the night before, the story goes, so as not to have to cook on the Sabbath. The tradition stuck in part, I imagine, because of the cozy familiarity of the meal, that delicious, cheap, nourishing, stick-to-the-ribs quality: It makes you want to hunker down with friends around a long table and just dig right in.

Brown bread has been the traditional accompaniment to beans for a good long time. Like most local food traditions, its origins are born of thrifty necessity. In other words, early New Englanders had more cornmeal and rye flour than wheat flour; the three were combined in bread, helping to conserve precious stores of wheat. Many settlers in New England cooked their meals in fireplaces, instead of ovens, so they came up with a way to steam bread in the fireplace, usually in a cylindrical metal or glass mold, a precursor to today's coffee can. They'd been taught by Native Americans, who also showed them how to use corn as a grain for bread. Cornmeal often was called "Indian." In her directions for making brown bread in the 1828 *American Frugal Housewife*, Lydia Maria Child wrote: "Put the Indian in your bread pan, sprinkle a little salt among it, and wet it thoroughly with scalding water. . . . Be sure and have hot water enough, for Indian absorbs a great deal of water."

"Brown bread is as old as our country," James Beard wrote in *American Cookery.* "Everyone seems to treasure an 'original' recipe, handed down from the founding families."

Brown Bread

One cup of sweet milk,
One cup of sour,
One cup of corn meal,
One cup of flour.
Teaspoon of soda,
Molasses one cup;
Steam for three hours,
Then eat it all up.

—*Old Yankee Cookbook*

The Folklife Center's archivist interviewed one Robert Campbell of Glenburn, Maine, who had been baking beans in a bean hole for nearly forty years. "Even when I don't need the beans," he said, "when Friday night comes it's just an urge comes over me to start that fire and start baking bean-hole beans."

In this same archive of interviews, Diane Conary of Old Town, Maine, recalled, "Mom always made them the same way. She always used white beans. Always picked over them first, 'had to get the little stones out.' My favorite was big beans. Dad liked either big or small beans. Mom preferred the little beans. To make the beans, use salt pork, onion, just a little bit of white sugar, and a little dried mustard. Parboil the beans on the stove first. Then put them in a pot, a special crock. Then they cooked in the stove, an oil stove, all Friday night. Mom would get up in the middle of the night and add water.

"They were done Saturday morning, but we didn't eat them until Saturday night. They stayed warm. Years ago, I guess about 85 percent of the people around here had beans on Saturday night. We always had bread. Mom didn't make brown bread. Sometimes she would get brown bread in a can with raisins. That was a real treat! We would spread butter on it."

The "bean suppah" seems to be a mainstay of the social life of churches during the summer and early fall; I see signs for them all through the byways of Maine, in towns and in the countryside, inland, in the lakes region, and up the coast. When my grandmother used to rent a house in Midcoast Maine every summer for herself and my grandfather, she went to all the local church rummage sales, and she would often stay for the bean supper afterwards. She loved them, although she deplored the fact that she couldn't get a proper cup of tea afterwards. (I can just see my tiny, literary tea snob of a grandmother squinting askance at the inferior tea of rural Maine, her stomach full of excellent local beans.)

As a sign of the changing times around here, the Maine Council of Churches has provided a page on their website aimed at making these traditionally socially sanctioned calorie- and fat-fests healthier and more locally conscious, creating a downloadable resource kit for churches and other groups that are interested in offering a new version of the traditional bean "suppah" or other community meals. "We have suggestions for healthier versions of favorite recipes," they promise. "We've also included local sources for produce and other goods so your meal will support your community farmers and other local businesses. Locally farmed foods are generally better for the environment, as the goods do not travel thousands of miles to reach our dinner plates. And many local farms practice organic and other environmentally friendly methods of production."

Now that's Christian fellowship, Maine style.

Chapter Eleven

Rock Farmers and Stone Soup

"Life in the Maine frontier was serious business," writes Colin Woodard in *The Lobster Coast*, "and those who survived under these conditions had to be stubborn, self-sufficient, and able to endure considerable physical and emotional punishment." During an unspeakably violent, decades-long era in Maine's history, "at the close of the fourth Indian war in 1726, Midcoast Maine was a desolate wasteland" of "burned and looted farms, villages, fishing camps, and, undoubtedly, the remains of people who once lived in them." Farmland and pastures and cleared fields returned to scrub and saplings; long-abandoned towns were covered in forty-year-old forests. The region was described as a "howling wilderness."

The Indians had nowhere else to go; they died on their own land from the diseases the newcomers had brought, against which they had no recourse, despite all of their brilliantly adaptive traditions, strength and skill, knowledge of the land and sea, and fierce ability to hold their own in warfare.

"Maine's true natives had lost the coast to newcomers," Woodard writes. "Now it would be the newcomers' turn to defend their homes from covetous and powerful outsiders."

And so the ongoing class wars of Maine began, during which generation after generation of scrappy, hardscrabble, struggling Mainers stoically endured and protested against and became resigned to and fought against and were the victims of the incursions of rich speculators and greedy political figures. Now, they're the seasonal moneyed vacationers, at best known locally as "summer people," or, at worst, "Massholes," so called in honor of the hundreds of years of a northward-encroaching human tide that seems hell-bent on destroying everything the locals most treasure and love, with their money, proclivities, and demands, even as local economies benefit from and depend on them.

After the fourth Indian war devastated everything in sight from 1722 until 1726 or so, the "Great Proprietors" of Massachusetts, rich land speculators, began casting their acquisitive eyes on the now-desolate, depopulated Maine's natural resources. But their newly hatched plan to become New England's landed aristocracy was foiled by the Crown, who wanted Midcoast Maine for itself. And so the English government, in the person of one Colonel David Dunbar, a proud, ambitious Scotsman from Northern Ireland, annexed the region to Nova Scotia in 1729, seizing it from Massachusetts by right of conquest.

Dunbar's scheme was simple: He needed settlers to repopulate the area and farm the land, and he knew just where to find them: his own homeland. Conditions were desperate for the Scottish in Northern Ireland, who'd relocated there in search of a better life, but had found the same strife and hardship they'd left behind.

The scrappy adaptability of these hardy souls turned out to be exactly the quality that was most useful for the struggle of making a living out of the earth and sea in Maine. Many of their descendants are still here today, farming, fishing, foraging, and hunting, using methods handed down through the decades and centuries. Others of like mind and spirit have joined them from away, buying a few acres, a trawler, applying for hunting licenses, working long, hard days, year-round, to stay afloat.

These are the true Mainers, the people whose heels are dug into the soil, whose livelihood is tied to the fates and fortunes of the land and its vicissitudes, to the fish, lobster, oysters, shrimp, and crabs who live in the waters along the coast of Maine. These die-hard, self-sufficient survivors proved that it wasn't impossible to survive here, and they served as exemplars for the rest of the country.

ee

In more-recent years, the most famous proponents and practitioners of the "back-to-the-land" movement were a pair of idealistic intellectuals named Helen and Scott Nearing. In 1932, they found themselves broke when Scott was blacklisted from academia for his pacifism. Tired of the struggle of surviving in New York City, they left and bought a farm in southern Vermont, setting out to live an almost entirely self-sufficient life.

The Nearings cut wood from their own trees for heat and cooking; built houses, outbuildings, and walls from stones they dug out of their own land; composted soil and rotated crops for maximum yield and health; tapped their maple trees, boiling enough syrup to sell to pay unvoidable expenses; preserved enough food to get themselves through the winters, always spending half the day in leisure: reading, playing music, writing. Committed vegans, they ate no meat and kept no animals; in their gently and benignly crackpotty opinion, any domestication of animals, even as pets, was a form of slavery (although

Helen Nearing apparently had a pet cat or two that she never wrote about, and she and Scott eventually succumbed to the siren song of dairy consumption). Like Thoreau, they deplored capitalism, but unlike him, they paid their taxes. Their account of their decades-long experiences, a now-famous book called *Living the Good Life: How to Live Sanely and Simply in a Troubled World*, inspired countless young, searching, idealistic people to follow in their footsteps.

In 1952, when the area around their Vermont farm became too crowded and developed, they sold it and bought land in Harborside, Maine, moving their whole operation to the Midcoast region, where they started over. Their Maine farm soon became overrun with followers and acolytes, most of whom wanted to shoot the breeze instead of work, but there were a few who proved worthy of the challenge of farm life and stuck around to become part of the Nearings' world.

Eliot and Sue Coleman, a young, college-educated, well-bred couple who wanted to settle and farm in Maine, took over a sixty-acre parcel of the Nearings' land, which Helen and Scott Nearing sold to them for $2,000, just over $33 an acre, in 1968.

"It was not the dream farm Papa had in his mind's eye during the search," their daughter Melissa wrote in her memoir, *This Life Is in Your Hands*, about growing up on her parents' farm, "lacking as it did cultivated fields and a pond. But none of that mattered; it was their ground on which to stand, unbeholden to a mortgage or bank, and it was up to them to make it into the dream."

The Colemans cultivated, enriched, planted, and harvested the land for many years, until they divorced and left Maine. But Eliot Coleman returned in 1990 to the now-renowned Four Season Farm, remaking it into a thriving enterprise that has become a model farm for aspiring farmers.

The Nearings and Colemans proved that organic farming could be done in Maine without any newfangled techniques or equipment.

Their success in providing themselves and their workers and families a year-round subsistence with crops raised on the glacier-eroded, thin Maine topsoil was due to their understanding of time-honored ways of farming that go back to the Wabanaki. They enriched the soil with diligent nurturing, composted and mulched through decades of work with patient ingenuity, layering seaweed and lime, using every bit of cast-off organic matter from the farm. Crop rotations and plantings were designed with painstaking precision every year, and each year's results were recorded in a series of notebooks.

Eliot Coleman is, by any standard, a genius of a farmer. His methods and ideas are widely admired and applied by many younger farmers, to whom he is a kind of guru, a major rock star in a state where farmers can achieve that kind of legendary status—and with good reason, since farming in Maine is such a tricky, arduous, heart- and backbreaking undertaking. Even now, Maine's climate is a challenge to the most seasoned farmer.

Mary Pols and Meredith Goad wrote about the struggle in the *Press Herald*'s Source section in April 2014:

> Maine farming may never return to its heyday in 1880, when 64,000 farms were spread across 6.6 million acres. But the state is not just adding young farmers; it is adding acreage. Eight percent more of Maine's 19.1 million acres are farmed now than were in 2007.

> Numbers like these suggest Maine is headed into a future that may resemble the state's deep past, a time when a family's very survival depended on self-sufficiency and constant adaptation, now aided by new technologies and wisdom gleaned from two full generations of back-to-the-landers.

> Maine is bucking national trends by attracting younger farmers. The average age of farmers nationally is 58, according to the 2012

census. But from 2007 to 2012, the number of farmers ages 34 and younger in Maine increased a whopping 40 percent, a federal census found. Farming has become hip.

From all indications, the concept of eating fresh, local foods as a means to build not just bodies, but economies, has gone past trend and is here to stay.

ℓℓℓ

In August 2013, Brendan and I persuaded Melissa, now our friend, to invite us up to Four Season Farm in Harborside for a night. Having heard and read so much about the place, I was excited to see it firsthand, and to meet Eliot.

We drove up the coast on another perfect summer day. After winding down the cape on a two-lane road, we turned in at the Four Season Farm sign and beheld a vision of a farm: lush late-summer rows of vegetables and flowers; sturdy greenhouses and chicken pens; fields stretching back to dense woods. Beyond the first field, back toward the forest, was the farmhouse. The late-afternoon light was golden, with a fine veil of ocean mist hanging in it.

After we parked and got out, we found Melissa's nine-year-old twin daughters, Heidi and Emily, swinging on the rope swing over the pond, fighting over whose turn it was. Whoever's turn it wasn't was distracted from pummeling her sister by the little frogs their mother caught in her cupped hands, then let go. Next to the pond was a hand-built wood-burning sauna; Melissa told us that a few friends sometimes gathered here to sweat naked together. It reminded me of my adolescence in the 1970s, when my mother and her artist and hippie friends would do that very thing in Jerome, Arizona, down in the Gulch at a sculptor named Gary's place, and I would either stay at home or reluctantly go and keep my clothes on and get teased for my prudishness.

It turned out that the idea of a communal naked sauna still elicited the exact same response in me now, all these decades later.

Melissa brought us up to the farmhouse, where we met Eliot, a wiry, bright-eyed, handsome man who looked like a French movie star, and his wife, Barbara Damrosch, slender and dark-eyed, at first glance obviously fiercely intelligent. They were both in their seventies, but they had the energy and youthfulness of people many decades younger.

Evidently, we were all going out to dinner at a nearby farm and pizza bakery rather than eating produce from the farm, cooked in the farmhouse kitchen.

"We're taking the summer off," Eliot told us with puckish cheer as we walked out to the cars. "Our farm stand is closed for the first time in ten years. It's a sabbatical for us and for the farm."

"Not for me," said Barbara, laughing. "I'm not taking a sabbatical."

Several miles up the peninsula, we parked in front of a rambling barn and walked through Tinder Hearth's long bakery room with its enormous wood-burning brick oven.

The young owner, Tim Semler, was baking pizzas.

"Who built your oven?" Brendan asked him.

"We built it ourselves," he said.

"Where does your flour come from?" I asked.

"Mostly organic farms up in Canada," he said. "We use a variety of flours, some spelt, some winter wheat, and some heirloom varieties of wheat."

Tinder Hearth is renowned throughout Maine and beyond for its bread in particular, considered by many to be perfection in loaf form. Given the provenance of the flour, I had a strong feeling that I could probably eat this pizza without getting too bad a reaction, but no matter how tempted I was, I didn't want to take the chance. If I got foggy-brained and crabby now, it would ruin the whole visit. So I decided, reluctantly but without allowing myself any regret, to abstain.

We sat out back at a wooden picnic table. The pizzas looked delectable, the crust charred and crisp, the toppings generous—kale and basil, sausage and mushroom. Brendan, who ate six or seven slices in all, confirmed that they were indeed spectacular, but I still didn't eat any; it wasn't worth the price I'd have to pay for eating gluten.

Instead, I dismantled the head of celery Eliot had picked as we drove out of the farm. I dipped the stalks in the almond butter Eliot had fished out of their fridge, feeling like a special-needs child but not really caring. The fresh-picked celery was peppery and crunchy and fibrous. The almond butter was rich and nutty. I was fine, I told myself as Brendan moaned his way through another piece of pizza.

We adults drank wine out of plastic cups, a Rioja we'd brought from Portland and a bottle of the organic red Eliot likes.

"No sulfites," he said. "Doesn't keep me up at night. No hangover the next day. At my age, that's a good thing."

Heidi and Emily had run off to join a tribe of midsize kids climbing trees. At one point, a nearby tree sprouted eight or nine pairs of small, dirty bare feet that dangled from the leafy boughs. This, too, brought back memories of my own childhood, when we kids ran wild outside in a pack at parties while the grown-ups had their own fun and let us roam free.

Later, Heidi and Emily ran back to our table, their hands filled with blackberries they'd just picked. We all ate some.

"I don't think they really want you to be picking those," said Melissa.

"But there was a path that led right to them!"

Back at the farmhouse, Melissa took pity on me and insisted on cooking me a proper supper. Brendan and I sat at the long kitchen table with more glasses of wine while she scrambled several rich, orange-yolked eggs from the farm's chickens in butter and set out a block of cheddar and flaxseed crackers. That would have been enough, but she insisted on warming up the duck soup Barbara had made the day before. I ate an enormous bowl of it; so did Brendan, even after all that pizza. The broth was glossy with duck fat, the pieces of duck, tender and sweet. The rice melted in my mouth. It was superb. I forgot all about the pizza I couldn't have.

We three stayed at the table, talking and laughing, while the girls played upstairs and Eliot and Barbara watched a movie.

Just before midnight, Eliot came into the kitchen and kissed the top of his daughter's head. "This reminds me of when you and your friends from school would hang out," he said.

"Remember that night when I stayed up with two apprentices and got them drunk?" she said, laughing.

"Ha! Yes. That was very bad of you," he said with a smile.

Four Season Farm is known for its rotating crew of healthy, hard-working young apprentices, so uniformly and staggeringly good-looking that every morning when they emerge from each outbuilding, it's as if a J.Crew catalog has come to life.

And indeed, the next morning, after the chickens had woken us up with their soft, wheezy harmonica chorus and we had all had a good, strong cup of coffee, I was washing vegetables at the pantry sink when I glanced up and saw a young apprentice emerge from the greenhouse door carrying a wire basket full of eggs he'd just gathered. He was shirtless, his muscular chest gleaming, his biceps bulging, his jeans slipping below the waistband of his boxer shorts to show off his tanned washboard abs. Taking in his tousled chestnut curls, sun-kissed face, and pouty bee-stung lips, I laughed out loud.

"What's so funny?" Brendan asked.

"Nothing," I said.

He followed my gaze, took in that paragon of youthful grace and beauty, and then he laughed, too.

("Honestly, looks aren't a factor in our hiring," Barbara assured me when I told her this. "We often do it sight unseen, through good referrals and résumés. I chalk it up to farmy types being especially robust and healthy-looking.") Maybe that explains why Mainers in general are so good-looking.

We spent the rest of that morning in the kitchen prepping vegetables for a huge lunch for twenty-five people. We minced many bunches of cilantro, pounds of onion, mango, tomato, red pepper, and avocado, and juiced a heap of limes, talking to Barbara about her life and work. She's a writer and a native New Yorker who used to write for a number of publications, including the *Village Voice*, and was a college English professor. She had an organic garden and a landscape consulting firm in Connecticut in the late 1970s and '80s.

In 1991, on a visit up to Midcoast Maine to see her mother, who had retired to Blue Hill, Barbara went over to Harborside to meet Helen, and there was Eliot Coleman, tying up tomatoes in Helen's greenhouse. Barbara and Eliot had been corresponding a bit and knew of each other's books. They were instant soul mates: It was love at first sight for her, and the feeling was mutual. She moved in with Eliot not long afterward, and they have been inseparable ever since. She now works closely with her husband in their many joint ventures; in addition to farming and writing, they travel extensively, all over the world, giving lectures and consultations.

Barbara also writes a regular column for the *Washington Post* on gardening and cooking called "A Cook's Garden." I asked her what the latest topic was (she'd written a draft before dawn that morning), and she answered with succinct wryness, "Voles."

Over a second cup of coffee and a bowl of granola and yogurt with blueberries, I took a break from chopping and paged through Eliot and Barbara's new co-authored cookbook, *The Four Season Farm Gardener's Cookbook*. The book was filled with incredibly beautiful, true-to-life photographs of the farm, one of which had a handwritten quote superimposed: "After washing up we fix a simple supper, much of it harvested before, still alive and flavorful. We feel like the luckiest people on earth." The book also contained a thorough compendium of gardening advice and a resource section.

I pawed through the recipes avidly. Chicken Stew with Horseradish Cream looked delectable. Fish Soup with Tomatoes and Fennel looked like a light spring bouillabaisse I needed to make. I would have liked to dive into the book for a good long time, but there were onions to chop, and I didn't want to be a slacker, so I promised myself I'd buy a copy, read it at my leisure, and try out that beautiful-looking fish soup.

"Flash-pickling," I said, thinking aloud, watching Barbara pickle red onions and cabbage for the fish tacos.

"What's flash-pickling?" she asked. "I've never heard of that."

"That's what they call it in Brooklyn," I said.

"I don't know; I'm just throwing these into some vinegar," she said.

"It's all the rage among hipsters," I said, and we laughed.

ella

Barbara Damrosch's Chicken Stew with Horseradish Cream

(adapted from *The Four Season Farm Gardener's Cookbook*)

According to Barbara: "This rustic dish of chicken and vegetables, perfect for a family supper, is light but rich in flavor. A complete meal in itself, it's easy on the stomach at times when you're not feeling well, or when you are recovering from heavy holiday fare. I often make a lot of it, then eat it for several days. Since the solids and the broth are served separately, each diner can pour or ladle in as much broth as they like. A horseradish topping adds even more flavor and a bit of zip."

1 whole chicken (4 lbs.)
2 large carrots, scrubbed but not peeled, sliced diagonally into 1-inch-thick pieces
2 medium ribs celery, cut into 1 1/2-inch lengths
1 medium-size onion, peeled and quartered
3 medium leeks (white and light green), split lengthwise, well rinsed, cut into 2-inch sections
4 to 6 small white turnips, about golf-ball size, unpeeled and left whole
1 quart (4 cups) chicken stock
1 cup dry white wine
2 bay leaves
4 whole cloves
1 tsp dried tarragon or 2 tsp chopped fresh tarragon
1/2 tsp dried thyme or 1 tsp fresh
1 tsp salt (less if broth is salty)
Freshly ground black pepper, to taste
1/2 cup sour cream
1/2 cup whole-milk yogurt
1/4 cup prepared white horseradish (not creamy style)

Cut chicken into pieces, separating drumsticks from thighs, severing wings, splitting breast down middle with a knife or poultry shears. Cut the breasts in half crosswise to make 4 pieces. Cut back in half. Remove skin from all pieces except wings.

Place carrots, celery, onion, leeks, and turnips in large soup pot. Add all the chicken pieces, including giblets (minus liver). Pour in the stock and the wine. Bring just to a boil over high heat, skimming off any thick foam that floats to the surface.

Reduce heat to simmer. Add bay leaves, cloves, tarragon, thyme, salt, and pepper. Simmer, uncovered, until chicken is cooked through and vegetables tender, 1 hour or a bit more.

Meanwhile, whisk sour cream, yogurt, and horseradish in small bowl. Spoon horseradish cream into small serving bowl. Set aside at room temperature.

When stew is done, taste for salt and add more if needed. Using slotted spoon and/or tongs, lift out chicken. Remove meat from bones (discarding bones). Using slotted spoon, transfer vegetables to large warmed platter. (If a few bits of vegetable remain in broth, that's okay.) Discard bay leaves. Add chicken to platter.

Pour broth into warmed soup tureen or Dutch oven and serve alongside meat and vegetables. Give each person a generous soup bowl and have them help themselves to stew and broth. Pass horseradish cream. Serves 4.

ᘓᘓ

When just about everything was chopped that needed chopping, Brendan and I went off for a walk. We headed down the road that snaked along the coastline and came to a large, clean, rock-rubbled beach on a wild, secluded cove, where we picked our way over the sand to sit on the tallest rock and look out to sea for a while. It was easy to lose track of time there in the fresh strong breeze and sunlight, inhaling the smell of kelp left on the rocks when the tide went out, looking out at sailboats plying the choppy waves. I didn't want to leave.

But eventually, we headed up the rickety wooden staircase back up the bluff to the road and through the woods to the Nearings' property. As we approached the stone house, the solid-looking chalet that Helen Nearing had designed and built by hand using rocks from their land

and hand-mixed mortar, a ruddy-cheeked young woman wearing stretchy pants came out and said, "Welcome to the Good Life Center! We're about to have yoga, but we're open for visitors from one to five."

We smiled at her, thanked her, and went on our way, happy to have had at least a small gander at the famous place. As we bush-whacked our way back to Four Season Farm, I chuckled to myself at the aptness of our encounter. I almost wished we could have stayed for yoga, but lunchtime was approaching.

While Barbara grilled marinated haddock and cooked spicy ground beef and warmed corn tortillas in the oven, Brendan and Melissa and I heaped the table in the long great room with plates and bowls of the taco fixings we'd prepped: sautéed onion, mango salsa, tomato salsa, cilantro, pickled cabbage, pickled red onion. We set out a board of cheese and crackers festooned with grapes and leaves from the vine right outside, and a plate of fresh spring rolls a neighbor had made. We opened bottles of cold white wine and poured some for ourselves.

Promptly at noon, the other guests arrived, most of them writers in this case, as well as a farmer and a painter; there's no "fashionably late" in Maine, as we'd learned years ago when we first moved here. If you say noon, you can expect all your guests to assemble well before 12:05, barring acts of God and kidnapping.

We all piled our plates with tacos and then sat around the long table under the grapevine pergola on the granite cobblestone terrace, which was reached through double French doors off the long main room of the house. On that hot, dry summer day, it felt as if we were in Tuscany. It could have been a commercial for the idyllic Maine farming life. Young green bunches of grapes dangled overhead; the flower garden beyond the terrace was in full bloom. Healthy, happy chickens roamed and pecked through the shady woods beyond. The sky was a deep blue and the sun shone. As I looked around the table at the attractive, smart, interesting group, I thought all we needed was a superimposed caption: MAINE: THE WAY LIFE SHOULD BE. I felt a wave of gratitude toward Eliot and Barbara for generously hosting Melissa's writer friends and serving such a lavish meal for our benefit.

The other writers owned summer houses in seaside villages about forty-five minutes from Four Season Farm, and lived in Brooklyn or California the rest of the time. As soon as they realized that Brendan and I lived in Maine year-round, they interrogated us, asking how we'd done it, how we managed to make a go of it.

"We moved here on a whim," I said. "I don't know how we make a go of it. We're writers, so I guess we can live anywhere. You can do it, if we can."

"We want to," they all said hopefully. "We'd love to live in Maine year-round. Maybe we will. Maybe we can figure out a way."

One of them, Heidi, was a Portland native who grew up here in the 1970s in a house on the Western Prom.

"I went to Reiche Elementary," she said.

That's the public school a couple of blocks down Brackett Street from our house, whose educational reputation is not the highest, to put it mildly, but whose enrollment is interestingly racially and culturally diverse for such a predominantly white town.

"We were not rich," Heidi told me. "We lived in an old house, and the Prom was a dicey place. The West End was run-down and gritty back then."

I laughed. "Really?" I said.

"Oh, yes," she said. "I know it's hard to believe now."

Now, of course, the West End, especially the Western Prom where Heidi grew up, is the richest neighborhood in town; Portland has changed a lot since the 1970s, clearly. I've heard that many teenage kids who live there and go to Waynflete, the tony private school on the West End, aren't allowed by their parents to walk home, even in groups, after nine at night because of the "hobos" who might be lurking.

Heidi told me she used to be allowed to walk home alone, at all hours, even though it was such a bad neighborhood in those days. We reminisced about how back then, we kids were all allowed so much freedom to roam at will outside.

Portland's not the only thing that's changed.

ℓℓℓ

At the end of the lunch, after the rest of the guests had left, Brendan and I stayed at the table with Eliot. I was interested to see that he didn't adopt a rock-star persona, even though he was the Mick Jagger of Maine farmers. He was self-effacing, personable, and forthright.

He told us about wintering his flocks of chickens in mobile greenhouses that he would roll through the organic grain fields, ten feet per day. The chickens pecked at the fallen organic corn and wheat and other grain left there, and meanwhile, they fertilized and aerated the soil. So the chickens and the soil took care of each other, according to both the theory and the practice, and by the spring, he had saved a bundle on organic chicken feed, which was prohibitively expensive, and his fields were ready to go. He was trying this method not only for his and Barbara's own benefit, but for the younger farmers who learned from them and turned to them for advice and knowledge about how to make it in organic farming in this climate, with its "Zone 4 winters," as he called them, and the tricky soil.

ℓℓℓ

While Eliot and Barbara had clearly taken up the Nearings' mantle as the farmer-gurus of New England, dedicating themselves to helping younger farmers make a go of it up here, inspiring and aiding the next generation of Maine organic farmers, Four Season Farm looked to me like a model of fully achieved success, with its beautifully honed methods, magazine-model apprentices, Tuscan terrace, and bursting-with-health chickens.

But, as Melissa pointed out to me when I told her how amazing Four Season Farm looks to a visitor's untrained eye, every farm has its challenges, including this one, and learning how best to overcome them is the key to making it look easy, even though it's far from it.

Months later, when I asked Barbara what that "sabbatical" summer had been like for her, she told me, "Essentially, we didn't take a sabbatical; we simply put more effort and space into growing crops for the eight-month retail season that goes from mid-September to mid-May. This is the way we operated in the nineties, and into the next decade. We currently sell at a winter market in Blue Hill during that time, as well as to various wholesale accounts. During last summer we managed a full crew (larger than our winter one) to grow those crops. We did a small amount of wholesale business as well—vegetables, eggs, and, in my case, a full-time wholesale business in fresh-flower bouquets which I grew, harvested, and delivered three times a week, along with the eggs and whatever else we were selling.

"The difference was the closing of the farm stand and lack of participation in local farmers' markets. That made it somewhat more restful for Eliot, so that he was able to do a bit more writing and research. For me, it was nonstop work. I plan to continue with the flowers (but perhaps not all those deliveries), and we are adding in some more wholesale summer crops that other summer farmers don't specialize in. But I think we will stick with this emphasis on winter, at least for now. It also gives us a chance to rotate pastureland with both cropland and green manures, for better fertility, thus continuing to fine-tune our system."

Amazed by the amount of physical labor that goes into maintaining and sustaining even a farm as established as Four Season, I was curious to see firsthand what it's like to try to get a small, self-supporting organic farm off the ground in the first place. I decided to visit a newer farm with a younger farmer, a seat-of-the-pants, in-progress, scrappy, down-to-earth scenario, so I could find out what a less-established Maine farm looks like.

ℓℓℓ

I first met KJ Grow on a rainy day in the spring of 2013, just outside the glass doors leading into the skyscraper-like building that houses Doubleday, on West Fifty-Third Street near Times Square in Manhattan. She was part of the online media team I was meeting with, along with my editor, to determine how they could help promote my memoir, *Blue Plate Special*. We'd arranged to have lunch. I'd just come from LaGuardia Airport in a cab, having flown down from Maine.

We—KJ, her colleague, her boss, my editor, and me—walked together to a place they'd suggested, and which I'd preapproved, because the restaurant owner, a well-known chef, famously had celiac and was therefore gluten-free. From years of hard experience, I knew well that this was a rare thing in restaurants in New York. And if I had to go back to there again, I wanted a good lunch.

The five of us seated ourselves around a high table, perched uncomfortably on high, trendy stools. When I asked the waitress for a gluten-free menu, she looked blank. When I asked which dishes on the menu were gluten-free, she told me the green salad was, if I got it without dressing. Nothing else.

It was a Korean restaurant, and I'd been doubly excited to eat gluten-free Asian food in New York. The heartbreak for the gluten-intolerant or the celiac is that soy sauce is made with wheat, as are many of the sauces, and therefore, almost nothing in Chinese, Korean, or Japanese restaurants is safe, when those cuisines should, technically, be a gluttonous haven for us. Sitting there, daunted, unwilling to give up, I asked the waitress if the chef could make me a dish, anything, without soy sauce.

She looked consternated. "No," she said. "He doesn't do anything special for anyone. Sorry." She seemed, on the whole, not sorry in the least.

Granted, the place was jammed, but I was starving. I'd left home that morning without breakfast in anticipation of the amazing lunch I'd have when I landed, but why should she give a damn that I was ravenous? No reason whatsoever; but in Maine, the waitress would have cared. They always do, in every restaurant.

Welcome back to New York, I said to myself as I meekly ordered the green salad, no dressing. I snarfed it as I watched the apologetic, chagrined Doubleday online media team and my editor slurp and moan their way through pork dumplings and BBQ chicken wings and other amazing things I couldn't even bear to look at because I was afraid I might cry. Honestly, I was a grown-up, and it was only one lunch.

During the lunch, KJ kept looking over at me with an expression of genuine sympathy. I liked her instantly.

On the way back to the Doubleday offices, I fell into step next to her. It was a rainy day, but neither of us carried an umbrella; we both preferred to get rained on. Around us, traffic honked and snarled. We jostled through the lunchtime midtown crowds, keeping pace with each other, dodging umbrellas. She was tall, slender, chic, pale, lovely, bespectacled, and very, very nice. She still felt terrible about my lunch.

"It's okay," I assured her. "I have time before my flight home to eat a big lunch somewhere. I'm taking myself out as soon as we say good-bye."

She asked about my life in Portland and confessed ("Don't tell my boss," she whispered) that she was yearning to quit her job and move up to Maine, work on a farm as an apprentice, and eventually start her own farm. Her life in New York was just about perfect: She had a great job, a beautiful apartment, wonderful friends, and had made the most of the city since she'd arrived almost a decade ago. She'd experienced so much and had had so much fun.

But she was itching for a change. She didn't like to stay still, and she wanted to farm, as her family had done before her—but not in Montana, like them, but up in Maine. Something about Maine was calling out to her.

I looked closely at her. Her expression held something I recognized in myself—curiosity, impatience with standing still or being stuck, a sense of adventure, a hunger to live as fully as possible. She was a kindred spirit.

I gave her a big hug good-bye and wished her luck. Just before she went back into the gleaming corporate lobby to be whisked up to her office by the high-speed elevator, I called out, "See you in Maine!"

I didn't fully believe she would do it—at least, not so soon, but less than one year later, KJ quit her job, left her apartment, packed everything she hadn't given away, said good-bye to all her friends, and drove the six hours up to Maine with all her belongings.

Shortly after she arrived, she started a blog called Branching Out about her new life at Black Kettle Farm in Lyman, forty minutes southwest of Portland. I loved reading the unfolding story of a young New Yorker farming in Maine so much, I asked KJ's permission to stick a chunk of it in this book. Luckily she agreed, so here it is:

Excerpt from *Branching Out* by KJ Grow

Black Kettle Farm is run by Laura Neale, a kind of farming dynamo, and real community builder in the area. She's young and funky, goes to yoga and spinning classes and listens to reggae, and grows some of the most beautiful and tasty veggies in the area. She raises pigs and runs the farm all on a twelve-acre plot she purchased a few years ago. She's business-savvy and a compassionate person, and I have a lot to learn from her.

I'm living in a tiny camper with no heat, no electricity, no water. I gave away all of my possessions except what would fit in my car. When this apprenticeship ends in November, I have no clue what I'm going to do. And all of that feels very different and very free.

Last night after I'd moved into my camper, Laura threw a dinner party for the crew and friends of the farm. About a dozen people showed up, decked out in wool sweaters and Carhartts, all ruddy-cheeked and hale-looking. Laura served up cuts of pork from last year's pigs that she'd brined all day. I brought a bottle of Rioja given to me by friends in New York; a sheep farmer brought rum and pineapple and made rounds of Mai Tais for everyone. And despite being the new kid, I didn't feel like a stranger in a strange place. I felt home.

One week in, I am starting to get a feel for the rhythm of the farm and living in my camper. Here's how the days typically unfold:

5:00 a.m.—Dawn breaks and the birds starting singing. I lay still in my bed, eyes wide open, cocooned under many blankets until I am ready to throw off the covers and bear the early-morning chill of my camper. Winter is slow in retreating this year, and a handful of nights have been below-freezing temperatures.

5:30 a.m.—I bundle up, step into my rubber boots, and stomp through the muddy field over to the yurt. This week, the crescent moon has still been visible in the sky as the pink sunrise begins to filter through the trees. I do a twenty-minute yoga routine in the yurt, fully bundled, and begin to wake up my body.

6:00 a.m.—I return to my camper, stream NPR *Morning Edition* through my phone while I prepare coffee and breakfast. In the early season, farm work begins at 8:00 am, so I have plenty of time to sip slowly, wash up, and get ready for the day.

7:45 a.m.—I commute to the barn via a five-minute walk through the field, and I check in with the crew for our game plan for the day. The work is varied and continuous: My first week of tasks included trimming about 1,000 onions, repairing the high tunnel, digging holes for new trees, clearing a thicket of brambles, potting up tomatoes in the greenhouse and thinning brassicas, and assembling a shelving unit. Some of the work is quite physical and repetitive, and some is very focused and detailed. I find that I am quickly able to get "into the zone," and love the tasks that for some would seem tedious. I can work with little seedlings for four hours at a stretch and feel a deep sense of presence and peace.

12:00 p.m.—We break for lunch. I generally retreat to my camper and prepare something quickly—a sandwich wrap, or heat up some soup. If it's nice, I'll sit outside on my "porch" for a few minutes, or if I'm tired, sneak in a ten- to fifteen-minute nap. On Thursdays, someone from the crew cooks lunch for everyone.

1:00 p.m.—We work for another four hours, solid.

5:00 p.m.—Day is done. I cook dinner in my camper and then spend most of the rest of the evening in the yurt, where there is a woodstove and I can stay warmer. I build myself a fire, heat up water for a cup of tea, light candles and the oil lamp. I cuddle up on the sofa under a wool blanket and read for about two hours. Then, around 9:00 p.m., I do another twenty minutes of yoga and make my way back to the camper, using my headlamp to light the way. I'll often spot deer leaping through the fields at night, and I always marvel at the abundance of stars. I quickly get into my long underwear and pajamas and burrow under a sleeping bag and four blankets, nodding off around 10:00 p.m.

And when I wake and hear the birds start singing again the next morning, I smile and think, "It's so good to be here. This is the way life should be."

But life on the farm was by no means a romantic fantasy:

It was cold and damp, the kind of cold that settles into your bones and only a hot shower can cure. Nights dipped down to the 30s, and while I felt fairly confident in my fire-making skills a week ago, there were nights this week that I simply could not get anything to burn. One night when I desperately needed a roaring fire, I failed repeatedly, and cracked open a bottle of whiskey instead in a last-ditch attempt to warm up. I burrowed into my sleeping bag as soon as the sun went down. I missed my city friends and my cozy apartment intensely that night, feeling frozen and alone.

And when the weather is spotty and spring is slow in coming, things get stressful on the farm. With one eye on the ground and the other on the skies, Laura has to make real-time decisions about the operation that are critical for the timing of planting and harvest. On Wednesday, a chilly, overcast day with rain looming in the forecast, we hustled to get our first round of crops into the ground: rainbow chard, three kinds of kale, and napa cabbage. Right now, we are a crew of three—Laura, Abi, and me. Another apprentice will join us in a few weeks and we'll get some additional labor help from CSA work-share members. But that day the three of us transplanted about 3,000 seedlings into the ground. Calculate how many squats that is per person and you'll wince, or cry.

Needless to say, I was a little stiff the next couple of days. But along with the soreness also came a few moments of humility that bruised me too. It goes without saying that I'm new at this, and any apprentice is going to make mistakes as they develop and grow. But I really, really hate making mistakes and am hard on myself when I slip up. I'm trying to get better at shaking off those errors and just seeing them as they are—opportunities to learn—but I often allow them to build into rain clouds that hover over my psyche the rest of the day.

But as Jane Kenyon says, "How much better it is to carry wood to the fire than to moan about your life." And it's true and a little bit miraculous what a good day of hard work and a spot of sunshine can do to turn your attitude around. By the time the skies cleared on Thursday afternoon, I had let go of my self-doubt and felt grateful to be exactly where I was.

In late August, almost five months after KJ had arrived, Brendan and I drove out to visit KJ and get a tour of the farm and see her new life. The drive from Portland was just under an hour. We headed down the interstate, then turned inland before Kennebunk and drove along rolling country roads, past farms and through woods and rustic small towns. It's amazing how quickly the city gives way to the countryside outside of Portland.

Black Kettle Farm is located in Lyman, Maine, on twelve acres of land, four and a half of which are cultivated. It sits atop a ridge nestled between the foothills of the White Mountains and the seacoast, surrounded by birch woods and stone walls.

As we turned in at the farm and parked in front of the farmhouse, KJ came out with a jar of beautiful flowers; my birthday had been the week before. I hardly recognized the chic, urban, pale, professionally dressed young woman I'd walked through the rain with in Times Square. Now, she was tan and muscular, glowing with health and well-being, vitality and energy. She wore work clothes and boots. She looked gorgeous.

"Life in Maine seems to agree with you," I said, after we'd exchanged greetings.

"Oh, I love it here." She showed me her wrist. "A few weeks ago, I did a small thing that made a big difference. I took off my watch. At first, it was simply to get rid of the tacky tan line I'd developed, but then I noticed how it altered my sense of time. It changed my perception of the day from 'What's next?' to 'Where am I now?'"

Just then, Dingo caught sight of a cat who'd come over to see who the hell he was. Dingo lunged at him, snarling with murderous bloodlust, but was luckily brought up short by his leash.

"That's Steve," said KJ. "One of the farm cats."

Steve didn't seem in the least bit scared of Dingo, who had started to foam at the mouth and make hoarse, guttural sounds in his throat. Brendan put the agitated dog back in the shaded car, with the windows open.

We wandered off to see the place. Four young women ran Black Kettle Farm. The farmer, Laura, was thirty-seven. Her full-time employee, Abi, was thirty-six. KJ had just turned thirty-four, and Shannon, the other apprentice, was twenty-three, just out of college. They ate one meal together a week, a staff lunch; otherwise, they worked together all day and were on their own every morning, noon, and evening. It was a Saturday, and the other three women were either taking the day off or at the Portsmouth farmers' market, selling produce. It was KJ's turn to mind the farm, so we had the place to ourselves.

"One of the things that really appealed to me about Black Kettle, when I was applying for apprenticeships, was the solitude," said KJ. "Other farms promote constant togetherness among the workers. I love having a lot of time to myself before and after work. And also, it's the size of the farm I can see myself having someday: small enough to be manageable, but large enough to be productive and solvent."

She told us that with the money from a hundred or so families who have CSA shares, plus the produce they sell to many local restaurants, including a few of our favorites in Portland, Laura managed to make a small but decent living and pay her workers a fair wage. I was impressed.

The small farmhouse was simple; the barn, too—unpretentious New England structures, weather-beaten and sagging a bit, but well-tended.

"Laura's been making the house her own, little by little," KJ told us.

We headed over to the barn where, hanging on a hook by the big door, was the old black kettle of the farm's name.

Downstairs, the barn was orderly, the plank tables and shelves almost empty, the chalkboard next to the scale listing that week's haul in neat lettering: kale, lettuce, herbs, potatoes, sweet peppers, broccoli, eggplant, sweet peppers, and tomatoes, none of which were in evidence. The farm's CSA members had recently come to pick up their weekly boxes, which explained the provisional, fleeting-feeling emptiness downstairs.

But upstairs in the hayloft, KJ and the other apprentice, Shannon, had hung rows of newly harvested garlic, several varieties, all sorted and labeled. The garlic looked very fresh, with clean white papery skin and pleasingly fat bulbs. The strong, appetizing smell of fresh garlic filled the air.

Beyond the small parking lot, near the farmhouse and barn, KJ showed us the half-acre perennial garden where they grew sage, oregano, thyme, chives, lavender, and mint, as well as medicinal herbs like echinacea, yarrow, and St. John's wort, which they sold to restaurants and at market. A neighbor kept her beehives nearby, so the flowers provided nectar for the bees and were in turn pollinated. As we watched, buzzing bees hovered over the flowers, landed and drank, moving on. It was a peaceful sight, a perfect natural symbiosis in a small meadow by the road. I could have stood there and watched much longer; the smells of the herbs and flowers were heady in the sunlight, and the sound of the bees put me into an instant daydream.

The farm had two greenhouses, both of which Laura built herself. One was heated, consisting of rustic old pallets on cinder blocks; this was where the seedlings germinated until they were ready to be transplanted. The other, the high tunnel, housed several different varieties of tomato vines as well as peppers and basil. When we walked into this one, the smells of basil and tomatoes, concentrated in the solar-heated air, immediately transported me to an Italian kitchen and made my mouth water.

Beyond the greenhouses was the farm's main event—rows upon rows of vegetable gardens, four cultivated acres in all. Like the bottom part of the barn, the gardens appeared to be in a state of temporary, hard-won quietude; KJ told us that late August is an in-between season, when the spring shift is done and they're planting the fall shift. Many of the vegetables had been harvested, a monumental amount of work.

Imagining the long days spent bending and squatting in these fields in the sun and rain, I gazed out over the beautiful, meticulous, healthy, deeply colored rows of live, growing vegetables, among which were three varieties of salad mix planted cheek by jowl in a long row for maximum ease of picking and mixing, plus kohlrabi, broccoli, and Brussels sprouts. A patch of lettuces had been allowed to "bolt," or flower, which creates seeds. The plants were leggy and tall and blooming. Others sat in fat green globes, ruffling in the breeze.

"Do you do it all by hand?" I asked KJ.

"Mostly," she said. "But we do have some machines. My favorite farm tool so far is called the dibbler. When I first saw the thing, I thought it looked like some kind of medieval torture device, or something from a Renaissance fair. I'm sure there are fancier premade models available for purchase, but this one appears to be a cobbled-together contraption of PVC pipe and wooden spikes, set six inches apart in three rows. The idea is that Laura creates a bed in the field with her tractor, the tractor wheel treads becoming the aisles between where we will plant. Then she runs down the bed with a three-pronged implement attached to her tractor to create the lines in the bed; most of our plants are in two or three rows per bed. Then, we pull the dibbler down the length of the bed to create 'dibbles,' which are evenly spaced holes where we drop and plant our seedlings."

In one patch, they had planted "blue ballet" squash to attract insects away from the watermelon and delicata squash, which I thought was an ingenious way of avoiding the use of pesticides.

"Are there a lot of weeds?" I asked innocently.

"So. Many. Weeds," KJ said. "One week I spent hours upon hours pulling up weeds. It could make a person batty if you let it, but it can also be good therapy, to see a weedy patch fully cleared and the plants given new opportunity to produce and thrive."

We followed KJ back to the pigpen, a large fenced area with some shade, some sun, a shack, and all manner of huge plastic water containers. Six healthy pigs came over to greet us. They looked well-fed and plump, and—I had to admit to myself, being an avid eater of good pork—delicious.

KJ told us that the pigs' two favorite things to do, not surprisingly, are to root on the ground through ever-replenished heaps of fresh vegetable scraps from the farm, which are regularly thrown into their pen, and to wallow in the cool mud near their huge water containers, which is augmented by humans passing by and spraying their wallow with the hose, as KJ did. They also eat fifty pounds of grain a day from the grain dispenser set up in the middle of the pen.

Every spring, Laura started over with new piglets. After they're butchered in the fall, she distributes seventy-pound half-shares of each pig, along with any lard and innards, as people request them.

Despite this rapid turnover, the pigs all had names.

"The largest is Big Digs, or Dirk Diggler, because of his big wattles," KJ told us. He did indeed have large, pendulous growths on each cheek that reminded me of a pink, fleshy version of the side curls worn by Orthodox Jews, who don't eat pork (an irony I appreciated silently).

Pigs are appealing animals, even covered with mud, grunting, and wallowing, and these were the happiest pigs I'd ever seen. They appeared to be smiling. They clearly enjoyed butting up against one another, lying in puppylike heaps, and exploring the pile of leafy kale leaves and carrot tops with their snouts. Their bodies were robust and agleam with edible health. Yes, they'd be slaughtered in the fall, which was soon, but their short life was anything but nasty and brutish; from where I stood, in fact, it looked idyllic.

"A big thing to do on the farm at Happy Hour," said KJ, "is to hang out by the pigpen and drink beers. A local bakery gives us day-old baguettes. The other day, we stuck them on the pigs' backs and watched them run around with them. When they fell off, the pigs ate them. Big fun."

I laughed; it did seem like worthy entertainment. I would have sat and watched it myself for an hour or two. But the pigs didn't seem to feel the same way about us humans. Once they had ascertained that nothing exciting was going on with us, foodwise, they ignored us entirely and returned to whatever they'd been doing before we arrived, some in the mud, others in the shade. It was time to move on.

ello

KJ Grow's Pork Breakfast Sausage Patties

A few months after our visit, KJ told me the pigs had been slaughtered, and that she'd bought a share of Mr. Diggler. I asked her what kinds of dishes she was making with the fresh, organic pork, and she gave me the following delicious-sounding recipe, which she credited to Allrecipes.com.

2 lbs unseasoned ground pork

Mix the following spices and blend into the pork with your hands, then form into small patties:

2 tsp dried sage
2 tsp salt
1 tsp ground black pepper
1/4 tsp dried marjoram

1 T brown sugar
1/8 tsp crushed red pepper flakes
1 pinch ground cloves

Sauté patties in a skillet, 5 minutes per side, over medium heat. Serve with cheesy scrambled farm-fresh eggs and sautéed potatoes and onions for a hearty breakfast in any season.

ℓℓℓ

Back behind the pigpen, ringed by trees, was a flower-strewn meadow with a large, airy yurt on a wooden platform that served as a gathering place for the apprentices. They cooked on a propane stove and washed their dishes outside with water pumped out of a big blue barrel. Inside were a couch and a table with chairs, a rug and a woodstove. Behind that were the small old RVs where KJ and Shannon slept; Abi lived in an apartment in a nearby town. The inside of KJ's little camper was as shipshape and efficient as a belowdecks galley and berth of a sailboat. It didn't have a toilet; there was an outhouse nearby, and the apprentices showered in the farmhouse.

As we were leaving, KJ led us into the barn and handed us a heavy box.

"I picked some things for you guys," she said.

I peeked inside and saw a bounty of farm produce, including a bunch of fat orange carrots, kale, garlic, two kinds of tomatoes, basil, zucchini, green beans, spring mix, and peppers.

We drove home with our vegetables and flowers, back along the quiet country roads toward the coast, Black Kettle Farm receding behind us. In my mind's eye I pictured it as one integrated, wholly functional organism: plants, animals, people, dirt, buildings, and weather, all coexisting in a way that felt organic, both literally and in the deepest sense of the word.

Over the course of the next five days, we ate every scrap of vegetables from our box. They were all so delicious and flavorful and fresh, we ate as many of them raw and in salads as we could: a carrot salad, a caprese salad, a green salad with thinly sliced peppers and grated carrot. And one night, I threw together a delectable stew so filled with flavor it almost jumped off the plate into our mouths.

ℓℓℯ

Black Kettle Farm Vegetable Stew

olive oil
1 onion
a heap of chopped CSA box vegetables; for example:
6 cloves garlic
1 bunch kale
1 lb. green beans
2 medium zucchini
1 bunch basil
1 bunch parsley
1/2 to 3/4 cup chicken or vegetable stock
salt, black pepper, and red pepper flakes to taste
1 15-oz. can cannellini beans, drained and rinsed
1/4 cup toasted pine nuts
1 cup grated Pecorino Romano cheese

In a large skillet or saucepan, sauté the chopped onion and garlic in plenty of good olive oil. Add the rest of the chopped vegetables, season to taste, and add the beans. Continue to sauté, stirring often, adding stock as needed, until everything is soft and the flavors have melded, about 20 minutes.

Serve with toasted pine nuts, plenty of grated cheese, and more hot red pepper flakes. Serves 4.

Chapter Twelve

Into the Future

One July weekend in 2014, our friends Ethan and Lindsay invited us up to see their place near Popham Beach. They're a quintessential pair of young, native Mainers if there ever was one: She's a designer who works for L.L. Bean, and he's the sternman on his lifelong friend Lawrence's lobster boat; he also runs fishing and sightseeing charters in the summertime. They're in their late twenties and are both extremely naturally good-looking without being show-offy or self-conscious about it; they could be models straight out of some catalog, advertising the salubrious wholesomeness of Maine life.

Popham is a small lobstering and fishing village right on the water. It's wild and beautiful up there. We drove the hour north from Portland on a cloudless, golden early afternoon, turned off onto Route 1 in Bath, a curvy two-lane country road that took us down a peninsula through marshland, villages, and coastal forests.

After a low-key lunch at a half-decent clam and lobster shack right on the Fort Popham beach, we headed down the road to meet our friends at three o'clock, as arranged.

"We have a situation," said Ethan after we pulled up to the dock and parked. "My wife has been shanghaied by my father."

"That pirate!" I said. (It seemed appropriate.)

"We have to go and get her," he told us.

All of us, including Dingo and their dog Pepper, climbed into the *Guppy*, a large wooden dory with an outboard, the smaller of Ethan's two charter boats. We motored out through the harbor, past rocky, grassy islands.

"That's my mother there in that boat," he said, as we approached the narrow gut that led out into the open sea. "She and my stepfather live in that house, there." He pointed over to nearby Georgetown Island, to a shingled place with big windows on the cove.

Trying not to sound too depressing, but wanting the answer, I asked Ethan what the local lobstermen will do when global warming kills off all the lobsters in the Gulf of Maine; what would they catch instead? (Okay, there was no way *not* to make that sound depressing, but he answered with equanimity, and didn't seem offended. Obviously, it's something he thinks about.)

"Seaweed, probably," he said. "Farmed kelp."

Kelp, it turns out, has several uses. In addition to being edible in the form of kombu in soups, and as a thickener called alginate, and as a savory snack, garnish, and rice wrapper, its ash can be used in vast quantities for soap and glass production; its high iodine content makes it an effective goiter medication; and, since alginate blocks fat absorption, it can be used as a nontoxic diet aid. It also propagates fast, and its growth in the open ocean produces methane and ethanol, both renewable energy sources.

But no matter how oddly useful kelp is, we agreed, it will never replace the Maine lobster.

Out on Sheepscot Bay, we picked up speed and slapped headlong over the calm water. Ethan slowed when he saw another boat headed back toward the dock. He hailed them and spun around to meet them as they slowed down.

We pulled up alongside them, and for the next two hours, sat with our feet resting on each other's boats to keep us from drifting apart, and just hung out on the ocean. Ethan's father, Bill, who's also a lobsterman, had just won a lobster-boat race in Pemaquid, for which he'd "shanghaied" Lindsay and her friend, Jamie, a photographer who works with Lindsay at L.L. Bean, to be his "bow fluff," which is just what it sounds like, along with Ethan's lobstering partner and old friend, Lawrence, as crew.

We pulled out cold beer and wine and talked as the boats bobbed up and down on the waves. The sky was blue, the air warm, and there was no wind. Usually, Ethan told us, there was a breeze, and it was chilly and choppy on the water and partly overcast, but that afternoon was perfect.

Lindsay and I put our heads together and discussed our work.

I told her about this book, since the occasion for this trip was ostensibly research, and she described the magazine/catalog she wants to start, both print and online: well-written stories alongside beautifully photographed and designed pictures of various products made by hand in Maine. It would represent, she told me, the traditional, DIY, down-to-earth year-round reality of Maine, not the elitist, moneyed, summer-people bullshit that predominates in so many publications now. I told her I'd happily write for it anytime.

On our way back to the dock, we stopped off at Seguin Island, which boasts the second-oldest and tallest lighthouse in Maine. Ethan stayed on the boat to make some work phone calls while the rest of us jumped ashore and lifted Dingo and Pepper over the waves.

As we climbed up to the bluff above the rocky little beach to use the outhouse perched there, we ran into the caretaker, who was fixing the tracks for the little tram that hauled supplies up from the cove and beach for the lighthouse and living quarters. He knew Ethan and Lindsay because Ethan's ferry service took tourists over to Seguin, so even though it was after-hours, he generously offered to give us a tour.

We climbed the sandy path to the grassy plateau at the top of the island, where the main buildings are. The view was extraordinary from up there, over a hundred feet above the water on the last island before the open ocean.

The Seguin Island Lighthouse was commissioned by George Washington and installed in 1797. Its light is a modern-day electric bulb amplified by a many-petaled flower of very old glass, recently hand-polished by the caretaker. It sparkled in the late-afternoon sunlight. We walked around the catwalk outside the cupola; far down was blue water, all around us, in every direction. Close by, we could see Monhegan and other islands. The second inlet, far down the coast, was Casco Bay and Portland. It was a stunning view, intimate and yet full of grandeur.

We went back down to the beach and climbed back on board the *Guppy* and headed for the dock, where we got into our cars and drove to Ethan and Lindsay's place. They lived in an airy but cozy post-and-beam house on the water that Ethan's father built in the 1970s; he now lived with his girlfriend in a newer house just up the cove.

After we parked by the house and got out, Ethan went into the basement storage space. Dingo followed him and flushed a stray chicken out from her hiding place. "There she is," Ethan said. "I knew she was in there." He tossed her into the coop to join the rest of them, just settling in for the night.

In the buggy, darkening evening, we picked vegetables from their greenhouse and garden. They apologized for the weeds, which they told us they don't have time to pick, but we were too impressed by the bounty to notice.

While the men stayed outside and boiled the red potatoes Ethan had just dug from their garden on an old propane double-burner cookstove, in the same pot with the lobsters he had just pulled out of one of his traps, Lindsay and I stayed in the kitchen and cooked, like good women. She fried the rest of a striper Ethan had caught the day before. I made a salad with the vegetables we'd just picked: cucumbers, tomatoes, red onions, garlic, basil, green beans, and green pepper. Lindsay sautéed the zucchini and garlic we'd just pulled out of their greenhouse. We used olive oil from Ethan's brother's wife's family's place in Greece, which added a whole other level of homegrown to the mix.

"What should I do with the vegetable scraps?" I asked Lindsay. "Do you have a compost bucket?"

"Just throw them out the window for the chickens," she said. "They'll see it and get excited for tomorrow's breakfast."

On the counter were several large jars of beets that Lindsay had pickled that morning.

"They'll be good in the wintertime," she said. "We had so many all of a sudden from the garden."

The beets looked like big round jewels suspended in ruby red liquid. I was very tempted to open a jar and eat a few, but I admired them instead, contenting myself with a handful of raw green beans while I made the salad.

As we were setting the table, Bill, Jamie, and Lawrence arrived with the story of another adventure they'd just had; Jamie's knee was bandaged, but all was well. We all gathered around the table, heaped our plates, and feasted.

While we ate, I realized that this was a true foraged, fished, and garden-to-table meal. Everything in front of us was food that Lindsay and Ethan had grown or caught, gathered and served without fuss or fanfare. The meal was simple and perfectly delicious; the lobsters didn't need butter, and the vegetables were still alive.

Afterwards, we all sat out on their deck, looking out at the gleaming estuary while the full moon rose and the tide came in. It was one of the most magical days I'd ever spent, and I'll never forget it.

ℓℓℓ

"You're writing a book about food in Maine?" My friend Millicent Souris, a chef and baker and cookbook author who lives in New York, was unequivocal: "You have to meet Ladleah Dunn."

When I asked who that person with the interesting name was, Millicent promptly described her as "a cook, baker, grower of food, sailor, and native Maine person."

That would have been enough to catch my interest, right there, but she went on:

"The last time I was in Maine, two Augusts ago, I was staying with Ladleah in Lincolnville, where there's a sweet, somewhat public area to swim. According to Ladleah, it's also the only legal place to fish or clam, and sometimes there are razor clams, and the beach is full of lamb's quarter. Her husband was so bored by the ladies chatting with a cooler full of beer that he just dipped down and pulled up what we thought were quahogs for dinner. They were big. Very, very big. We did stuffed clams, and honestly, they were the best stuffed clams ever, because they were so big and could handle all the flavors. Ladleah had some pork belly squirreled away, and she makes bread, for fuck's sake, so we were set. She put them on the grill, then got guilted when a few of them tried to escape with that one foot of theirs.

"But clams be damned, we chopped everything up and ate them. And while we were eating them, she looked up how old they were. Eighty years old. Eighty-year-old clams! And we ate them! Which leads to a new mixture of 'Oh, man, we ate those truly majestic wise old clams' with 'Shit! They were old!,' and 'Man, that was good.' (Later, after some research, we found out that hen clams, are likely twelve years old at the most, but there was a pervasive sadness when we thought we were eating such ancient shellfish)."

When I wrote to Ladleah and explained the project I was doing, and the book's title, she wrote back, "My husband Shane is a moose hunter. He and his father have a tradition of going up to Newfoundland and meeting up with guides and native Newfoundlanders they've known for a long time and hunting for moose and caribou (if they are lucky to get a permit for the caribou). At home we hunt for deer, grouse, rabbit, and squirrel also."

Instantly intrigued, I asked her for some of her moose recipes. She described sausages and jerky and moose tacos, then added, "There really is no limit to what one can do with moose, as long as it's of good quality (like anything, I suppose), and is treated like grass-fed beef. That is to say, it is cooked rare, or all day. We *love* moose stroganoff made with a nice strong stock from our wild foraged dried mushroom stores—old-school, and so good. No nutmeg required, as our moose has a great spicy wildness to it, and with the chanterelles and black trumpets, it really is a hearty winter meal.

"Bolognese is always a winner. Fire-roast some tomatoes, kick it up with a little cinnamon, cloves, nutmeg, cardamom, an obscene amount of garlic, whatever root veg is hanging around, throw in some kale at the finish. Tourtière [meat pie], meatballs, burgers, curries, stews, tacos . . . treat it like a flank steak with a great chimichurri . . ."

Clearly, this woman knew how to cook a moose. And that turned out to be only the beginning of all the things she knows how to do.

Later that winter, on a frosty February morning, Ladleah wrote, "Come on up and hang in our greenhouse . . . it's about 70 in there right now . . . I have eight or so different varieties of kale, collards, escarole, celery, parsley, parsley root, carrots, raab, beets, chard, a bit of cilantro, leeks. The leeks have all been pulled, though, and I have baby lettuces, radish, spinach, and arugula coming up where they were."

She attached a photo of her bare feet resting on the earth, a mug of tea, a jungle of green things growing in the background, the walls of the greenhouse steamy with warmth.

I wanted to go up there that minute—or at least, that week—but things kept getting in the way: pressing tasks to attend to, work, a book tour, houseguests, deadlines, social obligations, daily life.

In March, she wrote to me, "We are going to smoke some moose jerky and make some moose chorizo. Care to come up and help?"

I cared very much to go up and help. But now, we were ensconced in the New Hampshire farmhouse with Dingo, and I was struggling to start a new novel, hoping to get it under way by summer so I could concentrate on this book then. The novel had taken over my life, as novels will. I wasn't ready to learn about moose yet.

So I put her off again, even more reluctantly this time.

Finally, in mid-September, it hit me that I absolutely needed to meet Ladleah and Shane and see their place. In fact, I couldn't finish this book until I did. They sounded like the living example of what this book is all about: the continuation of a centuries-long tradition of making a living off the land and sea, prime exemplars of this new generation of badass young DIY Mainers I've been getting to know since I moved here.

I wanted to make it up for the weekend of Ladleah's "Hurricane dinner," a fund-raising meal on Hurricane Island she was cooking, and to which she had invited Brendan and me, but once again, we had visitors arriving and things to do.

A few days later, after Brendan had gone to Los Angeles for a couple of weeks, I tried to find a dog sitter for Dingo so I could go up.

But no one could do it, and none of my cat-free, dog-friendly friends could take Dingo, either.

And then, a few days later, the stars finally aligned. Dingo went off for the night with our friend and Dingo's major crush, Angela Crabtree, a dog caretaker, artist, and longtime native Mainer. Before she took Dingo, she told me that her father had worked as a game warden in the Allagash for thirty-five years before he retired and moved back to Hope, his hometown, to become a private investigator.

"He has a million stories," she said. "He was held hostage at gunpoint by a couple of Canadian deer poachers he caught who tied him to a post in an empty camp and left him for dead. It took him days to escape."

"Holy shit," I said. "He should write a memoir."

After Dingo trotted happily off with Angela, I packed a small backpack with pajamas and toothbrush and change of clothes, went to our bougie local store for a bag of good cheese, red wine, flaxseed crackers, and chocolate to take to Ladleah and Shane, and gassed up the car.

And then, finally ready to go, I headed onto the interstate, up the coast toward Lincolnville, two hours north.

This was my first long solo trip since getting my first-ever driver's license the month before, and it felt appropriate that I was making my maiden solo voyage in order to meet two of the most resourceful people in existence. It was a scintillatingly clear, dazzling, early-fall day. The seawater in the coves was a deep, shifting, rippling blue; the trees lining the freeway were rich green underlain with delicate rust. As I drove past marshlands, I could see leaves on low shrubs turning their silvery undersides to the breeze. I listened to Top 40 radio and sang happily along with every song like a teenybopper as I bombed north at a racy seventy-five miles an hour.

Stopped in traffic at a red light in the scenic, touristy village of Camden, I called Brendan.

"I love driving!" I burbled. "Maine is so beautiful!"

"Be careful, baby," he said.

"Don't worry; I hear your bossy voice in my ear every minute: Check your blind spot! Be defensive! Never tailgate!"

"Ha!" he said. "I taught you well."

The directions from Ladleah were straightforward and clear: "There will most likely be a large boat out in front of our barn by the time you get here. Turn in after the boat."

I turned in at a driveway with, as promised, a sailboat propped on jack-stands, its hull resting on large wooden blocking, in front of an enormous, elegant boat barn marked KALLISTÉ YACHT SERVICES.

And there was Ladleah Dunn, at long last, sturdy and beautiful and smiling. Two elegant dogs surged around my car; I learned a few minutes later that they were wirehaired pointing griffons named Buckminster and Zubinelgenubi, Bucky and Zubi for short.

I parked next to Ladleah's car in front of the house and got out. After all this time, I felt we were already old friends who just hadn't met yet. I gave her a big hug.

"What do you want to do?" she asked. "Do you want something to drink? A bathroom?"

"I just really want to walk around," I said, happy as a kid to be there. "Show me everything! But first, how do you pronounce your name?"

"*LAID-lee*," she said. "It's Irish. My parents were a couple of romantics . . ."

While Ladleah showed me the boat barn, which she and Shane had built themselves from their own design, she told me about their business. They repaired sailboats; that was the way they made most of their income. The boat outside belonged to Shane's father. Ladleah's and Shane's sailboat, the one they'd lived on for three years between Florida and the Bahamas before buying this land and settling down, was stored in the barn. In the barn's smaller addition were two more boats they'd been paid to store for the winter. The boat barn was warm in the wintertime, Ladleah explained, because there was radiant heat in the smooth concrete floor and a wood-burning furnace that was so demanding, it was like having an infant to tend, with propane as backup heat.

Beyond the boat barn was a small flock of sheep with sweet, inquisitive faces, grazing in a small pine woods. They weren't at all woolly; their pelts were more like goats'.

"They're Katahdins," Ladleah explained. "We don't raise them for wool, just meat. I'm always really sad when the time comes to schedule the slaughter dates."

"I remember when they were lambing last spring," I said. "You posted pregnancy and birth updates on Facebook. It was like following a serial drama."

While we talked, a pickup truck drove in and a bare-chested young guy got out and conferred briefly with Ladleah, and then he drove away again.

"Avery's going to stack our wood," she said. "This is the first year we've hired someone to do it for us. He's the son of a friend of ours. He's gone to run an errand, and then he's coming back to work till dark."

Shortly after Avery drove off, Shane drove in. He introduced himself and shook my hand with a direct gaze and a firm grip. I liked him instantly, as I had Ladleah, both of whom radiated energy and purpose and trustworthiness and intelligence. We all climbed a wood ladder ("First one he ever built," said Ladleah, "but don't worry, it's sturdy") into Shane's father's boat and went belowdecks, where I admired the woodwork and the 1970s upholstery as I asked them about living on their sailboat for three years.

"Cruising was such an easy, mellow, fun life," Shane said. "We sailed off the coast of Florida, to the Bahamas. We drank rum, ate fish we caught, spent almost no money . . ."

"It was perfect, and then I started yearning for land—for a farm," said Ladleah. "I always thought I was going to be a sailor, not a farmer like my parents. But it turned out I wanted some land where I could grow food, put down roots."

While Shane went over to talk to Avery, who had just come back, Ladleah took me to the gardens and greenhouse. The planted rows were full of fall vegetables, kale and squash, and tall, stooped, nearly dried sunflowers. It turned out that they were "volunteers," grown from wayward seeds and not on purpose.

"The birds love them so much," Ladleah told me. "I never have the heart to cut them down."

"I think they're good luck, maybe," I said. "They're definitely beautiful."

The greenhouse was gridded with vertical strings, from the straw-strewn floor to the curved plastic ceiling, up which twined healthy vines filled with more varieties of tomatoes than I could count: mottled green gumball-size ones, inky-black medium ones, and cherry-red and fire-engine-red and maroon and crimson and orangey ones, of every size and shape.

"I test seeds for an heirloom seed company," Ladleah told me. "Some are better than others."

I sampled a few; the best, I thought, were the green gumballs, which were wondrously sweet and burst in my mouth with flavor and tomatoey juiciness. The inky ones were a disappointment; they looked as if they would be amazing, but they had hardly any taste at all.

"Yeah, I know, but people can't get enough of them," she laughed. "Probably just because of the color."

"So this is the greenhouse where you sit barefoot in the winter," I said, admiring its soaring, practical beauty. "It's so big. It's really nice in here."

"It's always at least ten degrees warmer in here than outside. We insulated it with a double layer of plastic and installed a small fan to inflate the two layers, creating an insulating air space. Sometimes in the winter on a sunny day it gets so hot I'm sweating in here."

"You built it, right?"

"We designed and built it ourselves, like all the buildings on this place except the house. It sits on tracks, so in the winter we slide it over what's now the outdoor garden and plant our winter vegetables directly in the ground."

We went outside again. Ladleah was right; it was much cooler outside than in the greenhouse. Right by our feet were several bean plants: Ladleah told me they were black beans, cannellinis, yellow-eye beans, yellow Indian woman beans, and a "mystery Arizona bean." Yellow Indian woman beans, she told me, had journeyed from Montana via Swedish immigrants; this was her first time planting them.

"I'm really excited to try them; they're supposed to have a great flavor and texture."

I asked her how she makes baked beans.

"It's important to use at least two whole onions in the bottom of the bean pot," she said, "at least for flavor, but I love them spooned on top in my bowl. Add plenty of mustard. And piccalilli with it."

I watched Bucky and Zubi romp around the garden until Ladleah gathered us all up and headed us in a herd toward the house.

I got my backpack and the bag of goodies out of my car and looked around. Next to the house was the garage, poultry coop, and sheep barn, one structure with three separate entrances and purposes. Peeking into the small garage I saw, on the clean floor, a neat stack of four kayaks next to a motorcycle and tractor; next to that was a bin of dried seed pods.

"Shane built the garage and sheep barn," she told me, "our first winter here."

In the fenced-in poultry coop were several Khaki Campbell ducks (a heritage breed, prolific layers who give an egg a day no matter what), and a couple of chickens, Buff Orpingtons, which are apparently sweet-natured but stringy to eat.

"There's a lot of fat on them," said Ladleah, "so they're perfect for stock. I love making stock. There's only two now, because a fox got the rest of them when they were outside pecking around."

Over the chicken coop grew a vine of squash and another of hops. Ladleah picked one of the little green balloons for me to crush between my fingers; it smelled resinous, richly skunky.

"You can tell they're related to marijuana," she said.

"Do you make your own beer with them?"

"We do," she said. "And we make red and white wine out of our grapes; the vines are on the garden fence. And we have lots of fruit and nut trees, too; we planted cherries, pears, apples, hazelnuts, almonds, peaches, and plums. We get lots of strawberries in June. We make cider from a friend's apples. We try for hard cider. Sometimes it's apple cider vinegar."

Then I saw the beehives in the corner of the yard, at the edge of the woods.

"And you have honeybees, too," I said with something approaching hero-worshipping wonderment. "Do you make your own cheese?"

"Oh yeah, I used to," she said. "But I stopped. There are too many amazing cheese makers in the area, and I just don't have the setup."

I looked beyond the garage to the woods.

"How big is your property? How far back do those woods go?"

"We own about three acres," she said. "But those woods go back a long way."

"It feels so remote here, so quiet," I said. "Even though you're two minutes from the main road, it feels wild here."

On the little porch were a couple of weathered Adirondack chairs and a bureau and a few small tables. Scattered around were baskets of cabbages ("for sauerkraut"), squash, cucumbers, a couple of different kinds of peppers, turnips, and tomatoes, and two gallon jars of cinnamon simple syrup. Another resinous-smelling vine covered with puffy green hops grew around the porch railing. A healthy ficus sat in its big pot by a small woodpile, and beyond the chairs was an old grill.

We went inside. Their house was shipshape and well-built, with sanded-down old wood floors, a small, efficient kitchen, comfortable old couches around a woodstove, and a mudroom full of work boots and coats. The bathroom had a claw-foot tub.

I followed Ladleah down to the basement, to the sweet guest room next to the laundry room, whose shelves were laden with put-up produce, jars and jars of various glowing jewel colors.

"I just made piccalilli and chipotle salsa," said Ladleah. "And I made elderberry liqueur and jam, and two kinds of relish, zucchini and cucumber."

She opened the big storage freezer in the corner to show me what was inside: packages of frozen homegrown heirloom-variety corn, cut off the cob ("The corncobs make great vegetable broth") and backstrap, sausage, stew meat, and flank steaks made from Shane's Newfoundland moose the year before.

"And we have some Maine shrimp in here," she said. "Maine shrimp are the best in the world. They're so small and sweet, you can eat the whole thing, heads and shells and all. Just cook them in butter and that's all they need; they're amazing. They're almost fished out, and the quotas are seriously reduced. The last time they were available, we bought twenty pounds. Now we're savoring the last few pounds."

I left my backpack on the guest bed and we went back upstairs to wait for Shane. We were all going out for a drink, and he had an errand to run on the way; then we were coming back here for dinner.

The house used to sit down on the ocean, Ladleah explained. It was a 1920s beach cottage that was moved up to this land in 2000, seven years before they bought the place. They weatherproofed and insulated it, renovated the kitchen, refurbished the floors, and opened up the upstairs so it's one big, airy room with a long L-shaped desk in the window alcove, where they spend forty-five minutes every morning, side by side on their computers, drinking coffee. (Ladleah pays bills, catches up on Facebook and e-mails and reads the news of the world or the latest food gossip; Shane looks at kayaks, hunting guns, motorcycles, and boats. "And then we go outside to work, and we're off the computer till the next morning," said Ladleah.)

Beyond the desks was a big iron bedstead ("We found it by the side of the road for $50"); a cat dozed on the coverlet, among the pillows.

ℓℓ

On our way to Belfast, we passed by a field strewn with big, round bales of hay.

"That's my hay," said Ladleah. "I'm obsessed with it! I've called them a few times about buying it, and they won't call me back. I really, really want that hay for the sheep this winter."

We stopped to see a friend of Shane's; evidently, Shane was buying his kayak. Ladleah and I waited in the car and watched the transaction: Shane and another earnest, thoughtful-looking young man conferred with their heads close together while they looked at the small boat, then they tied it onto the roof of the car together.

"Shane has this whole group of friends he goes white-water kayaking with," Ladleah told me. "They're all really nice guys, really excited about kayaking. Shane is almost philosophical about it. He thinks a lot about it; it's like poetry to him, an art form."

"You would never guess that guy works for the prison system, would you?" Shane said when he got back into the car.

"He looks like an English teacher," Ladleah said, laughing.

"He does," I said.

ℓℓℓ

The Three Tides bar sat on a wharf right on Belfast Harbor. There was a brewery right next door, with many kinds of fresh local beer on tap. We went to the outdoor bar and got drinks, then sat in a booth on the edge of the water. Behind us was an open-mouthed woodstove with a good fire in it, and there were couches and tables scattered around. My Dark and Stormy, made with Gosling's rum and local ginger beer, was spicy and sweet and delicious.

Belfast Harbor was a tidy little cove, filled with moored sailboats, ringed by shingled houses and small local businesses that appeared to be thriving. There was a lobster pound near the brewery. But it used to be a very different place, Shane told me. Until a few years ago, the fancy yacht-repair place on a hill above the bar was a chicken-processing plant. The water of the harbor was covered in feathers and a layer of chicken fat.

"Schmaltz," I said. "The essential ingredient in Jewish cooking."

"The sharks loved it," said Shane. "So did the crabs and fish. Then Perdue drove them out of business and the harbor fell into moribund decay until that boat-repair place opened. Now it's clean again here."

The Three Tides, which opened about ten years ago, was named after the legendary manner in which law enforcement used to dispatch the bodies of pirates they'd caught and killed: They let them dangle from the wharf for three tide cycles, during which the water rose and receded, and each time it rose, crabs would eat the corpses, and then when it fell, the townspeople got a good look at what would happen if they ran afoul of the law, themselves. An effective warning and deterrent, it sounded like.

As the sun went down, we moved to the couches by the fire.

I asked Ladleah about her childhood, her background and Shane's. Ladleah and Shane, both thirty-five at the time, were born six months apart, he in 1978, she in in 1979. "He likes to think he's older and wiser," said Ladleah, "but he's really just older and grumpier."

"What was your childhood like?" I asked her.

"My parents were hippie, organic, back-to-the-land farmers," she said. "They moved up from Massachusetts in the 1970s. I was born in Dixmont, Maine, on Peacemeal Farm, in a farmhouse with a river around it—hence my name, which means 'by the water-coursed meadow.' That's where I grew up. It was a diversified vegetable farm.

"But I was always going to spend my life and make my living on the sea, not the land. I worked as a sternman through high school for Larry Moffatt, who's a lobsterman and a painter. He teaches at the Haystack School from time to time. Then I went to the Maine Maritime Academy and studied biological oceanography where you qualify for a two-hundred-ton captain's license. I graduated magna cum laude, in three years instead of the usual four. So I graduated a year early, and I was planning to go to law school in the fall. I got a job with the Hurricane Island Outward Bound School when I was twenty-one, and that summer turned into five years. That's where I met Shane."

Shane had grown up in Western Massachusetts but spent summers in Maine, sailing with his father, and winters up in Newfoundland, hunting. He was also a trained chef who'd graduated from Johnson & Wales University's culinary school in Florida, as well as an excellent sailor and white-water kayaker and a skilled fisherman and hunter.

Naturally, these two exceptionally knowledgeable, smart, adventurous, intrepid people fell in love. "After burning out from pouring our hearts into the nonprofit, we took off to the Caribbean for those three years on our sailboat," said Ladleah. And then, seven years ago, they put every cent they had into their house and land, their yacht-repair business, their livestock, outbuildings, and their faith in themselves. And here they were. They'd built their life from a nervy willingness to take risks and work hard, a deep desire to be self-sufficient, to work only for themselves.

"I was going to be a lawyer," Ladleah said. "I wanted to change the world. But I discovered it's enough, it's even better, to do what I'm doing now—to live quietly in a beautiful place and work hard and build my life with my hands. Figuring out what to do every day is a process of triage: The place tells us what needs doing, what needs the most attention from us right then. I'm juggling plates all day long. I love it, I thrive on it. Some mornings it's cold, and I wake up and just dread getting out of the warm bed, putting my boots on, going outside, but then I feed the dogs and let them out and get out there and the sun is coming up and I feel the sheep's cold noses while I feed them and the dogs are with me and I'm suddenly so, so happy to be up early, with a day of hard work ahead. It's the best way to live."

లిలి

As we drove back to their place, I asked Shane and Ladleah about bear-baiting.

"I've heard both sides, and it's complicated," said Ladleah. "Ultimately, I think I'm against the campaign for repealing the law because I don't like where it's coming from: out-of-state money attempting to vilify hunting. The biologists who are for it argue that the population has to be controlled. Also, you can't hunt black bears; they're not like browns or grizzlies. They hunt you. They literally track the hunters. The only way to kill them is by setting up bait and waiting in a blind."

"What about the people who say it isn't fair to hunt them like that?" I asked, thinking aloud, remembering the blue plastic bear-baiting trap and tree platform we'd stumbled on when I was mush-room-hunting with Dorcas. "I've heard people say that baiting with donuts and waiting in a blind isn't hunting at all—it's cheating."

"Black bears are different in their habits and patterns," said Ladleah, "as opposed to grizzlies or brown bears, who are more offen-sive. Black bears are more catlike—stalking, hiding. Much more elu-sive. Therefore, the folks who want to kill them feel the need to lure them in, in order to ensure a clean kill. In this day and age I don't get the point of bear killing myself, but some say the meat is quite tasty. But death is a hard thing no matter what, and hunting can be ugly. There is no way to make it warm and fuzzy. I am a kill-to-eat hunter, never trophy."

"The bear's going to get shot either way," said Shane. "But this is the way it works the best. It's actually better for the bear: It's the cleanest shot, so the bear suffers as little as possible. They die instantly. Hunting bears the traditional way is just too risky. A lot of the time, the shot just wounds the bear, and it crawls off and dies slowly and painfully."

I listened, interested, reflecting once more on the complexities of hunting in Maine.

We stopped at a health-food store for quinoa spaghetti; Ladleah pocketed the receipt, since she was expensing tonight's meal, a recipe she was testing for Nancy Jenkins, the chef and cookbook author.

"Have you ever heard of sea moss pudding?" I asked as we drove the rest of the way back. "I found a great old book called *The Salt Book* that describes all sorts of Yankee practices—lobstering, building stone walls, snowshoes, even rum-running. And there's a section on harvesting 'sea moss,' which I guess is algae? They process it and make carrageenan out of it, but there's also a sort of recipe for pudding that uses cheesecloth."

"I love making sea moss pudding," Ladleah said. "I use the best cream and steep the algae in it after scalding the cream for fifteen to thirty minutes. Then I add the sweetener and pour it into the mold. The longer you steep it, the firmer it will be."

"Of course you make sea moss pudding," I said, laughing. "How did I know?"

ele

When we got back to their house, we opened the wine I'd brought and set out the cheese and crackers. Shane and I sat at the table and Ladleah started cooking dinner while Bucky and Zubi milled around.

"They're bird dogs," said Shane. "They point; they wear bells and go after the downed bird. There's a special relationship that exists between a hunter and his dog. There's nothing else like it."

While the pasta water boiled, Ladleah cut turnips into tiny cubes and caramelized them in olive oil and butter in a large skillet, then added minced shallots and chopped White Russian kale, garlic, and a spoonful of the powdered Aleppo pepper she keeps in a bowl by the stove, alongside the bowls of sea salt and black pepper. "I put this stuff in everything," she told me.

I asked Shane about white-water kayaking; his face literally alight, as if a bright fire burned in his head, he described the joy of being in a kayak alone in rushing water, the way it was like a dance between him and the river, a meditation, and a deep kind of wild fun.

We talked about hunting, his trips up north with his family, taking the ferry to Newfoundland, the guys he met up there, the hunting lodges and the experience of being out in the wilderness, looking for moose.

"We walk through a strange, marshy tundra," said Shane. "It's like ten layers of carpet in three feet of water. You sink down with every step into this soft, spongy mass." He added, "It's best to try for a young moose. It's the dichotomy of hunting: trophy versus meat— and I want the meat."

Then he gave me his recipe for moose jerky, which he got from a local Maine guy who worked at the marine supply store, who got it from a hunter and native Newfoundlander who had written it down as it was told to him.

ℓℓℓ

Newfoundland Hunter's Moose Jerky

1 cup soy sauce
1/2 cup Worcestershire sauce
2 T Tabasco ("If you're feeling really crazy, you can put in more Tabasco," according to the Newfoundlander)
1 tsp onion powder
1 tsp garlic powder
1 tsp liquid smoke (unless you're using a smoker)
1/8-inch-thick slices of 2 lbs. moose meat, any part, cut against the grain so it's short, a cross section of fibers (*Note*: Frozen chunks of moose slice easily.)
Methods:

Dehydrator: 5 to 6 hours

Smoker: 3 to 4 hours at 275 degrees

ℓℓℓ

Ladleah tossed the cooked pasta with the sauce and served it with a chunk of Parmesan and a hand grater. On the side, she served sliced, grilled moose sausage she'd taken out of the freezer to thaw that had been made by a Newfoundland hunter Shane had met on his last trip up there. The meal was amazing. The turnips, kale, and shallots melted in my mouth with the buttery, cheesy pasta. And the sausage was chewy and lean and rich and flavorful, almost but not quite spicy.

"We've tried to replicate his recipe," said Shane. "We can never get it right, and he won't tell us what he puts in there. He makes all different kinds, but this one's the best. He calls it Wild Game Sausage. I bet he gets the flavorings from a mail-order packet called 'Wild Game,' but I can't find it online, and I've googled it a hundred times."

"Maybe it's Old Bay," I said.

"Celery salt," he said, thinking about this as he chewed. "Maybe."

We got onto the topic of the Midcoast farm-to-table restaurant Brendan and I had visited a few months before, the one that had served $7 bowls of roasted, unhulled chickpeas and called it "ceci," the place that gave us class rage, and whose perfect little farm had made me coin the word *Foodsneyland*.

"Oh, we go there all the time," said Ladleah. "We're friendly with the owners. They work so hard. The chef lives and breathes her philosophies about food, and it's a truly worthy enterprise. You should go with us sometime in the off-season. We always eat and drink so well there. And the truth is, you can spend just as much money in any of the other area restaurants, but get fooled into a false economy."

I told her about our pink-cheeked, didactic waitress that night, who seemed to have drunk a little too much of the Kool-Aid.

"She was probably just new," said Shane. "Really, go back, go with us."

Now, in addition to bear-baiting, I was given good reason to rethink my strong initial knee-jerk reaction to one of the most popular restaurants in Maine. I promised Ladleah and Shane that Brendan and I would meet them there, one fall weeknight, and give the place a second chance.

℮℮

Ladleah Dunn's Moose Meatballs avec Black Trumpets

4 slices bread
2 lbs. ground moose (good grass-fed beef would work, too)
   (*Note*: If using moose, grate 1/4 cup of organic beef fat into the moose meat.)
1 cup dried black trumpet mushrooms, or 2 cups fresh
1 head of garlic, minced
1/4 cup minced parsley
1/2 cup grated Pecorino
1/4 cup raisins soaked in equal parts sherry
1/4 cup toasted pine nuts
1 1/2 tsp kosher salt
20 turns rough black pepper
4 large eggs
1/2 cup bread crumbs
1 glug of olive oil
1 cup boiling water

Good news for non-foragers, city dwellers, and off-season moose and mushroom enthusiasts everywhere: I *really* prefer using dried mushrooms in this recipe because you soak the mushrooms first in boiling water for a good hour, and then, once hydrated, place bread in a bowl and pour the mushroom liquid over bread. The soaking liquid gets incorporated back into the meatballs, which gives them a rich flavor.

Soak the mushrooms as indicated above, adding mushroom liquid to the bread. While bread is soaking, mince mushrooms and garlic. Sauté together lightly in a heavy pan coated lightly with olive oil, and salt and pepper to taste. Once fragrant, add the sherry from the soaking raisins and cook off the alcohol.

When the liquid has evaporated, but ingredients are not dry, remove pan from heat and add raisins. Stir together, then let mixture cool.

While that little pan of heaven is cooling, turn to the bread in the bowl and crumble it up with your fingers. Chunky is okay. Add the ground moose, cheese, pine nuts, eggs, and then the cooled mushroom-raisin mixture. Season once again with black pepper and salt. Add bread crumbs last to adjust moistness to taste. The mixture should be moist but not sloppy.

Shape and roll mixture by hand into 18 to 20 meatballs. Bake on a lined sheet for 25 to 30 minutes at 325 degrees F. You want the meatballs to be juicy and yielding, but cooked through. Serves 4

Serving suggestions: Try not to eat them all straight from the pan. I really love to serve these with a very soft boiled egg and braised greens. Another take would be to create a "one-pot wonder": Use a nicely buttered cast-iron pan to fry the meatballs, then add egg and greens. Cook together and enjoy. These meatballs freeze well once par-baked. I really don't recommend a red sauce here, as it just tramples the mushrooms. A little butter or olive oil and more Pecorino is enough.

Now try to not go out and get the stuff to make these right now. Hell, I think we'll make them this weekend.

ele

After dinner, Ladleah poured digestifs from a Mason jar over ice: Grand Marnier steeped in fresh-picked strawberries and put up last June. The resulting liqueur was addictively delicious and hot pink.

"This looks like what sorority girls drink to get into trouble," said Shane, chortling.

We stayed up talking and laughing until eleven p.m. I'd arrived at four o'clock, which meant we'd been talking for seven straight hours, and I still felt there was so much more to say, to learn from them, to talk about.

They showed me a couple of videos—a white-water kayaking video shot on the Little White Salmon River, and a cartoon by an outfit called O'Chang about a typical Mainer who talked in the thick Downeast accent. They'd been telling stories about local characters for the last hour or so, and the O'Chang cartoon reminded them again of the guy at the marine supply store with the jerky recipe, who apparently always offered you deer jerky that looked like it was five years old from a body-temperature plastic bag in his pants pocket; he also liked to tell a story of how he used to work with fiberglass without any respiratory protection and "that shit would bring your IQ right down to room temperature."

They told me about a registered Maine guide named Leaky Boot who could have been Willie Nelson's identical twin; the local politicians who'd given them grief about their business zoning, so Ladleah ran for local office and became a selectman herself, and is now the boss of those very local politicians; the tricky relationship between native Mainers and wealthy people from away who buy farms here and hire them.

Before we said good night, Ladleah said, "You need to write about the real Mainers. Write about what this place really is, not the bullshit image people buy into, not the rich people. The real Mainers, the real place."

I told her about Lindsay's idea to start a magazine that would showcase handmade products made by local people, beautifully photographed, with written stories alongside.

"Great idea," she said. "We need that."

ℓℓℓ

I slept so deeply that night in their comfortable guest bed, buried deep in blankets and duvets, my head nestled in soft pillows. I didn't wake up until almost eight o'clock, and felt as if I'd missed half the day. Ladleah had already fed all the animals, dealt with her e-mail and the day's paperwork, and was now on her way down to the boat barn because a two-hundred-pound mast had just been delivered, and she and Shane had to winch and hoist it against the side of the addition to store it.

I carried my mug of coffee outside into the warm summer morning and wandered around their property, looking in on the chickens and ducks, the sheep. The dogs kept me company. I went back by the beehives; the bees were active by now, as the sun got hotter, so I kept a respectful distance.

When Ladleah and Shane reappeared, we drank another pot of coffee in the kitchen and talked for two more hours. Before I left, Ladleah took me down to the greenhouse with a couple of quart containers, and we filled them with tomatoes. She packed them in a bag with four packages of frozen moose meat, a bag of Wabanaki heirloom hand-milled polenta from her neighbor, just-put-up jars of piccalilli, zucchini relish, chipotle salsa, and pickled garlic scapes, four cured bulbs of garlic, and a bunch of sweet purple grapes from their vine.

I hugged them both good-bye and thanked them fervently for their openness and generosity, their willingness to let a stranger into their lives to take nine dense pages of notes and ask them all kinds of impertinent questions and poke around their land.

"You're going to get that hay today," I told Ladleah just before I drove away. "Today is the day. I feel it."

I drove out of their driveway, past the boat, feeling warmhearted and inspired and happy.

During the two-hour drove back to Portland, I ate almost an entire quart of warm, ripe, soulfully delicious tomatoes while I listened to two writer friends discuss *Olive Kitteridge* on Maine Public Radio's book club show (a couple of times, I said aloud, "Excellent point!" or "Nicely put!"). I retraced yesterday's route through the Midcoast region, winding through Camden, inland along Route 1, over the bridge to Wiscasset, slowing down for the permanent traffic near Red's, past coves and inlets and farmland.

As I drove I thought about my life here, how happy I was—not an easy, superficial happiness, but the quiet internal daily joy of living in a culture based on authenticity and integrity, among people who valued hard work over glamour, honesty over style, quality over quantity.

It was an old-fashioned value system, one based on survival and sustenance, and it was reflected in Maine's food. Potatoes, blueberries, moose and maple, foraged mushrooms, lobster and clams: The ingredients from this place were perfect just as they grew in their natural state. They hardly needed anything done to them.

The same went for the people I'd met; there was an innate quality to all of them, a deep integrity that needed no dressing up or special presentation, that seemed to emanate from the land itself. I was even affected by it: I felt like a different person, a better one, since I'd come here just a few years ago.

I thought of a quote I'd read by John Bunker, Maine's foremost apple expert, when he tried to describe why he'd fallen in love with Maine at the age of eleven, then moved here as an adult and never left: "I just had a sense that this was the right place. I think maybe there was a recognition of something that spoke to the deepest part of my humanity."

Back in Portland, I turned the car up State Street to Congress, over to Walker, up to Brackett, into the alleyway, into the garage. And I was home.

Midcoast Tamale Pie

Simmer 6 boneless, skinless chicken thighs on very low heat, partially covered, for 40 minutes, in just enough water to cover, plus 1 inch, with 6 garlic cloves, 2 bay leaves, 1/2 tsp dried oregano, salt and pepper to taste. Pull the chicken from the broth and let it cool, then shred it into bite-size pieces with a fork and set aside. Reserve the broth, discarding the bay leaves.

Meanwhile, in 2 batches in the blender, liquefy a quart of very ripe heirloom tomatoes with 2/3 cup of chipotle salsa or a whole can of chipotle peppers in adobo sauce, plus a chopped raw onion and the garlic cloves from the chicken broth. You will have a thick, creamy, pinkish-brown liquid. Pour it into a large skillet. Add 1 grated large zucchini and about 1 tsp each paprika and cumin. Simmer on low heat, stirring often, until it thickens, about 20 minutes.

Add the shredded chicken to the skillet and mix well. Let it continue to simmer for 10 minutes, then turn off the heat.

Meanwhile, in 6 cups of the chicken broth, cook 2 cups of polenta (hand-milled from a neighbor's heirloom corn, ideally, but any kind will do), stirring frequently, till it thickens, about 10 minutes.

Pour the chicken with chipotle-tomato sauce into a large shallow glass baking dish, pour the thickened polenta over it, smooth the surface so it's even, and bake it uncovered at 350 degrees for 40 minutes.

Optional: You can also top it with 1 cup of grated pepper-jack cheese before baking; it's fantastic, either way.

Serves 2 people for 4 nights.

Bibliography and Further Reading

The northeast corner seems to have as many writers as it does farmers and fishermen. It would take many pages to list all of the wonderful, riveting books that have been written about this region, so I've contented myself here with the ones that particularly inspired me as I was writing this book. I encourage interested readers to use this list as a jumping-off place to dive deep into the rich sea of the literature of Maine.

Alice Arlen. *She Took to the Woods: A Biography and Selected Writings of Louise Dickinson Rich* (Down East Books, 2000).

Lura Beam. *A Maine Hamlet* (Tilbury House, 2000).

Jean Hay Bright. *Meanwhile, Next Door to the Good Life* (BrightBerry Press, 2003).

Melissa Coleman. *This Life Is in Your Hands* (Harper, 2011).

Trevor Corson. *The Secret Life of Lobsters: How Fisherman and Scientists Are Unraveling the Mysteries of Our Favorite Crustacean* (Harper Perennial, 2005).

Barbara Damrosch and Eliot Coleman. *The Four Season Farm Gardener's Cookbook* (Workman Publishing Company, 2013).

Paul J. Fournier. *Tales from Misery Ridge* (Islandport Press, 2011).

Helen Hamlin. *Nine-Mile Bridge: Three Years in the Maine Woods* (Islandport Press, 2005).

Thomas Hanna. *Shoutin' into the Fog: Growing Up on Maine's Ragged Edge* (Islandport Press, 2006).

Margaret Hathaway and Karl Schatz. *The Year of the Goat: 40,000 Miles and the Quest for the Perfect Cheese* (Lyons Press, 2009).

Bernd Heinrich. *A Year in the Maine Woods* (Da Capo Press, 1995).

The Home Comfort Range Cook Book, circa 1900.

Annette Jackson. *My Life in the Maine Woods: A Game Warden's Wife in the Allagash Country* (Islandport Press, 2007).

Sarah Orne Jewett. *The Country of the Pointed Firs* (Dover Thrift Editions, 2011).

Samuel Merrill. *The Moose Book: Facts and Stories from Northern Forests* (E. P. Dutton, 1920).

Helen Nearing and Scott Nearing. *The Good Life: Helen and Scott Nearing's Sixty Years of Self-Sufficient Living* (Schocken Books, 1990).

Kathy Neustadt. *Clambake: A History and Celebration of an American Tradition* (University of Massachusetts Press, 1992).

Lincoln Paine. *A Maritime History of Maine* (Alfred A. Knopf, 2013).

Michael Pollan. *The Omnivore's Dilemma: A Natural History of Four Meals* (Penguin, 2006).

Louise Dickinson Rich. *We Took to the Woods*, 2nd ed. (Down East Books, 2007).

Bill Roorbach. *Temple Stream* (Down East Books, 2014).

Terry Silber. *A Small Farm in Maine* (Anchor, 1989).

Andrew Smith, ed. *The Oxford Encyclopedia of Food and Drink in America* (Oxford University Press, 2004).

Keith Stavely and Kathleen Fitzgerald. *America's Founding Food: The Story of New England Cooking* (University of North Carolina Press, 2004).

Hank and Jan Taft and Curtis Rindlaub. *A Cruising Guide to the Maine Coast* (Diamond Pass Publishing, 1996).

Pamela Wood. *The Salt Book* (Anchor Press, 1977).

Colin Woodard. *The Lobster Coast: Rebels, Rusticators, and the Struggle for a Forgotten Frontier* (Viking, 2004).

Baron Wormser. *The Road Washes Out in Spring: A Poet's Memoir of Living off the Grid* (University Press of New England, 2006).

Acknowledgments

I owe a great debt of thanks to so many people who helped me in the writing of this book:

The Fitzgerald and Arshad families and Charlotte Brown: for welcoming me into the fold, taking such good care of Dingo, and feeding me so many excellent meals.

Our community of writer friends here: This is a famously idyllic place for writers. I've never felt so thoughtfully left alone and, simultaneously, so buoyed by moral support and excellent company.

Everyone mentioned and interviewed in this book: People in this part of the world tend to be private. Thank you all so much for allowing a newcomer from away to write about you, and for trusting me with your amazing stories. I'm inspired by and grateful to you all.

And my editor, friend, and Nordic sister, Genevieve Morgan, who asked me to write the book I most wanted to write at exactly the right time, and shepherded me through it with grace and wisdom, warmth and love: Thank you, thank you.

About the Author

Kate Christensen is the author of, most recently, *Blue Plate Special: An Autobiography of My Appetites*, as well as six previous novels, including *The Epicure's Lament* and *The Great Man*, which won the 2008 PEN/Faulkner Award for Fiction. She writes about food, drink, life, and books for numerous publications, most recently the *New York Times Book Review*, *Bookforum*, *Cherry Bombe*, *Vogue*, *Food & Wine*, the *Wall Street Journal*, and numerous anthologies. She blogs about food and life in New England at katechristensen.net.

Christensen lives in Portland, Maine, and the White Mountains, and is currently at work on a new novel.